✿ ✿ ✿

THE SANDMAN PAPERS

THE

AN EXPLORATION OF THE SANDMAN MYTHOLOGY

SANDMAN

EDITED BY JOE SANDERS

PAPERS

PUBLISHED BY FANTAGRAPHICS BOOKS

Fantagraphics Books
7563 Lake City Way NE
Seattle, WA 98115 USA.

Editor: Joe Sanders
Editorial Liaison: Gary Groth
Designer: Adam Grano
Promotion by Eric Reynolds
Published by Gary Groth & Kim Thompson

✦

For a free full-color catalogue of comics and cartooning, call 1-800-657-1100.
Our books may be viewed — and purchased — on our website at www.fantagraphics.com

Distributed in the U.S. by W.W. Norton and Company, Inc. (1-212-354-5500)
Distributed in Canada by Raincoast Books (1-800-663-5714)
Distributed in the UK by Turnaround Distribution (1-208-829-3009)

First Fantagraphics Books edition: April 2006

ISBN-13: 978-1-56097-748-3
ISBN-10: 1-56097-748-5

Printed in Canada

Acknowledgements:
"Of Parents and Children and Dreams in Neil Gaiman's Mr. Punch and The
Sandman" originally appeared in Foundation: The International Review
of Science Fiction, v. 71, Autumn 1997.

"Of Storytellers and Stories in Gaiman and Vess's 'A Midsummer Night's Dream'"
originally appeared in Extrapolation, v. 45, Fall 2004.

❧❧❧

❧❧❧

To Dick and Pat Lupoff
and Don and Maggie Thompson
for encouraging me to take
another look at comics.

And to all my students
who wouldn't let me stop looking.

❧ ❧ ❧

THE SANDMAN PAPERS

Table Of Contents

✦

❧❧❧

A NOTE ON TEXTS

✦

DC's collected edition of *The Sandman* is inconsistent in terms of pagination. Some volumes are numbered continuously; others simply reprint whatever first appeared in the monthly comic, with page numbers beginning anew each installment; sometimes, the page numbers are difficult or impossible to find. Consequently, documentation in these essays is inconsistent too, but parenthetical citations are as full *as possible* in order to help readers locate relevant quotations or images.

For the record, here are the volumes of *The Sandman* referred to in this volume:
- ✤ Gaiman, Neil. *The Sandman: Brief Lives*. New York: Vertigo/DC Comics. 1994. [*Sandman* #40-9]
- ✤ *The Sandman: The Doll's House*. New York: DC Comics, 1990. [*Sandman* #8-6]
- ✤ *The Sandman: Dream Country*. New York: DC Comics, 1991. [*Sandman* #17-20]
- ✤ *The Sandman: Fables and Reflections*. New York: Vertigo/DC Comics, 1993. [*Sandman Special* #1 and *Vertigo Preview*]
- ✤ *The Sandman: A Game of You*. New York: Vertigo/DC Comics, 1993. [*Sandman* #32-7]
- ✤ The *Sandman: The Kindly Ones*. New York: Vertigo/DC Comics, 1996. [*Sandman* #57-69 and *Vertigo Jam* #1]
- ✤ *The Sandman: Preludes and Nocturnes*. New York: Vertigo/DC Comics, 1992. [*Sandman* #1-8]
- ✤ *The Sandman: Season of Mists*. New York: Vertigo/DC Comics, 1992. [*Sandman* #21-8]
- ✤ *The Sandman: The Wake*. New York: Vertigo/DC Comics, 1997. [Sandman #70-5]
- ✤ *The Sandman: World's End*. New York: Vertigo/DC Comics, 1994. [*Sandman* #51-6]

ΦΦΦ

INTRODUCTION

by Neil Gaiman

✦

There's introductions and there's introductions and there's introductions, and then there's ones like this where I'm introducing a book that has some kind of connection to me, and I have no idea what I can really add to the book in your hand. Still, I need to try.

I once — at the International Conference on the Fantastic in the Arts, in Florida, some years ago — went to a presentation of three papers on my work (one of which is reprinted here), and after each paper was presented, I was asked if I would like to make some reply, which is honestly a bit like asking someone who has just undergone an autopsy if he'd like to talk about the experience. (My replies varied, at least in memory, from "Er, thanks. That was very nice of you," to an "Er, with respect, if you read the issue you've cited, I don't believe it actually says what you think it does." But possibly I just smiled and nodded.)

Those were, however — with the exception of pointing out the occasional objective mistake — simply my opinions, and I don't consider them to be privileged. Once you've written something it's not yours any longer: it belongs to other people, and they all have opinions about it, and every single one of those opinions is as correct as that of the author — more so, perhaps. Because those people have read the work as something perfectly new, and, barring amnesia, an author is never going to be able to do that. There will be too many ghost-versions of the story in the way, and besides, the author cannot read it for the first time, wondering what happens next, comparing it to other things that he or she has read.

So while I may, opinionated myself, disagree with some of the conclusions presented here, I am quite content for the opinions to exist; after all, the people who came to them read the work for the first time, which is more than I've ever managed. Sometimes I've had my eyes opened by papers on something I'd written, and noticed that there was something else there than I had intended. I've been praised for unintentional cleverness and damned for things I don't actually think I did. And I've always enjoyed it, perhaps because I've always had a healthy respect for academia. Even when puzzled by it, it treats art as if it matters. And for those of us who make art, that's a fine thing to experience.

I'm always particularly delighted by academic attention to comics — partly because I think we need the best critical minds to point to what we do and explain it to ourselves, and partly, even mostly, because it shows how much things are changing. (A decade ago I was invited to speak at one major American university by the art department, and was informed, apologetically, that the English department was, ah, boycotting my talk, because, after all, I did *comics*. These days the invitations *come* from the English departments ...)

One thing I know that I *can* say is that Joe Sanders (there are two people of that name in this book, just to confuse you. I'm talking about the editor) is not only a fine and perspicacious critic, and an excellent teacher, but he has also proved quite indefatigable in bringing this book into the world. I hope this book will prove to be only the beginning of the printed and collected dialogue between those who do comics and those who tell us what we did.

— Neil Gaiman
January 10, 2006

Indifatigable

✣✣✣

❖❖❖

PREFACE

by the editor

✦

Something more Viscera

First of all, this book's title may require some explanation. "Pa-pers" are relatively short critical/scholarly essays that usually are written to present at conferences.

The reason we write them — the reason the conferences exist — the reason for a lot of what goes on in college English departments — is that we need to share what's important to us. When we see something star-tling, we want to reflect on it, inhabit it more fully. We want to talk about it. Conversation, including in-class discussion, is exciting but often frustrating; it veers unpredictably, provoking unexpected insights while leaving other ideas underdeveloped. It is wonderful, but it evaporates too soon. Some observations deserve to be worked out more fully in writing, then shared. Frequently, it's not clear what one thinks until a cloud of observations settles into words, is reread, then spoken aloud and heard. Thus "papers."

And thus this book. Fairly early in *The Sandman's* run as a monthly comic book, readers recognized it as an extraordinary work. Even if the story's destination was unpredictable, it was fascinating. We wanted to talk about it. So papers about *The Sandman* began showing up at scholarly gatherings such as the annual conferences of the Science Fiction Research Association (SFRA) and the International Association for the Fantastic in the Arts (IAFA). I'd gotten in touch with Neil Gaiman while writing an entry about him for a reference book and had gone on to do several papers about his work. Then, during an IAFA event at which he was a guest, he casually asked if I'd ever thought of editing a collection of such essays. I hadn't, but it sounded like fun ... So, much later, here's a gathering of papers that discuss aspects of *The Sandman*, sometimes focusing tightly on separate sections of the work, sometimes observing themes that run throughout.

Since most of the essays were written independently, over several years, the coverage isn't comprehensive. In fact, there's some overlap as writers gravitate toward the same subjects: Shakespeare, sex, the Furies, death (and Death). It's interesting to see such shared concerns but also to see where the writers' interpretations diverge. Sometimes I disagree with parts of an essay; however, each finally convinced me that it was thoughtful and well-supported. As editor, I tried to encourage writers to develop their conclusions fully — oral delivery at a conference sets a strict requirement on length. I also encouraged direct, non-jargony writing. Beyond that, I've been surprised and pleased, as each individual essay came in, to see how it has increased my appreciation of *The Sandman*.

The first section of essays deals with parts of *The Sandman*, more or less in order of original publication. B. Keith Murphy sets up a literary-social context for Gaiman's work by talking about the traditions in prose fiction and comics that were waiting for Neil to adapt or ransack. My own first essay looks mainly at one of the most successful single-issue stories, the award-winning "A Midsummer Night's Dream," while David Bratman examines the challenging story arc *A Game of You*. The second-most celebrated *Sandman* short story is "Ramadan," the subject of Renata Sancken's essay. The last two major story arcs are the subjects of the final two essays, as K. A. Laity questions Dream's respect for female power in *The Kindly Ones* and Joan Gordon identifies Neil with Shakespeare's Prospero in the climax of *The Wake*.

Interest in Shakespeare carries over into the first essay in the book's second section, in which Alan Levitan uses *The Sandman's* insights to illuminate Shakespeare's writing. In similar fashion, the essays in this section examine *The Sandman* next to other pieces of Gaiman's writing and/or work by other writers. My own essay looks at Dream's behavior in light of characters in some of Neil's other comics. A comparison with Jorge Luis Borges's interest in variable realities is the subject of Lorena Soledad Sousa e Paula's essay. The next essay deals with how Neil and his sometimes-collaborator Terry Pratchett have adapted ancient myth for a modern audience; Stacie Hanes deals with Pratchett's witches, while I talk about Neil's. Dream's appearance — why those flowing robes? — catches the attention of Lyra McMullen, who sees how the look of the wardrobe contributes to the overall effect. And, finally, Joe S. Sanders concentrates on the use of language by characters whom readers first meet in *The Sandman* but who continue into the second miniseries about Dream's sister Death.

Looking at this list and reading the essays themselves, readers will notice how much is left out. Where's the essay on "Hob's Leviathan"? How did Neil use the limitations of a monthly comic book to his story's advantage? What about Dream of the Endless as opposed to Miracleman, the godlike character Neil inherited from Alan Moore? Etc. Where are *those* essays? Well, some promised essays never got written (or submitted), while some writers who had signed on early disappeared by the time the project finally was re-activated. There's a lot more to say about *The Sandman*, and this book is just an early, incomplete effort. That in itself is a good sign. When we discover a story that holds our attention and that deserves to be thought and talked about — and written about — with increasing pleasure, we know that we're in the presence of something that will continue to satisfy us for a long time. It's called literature. So I hope that you'll enjoy looking over these essays and thinking about *The Sandman*. I also hope that you'll then feel like sitting down at your own computer and joining the dialogue.

— *Joe Sanders*
Mentor, OH

EPISODES

&

THEMES

❖❖❖

THE ORIGINS OF *THE SANDMAN*

by B. Keith Murphy

✦

I t is considered by many to be the paragon of the comic-book
form. It's mentioned in the same breath with such comic icons as
Art Spiegleman's *Maus* or Frank Miller's *The Dark Knight Returns.* It is studied
as literature on college campuses and, years after the last new issue hit
the stands, the collected volumes of the comic are still among DC Comics' best-selling titles. It is Neil Gaiman's *The Sandman.*

The Sandman provided new life and a new sensibility to the comic book.
Yet it owes a great deal to both literature and comic forms that preceded
it. This essay is an attempt to trace the cultural history of *The Sandman*
from the original gothic horror traditions to comic books that aspire to
literary traditions far beyond that of the standard superhero fare.

Any genre of literature develops a set of generic expectations, a kind
of unspoken set of rules that define what is acceptable and expected in
that genre. Those shared expectations create a sense of community between readers.

> You see, we comics fans share a very special language all our own. We talk
> about continuity, meta-humans, and indicias, things most people have
> never heard of. Comics possess their own charming logic that is vastly
> different from the real world's — so different, in fact, that many of us
> quite often retreat from the real world into the "logic" of comics. (Eury)

This world of characters and jargon and narrative expectations creates a linguistic community of readers who share a language and a world view. By its very success as a medium, the commercial, "mainstream" comic book in America reached a pivotal point where generations of new artists and writers, raised on the comic-book narrative form, merely repeated the themes, forms, and ideas with which they had been raised. As such, many of the American costumed superheroes became cultural icons through the repetition of these successful forms. Unfortunately, this also meant that the American comic-book form, by the late 1970s, had become little more than a parody of itself.

Much of that changed thanks to the infusion of British talent that made up the initial waves of the British horror comic invasion. Interestingly enough, the roots of that invasion dates back to the earliest Gothic novels.

A HISTORY OF THE FUTURE. Horror is defined as a fictional narrative "which shocks or even frightens the reader, and/or perhaps induces a feeling of repulsion or loathing. The word *horror* derives from the Latin *horrere* 'to make the hair stand on end, tremble, shudder.'" The horror story can trace its beginning to the Gothic novel, which saw its heyday from 1760 to approximately 1820. The generic trappings of the Gothic novel can still be seen in modern ghost and horror novels, films, and comics.

> Most Gothic novels are tales of mystery and horror, intended to chill the
> spine and curdle the blood. They contain a strong element of the super-
> natural and have all or most of the now familiar topography, sites, props,
> presences and happenings ... The whole apparatus, in fact that has kept
> the cinema and much third-rate fiction going for years, is to be found in
> these tales. (Cuddon 406)

The elements include a brooding but attractive nobleman; dark family secrets; a quivering heroine; a vast, crumbling castle that's not as empty as it looks; and ominous supernatural portents.

The seminal Gothic novel was Horace Walpole's *The Castle of Otranto* (1764), which still survives in print. The genre peaked with Mary Shelley's *Frankenstein* (1818) but was more popularly represented by mountains of cheaply produced, quickly written formulaic works (Cuddon 382). By the early 18th century, British readers had tired of Gothic horror, turning instead to novels in which more fully developed characters such as Jane Eyre encountered situations that were outré but not quite macabre. Meanwhile, the Gothic had traveled to America, where

> … Charles Brockden Brown attained something approaching fame with a succession of Gothic romances … Brown was to influence Nathaniel Hawthorne, Mary Shelley and Edgar Allen Poe — one of the most Gothic of all 19th c. writers of short stories whose long term contribution to the horror story, the tale of suspense and mystery and detective story was immeasurable. (Cuddon 381-2)

Early in the 20th century, the Gothic in America drifted into a rowdier vein of horror explored in pulp magazines, where action and tight plotting were more important than subtle characterization or polished prose. The most literate, *Weird Tales*, kept grotesque mutilations to a relative minimum and sometimes, as in the work of Anglophile writer H. P. Lovecraft, achieved the level of art. In "The Outsider," for example, Lovecraft used Gothic horror conventions to present a first-person narrator who is as unjustly but absolutely excluded from human society as was Frankenstein's monster. All of the less restrained components of the Gothic and horror stories would, in time, travel back to Britain to reappear in a particular form of British popular fiction: Penny Dreadfuls.

PENNY BLOODS. In England's Victorian era, penny fiction represented the state

of the art of illustrated stories. "Bound in paper and cheaply printed. A penny, from the cost; dreadful, presumably because they were regarded as low, vulgar, sensational, etc." (Cuddon 696). These books were the "Victorian equivalent of the horror comic" (Perry and Aldridge 38). The Penny Dreadful followed the deeds of a primary character, usually a well-known and notorious individual: "Highwaymen and notorious criminals were popular characters,…[including] many fictionalized accounts of Dick Turpin, Jack Rann, Jack Sheppard, and Sweeney Todd, the demon barber of Fleet Street" ("The Barry Ono collection"). The Penny Dreadful was characterized by its sensational art and a format which emulated more traditional news sources of the day.

> A sensational cover drawing was always required, for publishers were already well aware of the value of point-of-sale display in raising circulation. *The Illustrated Police News* [a popular penny dreadful which chronicled the misadventures of Spring-Heel'd Jack] had a bogus air of respectability, mocking the sober *Illustrated London News* in style. It was, however, a magnificent opportunity for the presentation of scandal and sensation, put across with the Victorian penchant for retribution and punishment

indulged to the full. (Perry and Aldridge 38)

As a result, even as far back as the Victorian era, newspapers were generally barren of illustrative material, and books which incorporated pictures into storytelling were considered
"less than respectable."

In 1890, Alfred Harmsworth's Amalgamated Press introduced *Comic Cuts* and *Chips* in an
attempt to gain a foothold in the penny market; "he wanted to break into a market dominated by the penny dreadful, with its sensational serials and crude drawings. But his publication
was to be priced at a halfpenny — and later A. A. Milne was to say that Harmsworth 'killed
the penny dreadful with the ha'penny dreadfuller'" (Perry and Aldridge 47-8).

Because of the lack of a pool of British artists and writers, *Comic Cuts* (and contemporaries such as *Chips*) included a great deal of work "lifted" and adapted from American comic
strips. *Comic Cuts*, which consisted of gag strips interspersed with jokes, lasted over sixty-five
years. The mass marketing of these periodicals established the form of the comic genre in
Great Britain.

With the birth of the American comic book a few years later, the British and American
comic strip/book genres began to develop in separate directions. Until World War II, the
British comic industry continued to produce primarily humor books while America had first
discovered the superhero, then rediscovered the horror comic.

THE YANKS ARE COMING. Until the 1930s, the American comic-book
industry was also dominated by reprints of daily strips from newspapers. In 1933, Jerry Siegel
and Joe Shuster provided DC Comics with the formula that would make the American comic-book industry extremely profitable and influential for the next six decades. That formula
was the superhero genre, and it was typified by its first major character: Superman (Daniels
20). The superhero is an apparently ordinary man or woman who reveals extraordinary abili-
ties by donning a dramatic costume to assist the less able/competent authorities in protecting civilians. By World War II, the comic book and its superhero genre had become a staple
of American culture — so much so that comics were provided to American troops serving
overseas during and after the war. These American imports soon exposed the British to a new
and exotic form of literature

> which first arrived in Britain in any numbers with the GIs stationed there
> towards the end of the Second World War. These comics came from a
> tradition of publishing very different from that previously known in
> Britain, and were primarily aimed at adults. In the early days, they were
> directly imported in bulk, with titles such as *Eerie*, *Crime Detective*, *Crimes
> by Women* and, of course, *Superman*. (Barker 8)

During the latter part of this initial wave of American comic books into Britain, one American publishing house began producing books which echoed the British traditions of the horror genre but maintained a more rambunctious American style and sensibility: Educational Comics (later Entertaining Comics, or simply EC) Comics. The EC titles told highly literate tales (some were even adaptations of Ray Bradbury stories) with all the trappings of the gothic genre. The American addition to the genre came as a result of EC's unblinking point of view:

> EC had pioneered a new kind of horror comic based not in myth and fantasy but in the banal horrors that, just maybe, could be taking place behind the closed doors of any business or suburban home. These powerfully illustrated melodramas especially appealed to adolescents and young adults who may not have read other, milder comics ... The value system apparent in [writer/editor Al] Feldstein's scripts was one that had no shadings of gray, no ambiguity. Good people were totally good and evil people were irredeemable, consistently evil. (Goulart 178)

Beginning in April, 1950, EC debuted *Crypt of Terror* and *The Vault of Horror*, these titles were soon followed by *The Haunt of Fear, Weird Science,* and *Weird Fantasy.* EC's early publications are "what many consider the supreme works of the Golden Age of comic books" (Inge 117). EC had been founded by William Gaines, the son of Max Gaines (originator of many of the second tier of DC heroes including Flash, Green Lantern, and Wonder Woman) who, in 1941,

> convinced of the need to fashion the right products for their youthful readership began publishing *Picture Stories from the Bible.* In 1945 he [Max] sold the other titles (the superheroes) to National [DC], and began his own firm Educational Comics, Inc. There he continued *Picture Stories from the Bible,* adding *Picture Stories of Science, Picture Stories from American History,* and *Picture Stories from World History.* (White 31)

Needless to say, none of the titles created by Max made any money. When Max was killed in a boating accident a few years later, William took an interest in the company and began creating a stable of titles that would change the face of comic books on two continents.

> Among innovations the EC staff brought into comic book art were the use of highly literate and stylistically effective narrative captions, realistic dialogue which permitted characters to use blasphemy (though without obscenity or cursing), and engaging plotlines which always concluded

with an ironic twist or a surprise ending, and some of the most distinctive visual effects ever produced for the pages of comic books. Here was
creativity of the first order, an inspired blending of the visual and literary
media possible only when artists and writers are free to pursue their own
standards of excellence. (Inge 117)

In the United States, the EC titles were financially successful. They were equally successful in Britain. The EC books led the vanguard of the second wave of American books to hit
British soil. "By 1954 a new set of comics was being reprinted, deriving from a later development in the US industry: the horror comics. Although presaged in *Eerie* and the like, these
were different. *Black Magic, Frankenstein, Haunt of Fear* and *Tales from the Crypt* [the latter two
titles from EC] now graced many a newsagents' shelves or market stalls" (Barker 8).

The books were eagerly received by British youth. A physician, who would later be a vo-
cal opponent of American-style comics, reported that young patients of his hospital were
frequently seen trading the books from bed to bed. The appearance of these comics sparked
a firestorm of public reaction; "the conservative government, late in 1954, introduced a bill
to control them. Known as the Children and Young Persons (Harmful Publications) Act, it
became law in 1955. Within weeks, virtually all these comics disappeared. ... The Act ... was
renewed without discussion in 1965. It is still in force" (Barker 9, 17).

Thus, the Harmful Publications Act was intended to isolate the British comic industry
and its audience from the overwhelming majority of American comics and their influence. As
a result, juvenile humor books such as *Beano* and *Dandy* became the British standard. This
isolation, in combination with the anti-horror comic furor, negatively impacted the image of
comic books in Britain:

> In Britain, however, they [comics] were still generally regarded as junk:
> fodder for the illiterate and uneducated. There was persisting residue
> from the puritan past that regarded enjoyment without effort as worth-
> less, and for that reason visual perception in popular culture forms tra-
> ditionally took second place to the written word. Put another way, it was
> alright to read, but not to look at pictures. (Perry and Aldridge 7)

Despite this, the British comic-book industry, led by *Beano* and *Dandy*, developed its own
subversive traditions.

> They represented a new type of comic, powerful in gag humor and slap-
> stick, with a stubborn scorn for the higher virtues. The cartoon heroes in
> *Film Fun* had to turn out to be good natured at heart if only to keep within
> the libel laws. But no such scruples could possibly affect the cow-pie eat-

ing, steer-tossing tough guy Desperate Dan in *Dandy*, or the authority-
hating Lord Snooty of *Beano*. Schoolteachers, policemen, officials of any
kind were usually figures of ridicule to be thwarted at every opportunity.
(Perry and Aldridge 51)

This change in approach marked a clear departure from the American comic vision.
Where American superhero comics were generally morality plays in which the hero represented the virtue of authority, their British counterparts, like the American underground
comics phenomenon of the 1960s, championed the common man as an anti-authoritarian
force.

This dichotomy is equally evident in the typically British takes on the American superhero genre with such titles as *Captain Marvel*, later called *Marvelman* (*Miracleman* in the United
States), and *Judge Dredd*. The most American, at the beginning, was *Marvelman*, yet all of the
British titles retained a certain disdain for authority figures. As a result, the titles were finan-
cial successes.

> While superhero comics crashed in America after World War II, their
> English counterparts sold briskly. On August 19, 1953, Miller and Son
> launched weekly versions of *Captain Marvel* and *Captain Marvel Jr.* with
> glossy color covers and 32 page black and white interiors. Their success
> was immediate; the titles rapidly became Miller's best sellers demanding
> approximately 256 pages of material monthly. (Gore)

Marvelman (the name was changed after National sued Fawcett for copyright infringe-
ment) and his compatriots became the reading staple of avid comic-book readers in Britain.
The changes that were made initially to protect the publisher from litigation continued to
mold *Marvelman* into a purely British book until the book ceased publication in 1963. The
most "British" of those changes rested in the fact that the series' tone was very different than
the serious face presented in American superhero fare. "The tone of the *Marvelman* strip was
quite whimsical and relaxed. His many adventures were low key and his menaces perhaps
less frightening than most of his American contemporaries"(Humphreys).

Marvelman's importance to the British comic-book readers of the day is reinforced by
the fact that it was reborn in the British comics revival of the 1980s. In 1982, Quality Comics revived *Marvelman* in the pages of *Warrior* in an acclaimed series penned by Alan Moore.
Moore's genius lent itself well to the task. His reworking of the powerful character's silly
Golden Age origins revealed them to be a government experiment in super power and
mind control. Unfortunately, after 21 issues, pressure from Marvel Comics succeeded where
National's victory over Fawcett failed. *Warrior* dropped *Marvelman*. In 1985, however, Quality
exported *Marvelman* to the United States as *Miracleman*. This run from Eclipse comics con-

tinued sporadically into the early-1990s with new material by Neil Gaiman. *Marvelman's* success led, in part, to the advent of Judge Dredd and Dan Dare, the first purely British heroes (Murphy). Dredd, Marvelman, and Dare remained something uniquely "other" than their American counterparts. As such Marvelman, Dredd, and Dare are important influences on the creators who would follow (Holland). From these influences, as well as the long British tradition of more literate, character-driven horror fiction, the beast began to stagger from the swamp.

LIKE HAMLET COVERED IN SNOT.

The first shot of this British invasion was fired by a very unlikely hero: Alan Moore. Moore, born in 1953 in Northampton, was raised in relative poverty and was expelled from a conservative secondary school before he graduated. By 1971 he was untrained and unemployed when he began working for *Embryo*, a magazine founded by some of his friends. By the late 1970s he was freelancing as a writer for *Dr. Who Weekly* and *2000 A. D.* Moore's work began to get industry-wide notice when, in both 1982 and 1983, he won the British Eagle Award for Best Comics Writer ("Alan Moore Fan Site").

Len Wein, co-creator and editor of DC's *Swamp Thing*, solicited scripts from Moore. Moore says, "I believe I was just about the first British writer brought into American comics" (Daniels 161). Moore was paired with renowned artist Steve Bissette and inker John Totleben.

> The team of Moore, Bissette, and Totleben took flight at once. "We found out all we wanted to do the same thing with the character," says Bissette. "Alan immediately kicked it into gear with issue 21, 'The Anatomy Lesson.' I had never read a comic script like that in my life." Moore's inspiration, presented in unusually evocative prose, ... [was] a purposeful plant with strong ecological opinions, not the suffering scientist he describes as "a little bit like Hamlet covered in snot" (Daniels 161). [*Fig. 1*]

He also could be described as slime-dripping version of Bronte heroes such as Heathcliffe or Mr. Rochester. In any event, Moore's *Swamp Thing* is frequently cited as the first book in what would become DC's immensely popular, predominantly British-created Vertigo line of "sophisticated suspense." "Moore's *Swamp Thing* broke the mold of clichéd superhero comics and the perceived restrictions of the books, opening the envelope wide for all writers to diversify the comic universe" ("The Top 100" 62).

Moore found the "mold" of American comics easier to break than had those raised on them because, as with Gaiman, British writers' exposure to the books and their generic expectations/restrictions was limited, whereas American children who were inclined to become comic-book creators had been inundated with the powerful imagery and storytelling of the Silver Age of American Comics. American popular culture at this time, especially that

Fig. 1: Writer: Alan Moore Artists: Steve Bissette & John Totleben "Swamped"
Collected in *The Saga of the Swamp Thing* [©1983 DC Comics]

targeted at the young, was rife with the simple redemptive violence fantasies purveyed by both Marvel and DC comics. The big two comic publishing houses flourished in the wake of Stan Lee's re-invigoration of the comic medium with his work at Marvel. In the meantime, television had discovered the superhero and increased saturation level of this narrative form. Youngsters simply could not grow up in America in the mid-'60s through the mid-'70s without being very familiar with the superhero and all for which he stood.

Swamp Thing soon ran into trouble with the American version of the Harmful Publications Act, the Comics Code Authority (CCA). The CCA began to object to images and themes that were appearing in the books. "DC soon decided that the quality of *Swamp Thing* justified its continued publication without interference from the Comics Code. The label "Mature Readers" was eventually affixed, and the way was opened for an entire line of sophisticated comic books" (Daniels 161).

Karen Berger, who was to become editor of the Vertigo line of books credits Moore with laying the foundation for the eventual boom of British horror comics in the U.S.: "I think Alan was the first writer in mainstream comics who was writing for adults. ... He was writing a horror comic, but one with lots of humanity and soul" (Daniels 161).

Moore continued breaking the barriers of the genre when, in 1986, DC published *Watchmen*. *Watchmen* won nationwide notice and was reviewed in most national periodicals and newspapers.

> In *Watchmen* Moore posits the existence of costumed superheroes in the real world ... subtexts of the genre that stand revealed when placed in a realistic setting: the role of violence in determining a hero's purpose, the sexual energy overtly exhibited while simultaneously (even paradoxically) sublimated, the profound changes wrought upon a world by the existence of even a single super-powered being, etc. While doing so, Moore frustrates expectations at every turn, playing by the genre's rules only to the point where he can gain the most insight by altering the expected outcome. (Tice 50)

Although disguised as a superhero comic, *Watchmen*'s characters, motifs, and themes are all clearly taken from the Gothic horror genre. *Watchmen*'s plot centers around an unspeakable beast that has the power to destroy humanity. The main characters included a madman (Rorschach), a man whose humanity was destroyed by science (Dr. Manhattan), and a character who is a clear reference to the Jekyll/Hyde archetype (Ozymandius). Twisted around the primary plot, in a complementary plot that is a nod to both *The Rime of the Ancient Mariner* and EC Comics, is a tale of shipwrecked pirates who must fend off sharks and cannibalism. As a twelve-issue miniseries *Watchmen* pushed the development of the comic book in a new direction. "In its moral and structural complexity, *Watchmen* is the equivalent of a novel, and it remains a major event in the evolution of comic books"(Daniels 197).

ENTER DREAM. As a result of the success of *Swamp Thing*, DC president Jenette Kahn appointed Karen Berger DC's British liaison. Berger immediately hired freelance writer and former journalist Neil Gaiman to write a miniseries revamping DC's little known Silver Age heroine, Black Orchid. As a result, Neil Gaiman had achieved his childhood dream and had the opening to reshape the face of the comic book.

> Writing American comic books was Gaiman's childhood goal, much to the distress of his school's career adviser. "He said, `Well, how do you go about doing that, then?' And I said, `You're the careers adviser, you tell me.' And there was a long pause and at the end of it he said, `Have you ever thought about accountancy?' And I said, `No, I have never thought about accountancy.' And then we sat there staring at each other and I said, `Shall I send the next boy in?' And he said, `Yes, you may as well.' As far as careers advice and planning goes, that was mine."
>
> Fascinated as he was by American comics, Gaiman "never wanted to do the things that people had been doing with them," he said. "The problem with a lot of American comics writers is that they've grown up reading comics and nothing else." Gaiman set his sights higher. (Covert)

One of the reasons that Gaiman's sights are higher than those of his contemporaries is that he was a voracious reader as a young man. As Gaiman explains, "I was a reader. My parents would frisk me before family events. Before weddings, funerals, bar mitzvahs, and what have you. Because if they didn't, then the book would be hidden inside some pocket or other and as soon as whatever it was got underway I'd be found in a corner. That was who I was — that was what I did. I was the kid with the book" (White).

Gaiman claims that his early reading habits were critical to his development as an author because

> books encountered in childhood serve as the richest compost for whatever an author creates as an adult. He read H.P. Lovecraft, Michael Moorcock, T.H. White. (His children read Gaiman, which is a bit scary.) There is in his work, and even in his speaking voice, a kind of once-upon-a-time rhythm of enchantment; if he is not, perhaps, the most effective poet, the poetry of the fable lives in his prose. (Sutton)

Gaiman also admits being influenced by such authors as C.S. Lewis, Samuel R. Delaney, Harlan Ellison, and Roger Zelazny (Austin). Gaiman's reading background schooled him in the rich literary traditions of (primarily) British authors whose work challenged the reader by treating them as intellectual equals rather than patronizing the readership as does some popular culture. The work of the authors, and the narrative expectations of the British comics Gaiman read shaped his work into a form that was more literate, more intelligent, and distinctly British. As a result, Gaiman's work has always been more than the standard comicbook fare created by his American contemporaries. Where American comics tend to feature one-dimensional characters in shallow plots where violence trumps intelligence — and, if recent trends at publishers like Image hold true, images trump words, Gaiman's work reflects the literary tradition in that the characters are more fully developed and the plots are rife with meaning and symbolism.

Gaiman's unique vision was brought to comics courtesy of Alan Moore. Gaiman had been handpicked by Moore to replace him in Britain as the writer of *Marvelman*, and Gaiman credits Moore with leading him to comics: "What got me into comics was very much Alan Moore. The work he did for DC during the 1980s took comics places they had never gone before" (Daniels 206). As Gaiman told interviewer Brian Hibbs,

> because it was a medium that I loved. I'd read comics extensively as a kid, and wanted to write comics as a teenager. I drifted away in the late seventies when there was very little interesting to read. I would occasionally pick up and flip through a comic, then put it back down in disgust. Then one day in early '84 (or very late '83) I was on Victoria Station in London and they had a pile of comics at the newsagents, including *Swamp Thing*. It was a title that I had loved as a kid, so I picked it up, thumbed through it, and thought. "'ang on, this is literate, this is really interesting." But by this point I had a very deeply ingrained prejudice against comics, and put it back down. Over the next month or so I'd pick up the *Swamp Things*, flip through them, and put them back down again. And finally, I think it was *Swamp Thing* #28, I bought it and took it home with me, and that was that. I'd discovered Alan Moore, discovered what he was doing. I realized you could do work in comics that was as every bit as mature, and interesting, and exciting, as anything that was being done in mainstream fiction or in modern horror literature. It was like coming back to an old lover, and discovering that she was still beautiful. (Hibbs)

Gaiman and artist Dave McKean immediately picked up the renaissance where Moore had left off:

> In this tale [*Black Orchid*], something unanticipated happens. The man who has caught Black Orchid stands before her and says, "Hey, you know

something? I've read the comics ... I'm not going to lock you up in the basement before interrogating you ... then leave you alone to escape. That stuff is so dumb. But you know what I am going to do? I *am* going to kill you. *Now*." And then he does just what he has promised: He kills her — the woman who is the namesake of this book — in a brutal and unflinching manner. It is a startling moment ... because, in those moments when the killer tells Black Orchid that he understands how the rules of the super hero genre work, he isn't merely addressing an endangered heroine of a comic book drama: He is also addressing the readers of that genre in ways that we have rarely been addressed before. In effect, in this one moment the killer is a stand-in voice for the writer of this tale, Neil Gaiman, and he is informing us all that the familiar rules of comic book storytelling — all those rules that insure the hard-earned triumph and inevitability of justice — will not apply in this narrative. Enter this story, the author is saying, and you enter a place where all the accepted customs of the genre's mythology have been suspended, and a new mythology — much closer to the dark dreams and darker realities of modern-day life — is about to be constructed. In other words, we are not only at the beginning of a new story, we are at the beginning of a new *way* of telling such a story. (Gilmore)

While Gaiman was working on *Black Orchid*, DC began to get cold feet about investing so much in a book headlined by a female character. So Gaiman and Berger discussed their options. Gaiman characterized the discussion in this manner:

When Karen asked what I wanted to do next, I had suggested a *Sandman* graphic novel, featuring the old Simon and Kirby 1970s incarnation because there were a few things that I thought were really interesting. I liked the idea of a character who lived in dreams, who had no objective existence. So, later, she said, "Well what about that Sandman idea?" I said, Okay. She said, "Great, but make it a new one...." So I sat around for a few days just thinking. Trying to put together a character who could exist in the DC universe, which is what they wanted, and who would satisfy me. The kind of character I'd like to read about. Who could exist in a book that wouldn't be a "monster of the month" book. It wouldn't be a superhero book. It wouldn't be predictable. It would just go off wherever it wanted to go off, so I could write whatever sort of stories I wanted to write. So I figured I should just reduce it to the basics, and what I got when I reduced it to the basics was Dream. (Amado)

Gaiman's re-interpretation of the book was thorough:

> Now, the original Sandman, in the late thirties and forties, was a kind of
> Batman Lite. Millionaire Wesley Dodds, at night, would put on gas mask,
> fedora, and cape, hunt down bad guys, and zap them with his gas gun,
> leaving them to sleep until the cops picked them up the next morning
> — hardly the stuff of legend. So what Gaiman did was jettison virtually
> everything except the title. The Sandman — childhood's fairy who comes
> to put you to sleep, the bringer of dreams, the Lord of Dreams, the Prince
> of Stories — indisputably the stuff of legend. (McConnell)

It is in those first few issues of *The Sandman* that it becomes evident that Gaiman is not
playing by the same rules as anyone else. In fact, he's not even operating in the same horror universe as anyone else. One of the most poignant changes early on is his ability to take
flat stock characters from the DC universe and turn them into fully rounded characters that
become critical to the overall narrative he is spinning. A prime example of this are the characters of Cain and Abel, once relegated to the minor role of introducing DC's horror anthology
House of Secrets. Gaiman takes the pair and, in the space of a few panels, makes the reader care
about them and their continued plight. Gaimain does this by tying these characters to one
of the strongest mythic structures in the horror genre: the light/dark allegory. While this is
a simple metaphor to abuse, Gaiman utilizes it so deftly that instead of merely asking the
audience to despise the evil Cain, Gaiman leaves the reader in a more literate, complicated
space of pitying both Cain and Abel. [*Fig. 2*]

Gaiman also stays true to his Gothic horror roots. His realm of dreams and the waking
world are both filled with monsters of all sorts including some very human monsters. Terror
lurks in every shadow and something growls beneath every bed. What sets Gaiman's work
apart from the mountains of schlock is that he is entering a relationship with the reader. Instead of being a "monster of the month" book, Gaiman's work utilizes the tropes and motifs
of the Gothic horror genre. Gaiman himself admits to consciously adapting his work to the
strictures of this genre:

> There was a definite effort on my part, in the stories in this volume [*Pre-
> ludes and Nocturnes* which collects issues 1-8] to explore the genres avail-
> able: "The Sleep of the Just" was intended to be a classical English horror
> story; "Imperfect Hosts" plays with some of the conventions of the
> old DC and EC horror comics (and the hosts thereof); "Dream a Little
> Dream of Me" is a slightly more contemporary British horror story; "A
> Hope in Hell" harks back to the kind of dark fantasy found in *Unknown* in

Fig. 2: Writer: Neil Gaiman Artists: Sam Keith & Mike Dringenberg "Imperfect Hosts"
Collected in *The Sandman: Preludes & Nocturnes* [©1995 DC Comics]

the 1940s; ... (Gaiman)

In the first few issues of the series, Gaiman utilizes motifs such as the *ubi sunt* theme, a favorite of the Graveyard School of poets, which laments the transitory nature of life. (Murfin and Ray 412) He also provides readers with a rich tapestry of such gothic horror elements as the focus on decay (both architectural and physical), the supernatural, and the grotesque. Yet he does this in a very literate manner, relying as much on creating horror in the blank space between comic panels, and thus in the reader's mind, as he does on the artist's work within the panels themselves to flesh out the horror created by Gaiman's use of language. Gaiman respects the reader's intelligence, and he tests the very limits of that intelligence.

Gaiman's creation was, clearly, not from the mold of the spandex-clad heroes that made up the bulk of DC's production. In fact, *The Sandman* was such a departure from the norm that Gaiman expected a short life for his creation: "The biggest thing that I actually hoped for was to become a mild critical success. Bear in mind that this is 1987, when a critical success and a commercial failure were synonymous. I had sort of planned this huge, arching epic, but what I also expected was that we would be cancelled right off" (Savlov). Gaiman says that, when the book was not canceled, it financially came into its own with issue number eight: "I was very surprised when 'round about issue eight we were selling more than any horror comic had ever sold. I mean we were selling more than *Swamp Thing* had ever sold. We were selling more than any comic of that kind in the previous five years had sold, and that was astonishing" (Vaughn 58-9).

He also says that issue eight marked the point when he began to find his own voice as a writer:

> Just doing a story in which the Sandman and Death wandered around
> New York, and nothing happened ... I don't know. It was probably the
> first "Neil Gaiman" story. The other seven, you know, they're very com-
> petent, but you can look at them and you can see where they came from.
> You can see me doing Alan Moore, you can see me doing various other
> things. I think issue eight was the first issue that started to sound like
> me. (Vaughn 59)

What does a Gaiman story sound like? To begin with, it assumes the reader is intelligent. "I wanted to write a comic for intelligent people. I don't understand why people write down. Who are they writing down to?" (Daniels 206). Bryan Talbot, who worked on a number of issues of *Sandman*, points to the intelligent writing as the key to the book's success:

> In earlier publishing, where 95% of the titles concerned one guy in tights
> hitting another guy in tights, it definitely brought intelligence. It wasn't

the only one to do that, but I think that was one of the main things it did ... Neil created something new. That's quite a big thing in comics. It was something that nobody's done in the comic form before. The character was very different than any other character in comics. The whole sort of world that Neil created to go with it was quite unique. (Vaughn 64)

DC's Executive Editor [at the time], Dick Giordano, describes Gaiman's contribution to comics as a "writer's vision" (Vaughn 65). Giordano says that it is this writer's vision that led to the book's success:

Because it was offbeat, because the writer's viewpoint never changed. Because he dealt with whatever subject matter tickled his fancy for that moment so that, unlike most superhero books where you pretty much have a pretty good idea what this new storyline is going to be about after you have read the first four or five pages, you really couldn't tell with a Neil Gaiman story where it was going. Sometimes Neil didn't know where it was going. (Vaughn 65)

Giordano argues that Gaiman's writer's vision brought about not only more intelligent books but brought an entirely new audience into comic-book shops:

We have a considerable amount of proof that the people who buy most of her [Karen Berger's Vertigo line] books, especially *Sandman,* don't buy other comic books. [They] aren't regular comic book readers who happen to get off on the *Sandman,* but people who went to get *Sandman* because they heard about it and they hadn't been buying comics before. (Vaughn 65)

After seventy-five issues, *The Sandman* has become a comics legend. How great is the legend? Well, Robert Wilonsky tried to sum it up in a mid-2000 issue of the *Dallas Observer:*

Not long ago, a journalist asked Neil Gaiman how he feels about the fact that, despite his large body of work — novels, comics, children's books, short stories, and so forth — he will be remembered solely for *Sandman.* Gaiman sneers at the question, but it's not an entirely unfair one, and he knows it. After all, *Sandman* was a hit almost from the moment the first issue, *Preludes & Nocturnes,* reached the stands in December 1988. Even now, its bound collections — 10 in all — continue to rank among the best sellers in DC Comics' adult-oriented Vertigo offshoot, of which *Sandman* was the charter member.

The series spawned gushing praise: Norman Mailer wrote that it was a "comic strip for intellectuals, and it's about time." Tori Amos, whose songs often reference Gaiman, treats The Endless — the family of time-less gods who personify such forces as Death, Destiny, Desire, and, of course, Dreams — as though they exist in this world. ("On bad days I talk to Death constantly," she wrote in the introduction to 1994's collec-tion *Death: The High Cost of Living*.) The title won more awards than are given for comics; it was treated, in fact, like literature, as though it were too special to be included among the panels-and-balloons riffraff. In Sep-tember, DC will publish the paperback version of *The Sandman Companion*, a nearly 300-page book that explains every panel; no comic book ever received such elucidation. (Wilonsky)

The Sandman proved to be a unique and groundbreaking voice in the comic-book industry.

Gaiman's landmark contribution is "Sandman." It is one of the great-est stories in the history of the medium in terms of size (2,500 pages and 2 million words) and sophistication. The intricately interconnected tales concern Morpheus, lord of dreams, as he visits historical characters, mythical deities and creatures of his creator's prodigious imagination. Those include a hack named William Shakespeare who makes a dreadful bargain for genius; a man determined to live forever; the disembodied head of Orpheus begging for the release of death, a writer who keeps his battered muse locked in the attic and a murderers' convention whose guest of honor consumes his victims' eyes. (Covert)

In the wake of *Swamp Thing* and *The Sandman*, the Vertigo line has seen such British cre-ators as Garth Ennis and Grant Morrison found wildly popular titles. And now, American writers and creators who were raised on *Swamp Thing* and *Sandman*, like Steven T. Seagle, have begun producing Americanized versions of the British horror-comic form. Each of these "second generation" horror-comic creators are producing works that are highly literate and true to their gothic horror roots.

CONCLUSION. The development of the modern horror-comic genre owes a great deal to the cross-pollination of literary culture between Britain and America. From its earliest incarnation as a Penny Dreadful, to the Silver Age peak of the EC Horror Comics and their British reprints, to the modern line of Vertigo Horror comics, this genre has taken roots and formats from British literary tradition, applied a certain amount of American packaging and formalization, and created an art form that exceeds the sum of its parts.

Had British comic writers been exposed to the heavily formulaic American superhero comics as status quo rather than as rare import, it seems unlikely that Moore, Gaiman, and such contemporaries as Garth Ennis and Grant Morrison would have provided such a fresh and insightful approach to a rather old and tired genre.

Therefore, in one of those odd coincidences, the Harmful Publications Act, which was created in the wake of the success of EC's line of American horror comics in Britain, actually has served to protect young British minds — but not so much from exposure to the "harmful and dangerous" ideas and images of the genre. Instead, by protecting the young British minds from stereotyped American comic books, the Act allowed the modern version of this genre to blossom. Blossom it has. The Vertigo line is DC's second best-selling line of comics (only the Batman-Superman family of books outsells them). Gaiman and Moore's works have been recognized by the comic industry and the general publishing industry with numerous awards. *Sandman* has become such a popular culture phenomenon that it has spawned at least four spin-off titles (*The Endless: Books of the Dreaming, Death, Lucifer,* and *Books of Magic*). Popular musicians have recorded songs about either the book or its characters. A *Sandman* movie has been rumored, and Gaiman has embarked on a successful career as a novelist: writing modern gothic horror novels.

One of the common themes in both *Sandman* and *Swamp Thing* (as well as many of the EC titles) is karma and the endless cyclical nature of existence. Perhaps, then, it should be of little surprise that the Vertigo books are becoming increasingly popular in Britain. What goes around …

WORKS CITED.

"Alan Moore Fan Site: Biography." http:alanmoorefansite.com/olc__site/bio/index.html 9/16/00

Amado, Alex. "Following His Dream: Neil Gaiman talks about his past, present and future as a storyteller." http://www.maths.tcd.ie/~afarrell/things/interview.html 9/16/00

Austin. Jonathan D. "Neil Gaiman: Adults deserve good fairy-tales too." *CNN Interactive* http://www.cnn.com/books/news/9902/25/gaiman.neil/ 25 February 1999

Barker, Martin. *A Haunt of Fears: The Strange Story of the British Horror Comics Campaign.* Jackson, MS: University Press of Mississippi, 1984.

"The Barry Ono collection of penny dreadfuls." The British Library's Online Information Server. http://www.bl.uk/collections/epic/onweb.html› 7/11/00

Covert, Colin. "The Dream King." http://www.hollycow.com/dreaming/lore/article__ 01.html

Cuddon, J. A. *The Penguin Dictionary of Literary Terms and Literary Theory.* London: Penguin, 1991.

Daniels, Les. *DC Comics: Sixty Years of the World's Favorite Comic Book Heroes.* Boston: Bullfinch Press, 1995.

Eury, Michael. "Inside DC (21): Screaming at the Screen." *Outlaws*, 8 April 1992, np.

Gaiman, Neil. "Afterword." In *The Sandman: Preludes and Nocturnes*. NY: DC Comics, 1991, np.

Gilmore, Mikal. "Introduction." In *Black Orchid*. NY: DC Comics, 1991, np.

Gore, Matthew H. "The Origin of Marvelman." http://www.geocities.com/Hollywood/Hills/6569-marvelman/ 9/18/00

Goulart, Ron. *Over 50 Years of American Comic Books*. Lincolnwood, IL: Mallard, 1991.

Hibbs, Brian. "Gaiman Interview with Brian Hibbs." http://www.holycow.com/dreaming/lore/interview1.html

Holland, Steve. "One Small Step." http://www.dalmatia.net/lupic/dandare/mthrfam/step.htm 9/18/00

Humphreys, Brian. "MM – The Original Big Blue." http://www.marvelman.freeservers.com/page3.html 3/28/05

Inge, M. Thomas. *Comics as Culture*. Jackson, MS: University Press of Mississippi, 1990.

McConnell, Frank. "Preface." In *Sandman: Book of Dreams*, ed. Neil Gailman and Ed Kramer. NY: HarperCollins, 1996.

Murfin, Ross and Supryia M. Ray. *The Bedford Glossary of Critical and Literary Terms*. Boston, MA: Bedford, 1997.

Murphy, B. Keith. "Apocalyptic Pop: Judge Dredd and the British View of American Cultural Decay." Presented at the Southern Conference on British Studies/ Carolinas Symposium on British Studies, 13 November 1998.

Perry, George, and Alan Aldridge. *The Penguin Book of Comics*. London: Penguin, 1989.

Savlov, Marc. "A Sort of Legend." *The Austin Chronicle*, http://www.austinchronicle.com/issues/dispatch/1999-09-10/books__feature.html 10 September 1999

Sutton, Terri. "Once Upon a Time." *City Pages*, http://www.citypages.com/databank/20/944/article6924.asp) nd.

Tice, Steven. "Botched? I Think Not." *Musings*, May 1993, 50 - 51. "The Top 100: The Most Important Comics of All Time." *Hero Illustrated: Special Edition*. May, 1994.

Vaughn, J. C. "Dreams." *Fan*, January 1996, 58 - 67.

White, Claire E. "A Conversation with Neil Gaiman." *Writers Write*. http://www.writerswrite.com/journal/mar99/gaiman.htm March 1999, 19-39.

White, Ted. "The Spawn of M.C. Gaines." In *All in Color for a Dime*, ed. Dick Lupoff and Don Thompson. Iola, WI: Krause Publications, 1997.

Wilonsky, Robert. "DreamWeaver." *Dallas Observer*, 7 July 2000. http://www.dalasobserver.com/issues/2000-07-20/stuff.html

⚜ ⚜ ⚜

OF STORYTELLERS AND
STORIES IN GAIMAN AND VESS'S
"A MIDSUMMER NIGHT'S DREAM"

by Joe Sanders

✦

In 1990, when "A Midsummer Night's Dream" (AMND) appeared in the nineteenth issue of *The Sandman*, Neil Gaiman was seeing how far the comics' medium would stretch to fit difficult subjects. About half-way through the script that he was about to e-mail to artist Charles Vess, Gaiman paused to make the following half-joking, half-serious comment:

> This is a really fascinating comic to write. I mean, ei-
> ther it'll work really well, or it'll be a major disaster. Not
> just a disaster. I mean people will talk about this in the
> list of great interesting failures forever. They'll say things
> like "Cor! You call *The Hulk Versus the Thing in Three-Dee Pop-
> Up Graphic Novel with Free Song-Book* an interesting failure?
> You should have been there when Gaiman and Vess made

idiots of themselves on *Sandman!*" Or, like I say, it may work. (It's a million-to-one shot but it might just work.) (Script 16)[1]

As it tuned out, the story was extremely successful, convincing many people — even, briefly, the judges for the World Fantasy Award — that comics have potential for real accomplishment. It's worth examining, therefore, both to show some of the ways Gaiman and Vess together made the story work and also to consider what Gaiman was trying to say that utilized the comics medium so thoroughly and so well.

The story's surface action is deceptively simple: The Sandman is one of The Endless, supernatural beings who represent basic categories of human thought. The Sandman is the lord of dreams and he has made a bargain with William Shakespeare to write two plays on demand. In return, Shakespeare has been given access to the great stories he can turn into other plays.[2] Shakespeare and his acting company have been summoned to perform the first commissioned play, *A Midsummer Night's Dream* (*AMND*), in 1593 at the foot of a hill in the Sussex downs for the Sandman and his invited guests, the king and queen of fairies and their retinue.

With Auberon, Titania, Puck, and the other fairies watching their impersonators perform, one potentially confusing aspect of AMND is keeping track of different aspects of the action. Gaiman comments to Vess that "it's a little like choreography, holding it all together, since the action is occurring on four levels: backstage, on stage, with the front row, and back in the peanut gallery" (Script 10). He later adds, as events gather momentum within the same setting, "Okay, we're looking at Burbage, playing Auberon, and Puck, playing the actor playing Puck. (Oh God this is getting complicated. Welcome to Infinite Mirror Comics"(Script 22).

Obviously, the "levels of action" Gaiman is concerned about are not simply locations but elements of the story. Another way to try separating different concerns is by moving from apparently minor to larger aspects. One small part of the story is the play within a play, *Pyramus and Thisbe*, which the uncouth villagers rehearse and perform for the aristocrats' amusement. Gaiman would dispute, however, whether the "rude mechanicals" are a minor element since he describes the scene in which Bottom awakens after his enchantment as "in some ways, the core of the play" (Script 24). In any event, surrounding that portion of the play is the main action with its complex echoing of passions and schemes. Enfolding the play-as-written is the drama of its first performance, which depends on the interacting personalities of Shakespeare and his cohorts. In addition, the fairy folk and the Sandman do not watch passively but incessantly react to and comment on the play and actors. [*Fig. 1*] Finally, of course, readers respond throughout the spectacle, both awed and exasperated by Shakespeare, alternately intimidated by and pitying the Sandman.

As these attempts to separate "levels" in the story show, the levels resist separation. They *want* to blur into each other, smearing together roles, personalities, and motives, so that we see the same human concerns from different angles, in different shapes. Even so, especially

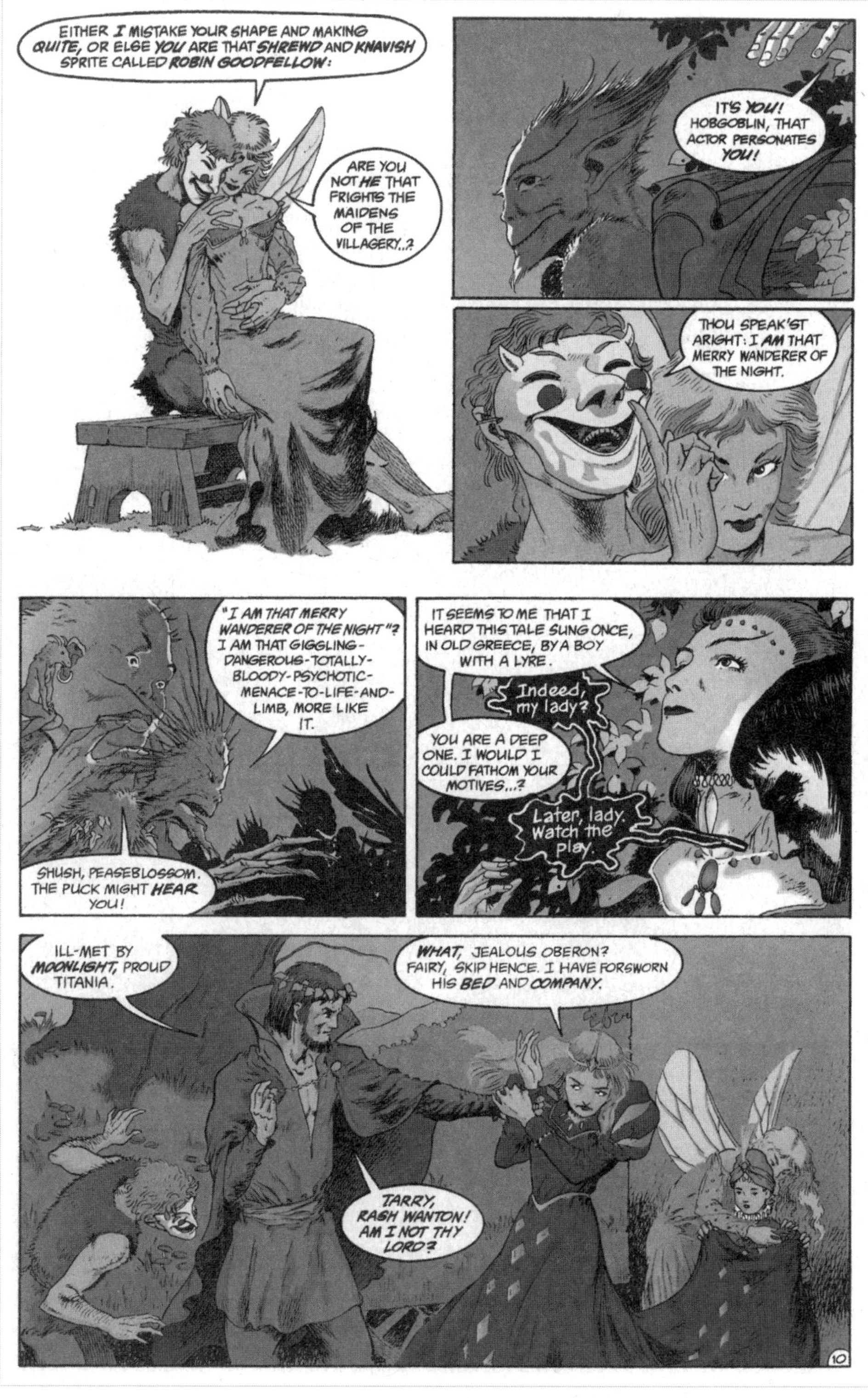
EITHER I MISTAKE YOUR SHAPE AND MAKING QUITE, OR ELSE YOU ARE THAT SHREWD AND KNAVISH SPRITE CALLED ROBIN GOODFELLOW:
ARE YOU NOT HE THAT FRIGHTS THE MAIDENS OF THE VILLAGERY..?
IT'S YOU! HOBGOBLIN, THAT ACTOR PERSONATES YOU!
THOU SPEAK'ST ARIGHT: I AM THAT MERRY WANDERER OF THE NIGHT.
"I AM THAT MERRY WANDERER OF THE NIGHT"? I AM THAT GIGGLING-DANGEROUS-TOTALLY-BLOODY-PSYCHOTIC-MENACE-TO-LIFE-AND-LIMB, MORE LIKE IT.
SHUSH, PEASEBLOSSOM. THE PUCK MIGHT HEAR YOU!
IT SEEMS TO ME THAT I HEARD THIS TALE SUNG ONCE, IN OLD GREECE, BY A BOY WITH A LYRE.
Indeed, my lady?
YOU ARE A DEEP ONE. I WOULD I COULD FATHOM YOUR MOTIVES...?
Later, lady. Watch the play.
ILL-MET BY MOONLIGHT, PROUD TITANIA.
WHAT, JEALOUS OBERON? FAIRY, SKIP HENCE. I HAVE FORSWORN HIS BED AND COMPANY.
TARRY, RASH WANTON! AM I NOT THY LORD?
10

Fig. 1: Writer: Neil Gaiman Artist: Charles Vess "A Midsummer Night's Dream"
Collected in *The Sandman: Dream Country* [©1995 DC Comics]

while the play is being performed, readers need to appreciate the original separateness of elements that strongly resemble each other. Realizing this, Gaiman attempts to indicate clear separation of parts in his instructions/suggestions to Vess: Each page should have long, horizontal panels at the top and bottom to contain whatever is happening onstage; the middle of the page can thus be used for four panels "focusing on other areas of the action" (Script 11). Moreover, responding to his editor's comments on an earlier draft of the script, Gaiman suggests "putting a heavier black border around each panel set on the stage to indicate, almost subliminally, that these are discrete units" (Script 12). He leaves final decisions up to Vess, however, as the artist who must actually turn the script into a comics story.[3]

In the published story, Vess uses Gaiman's suggested layout briefly as the play begins, on pages 8 and 9. Even here, though, the discrete units are escaping their boundaries. On page 8, panel 2 is superimposed on panel 3. To a lesser extent, panels 1, 4, and 5 also intrude over the upper and lower edges of the page. On page 9, actors are performing in the borderless panel 4, not just in the horizontal panels at top and bottom — which, with Gaiman's encouragement, show not only what's happening in the performance onstage but also action behind the backdrops (which themselves resemble overlapping comics panels), along with a *from*-backstage view of the fairy audience responding to Bottom's clowning.

The next two pages virtually abandon the static layout that was intended to help readers keep track of the story's momentary focus. Page 10 uses a horizontal panel at the bottom; page 11 has one at the top. But what might have been one long onstage panel at the top of page 10 is interrupted by Auberon's offstage comment to Puck, while a long vertical panel on the right side of page 11 replaces a long horizontal one at the bottom containing stage action. Even while he was suggesting how to keep readers from becoming confused, Gaiman observed that "I think they'll be able to cope" (Script 12), and a verbal description of the unfinished pages is more confusing than they are themselves when seen. Vess is able to use other devices besides panel layout to avoid confusion.

One such device is the depiction of characters themselves, how "realistic" they appear. Gaiman's directions stress the otherworldliness of the Sandman and of Auberon, Titania, Puck, and the other fairies. Vess's art intensifies that strangeness, so that combinations and exaggerations of physical features clearly separate fairies from humans, even actors in costume. We know where we are by recognizing whom we're seeing.

Another device Vess uses to help readers recognize discrete units is his choice of color, both in kind and intensity.[4] Onstage scenes are in bright, lively colors, apparently viewed by daylight; this includes scenes that emphasize the painted canvas backdrops, wagons, and other evidence that we are watching a performance of a play, not real-life action. This color scheme indicates which portions of the story are occurring in this world. In the front stage, however, the colors grow darker and the atmosphere dimmer.[5] As Titania tells Hamnet Shakespeare during the play's intermission, "There is no night in *my* land, pretty boy, and it is forever summer's twilight"(AMND 16). Scenes in the royal arbor or further back in the crowd of fairies are immediately recognizable by this different color scheme.

In addition, Vess adds his own elements of design to vary pages' layout while keeping areas of action distinct. On page 11, where the lively-colored onstage panels butt into each other and might simply merge,[6] the onstage Titania's speech balloon in the top panel swirls down and to the left, to meet the genuine Titania's words in the top of four panels that focus on the Sandman and the fairy queen. Thereafter, the curving light areas in the faces of Titania and the Sandman, along with her white word balloons, draw readers' eyes from side to side and down rather than across the page. When the bottom of the page is reached, then our eyes are released back to the vertical panel at the right. Titania's last query, bottom left, also directs our attention back to the play's action, and her remark at the bottom right actually completes the page's content. [*Fig. 2*]

Vess appears to have felt that Gaiman was being overanxious, that there were other ways to separate things that needed to be apprehended separately — and that, in fact, it would be a mistake to keep aspects of the play absolutely separate. In this, he justified Gaiman's willingness to trust the artist's intelligence, for Vess was responding to and serving faithfully the spirit of a script, in which roles, personalities, and motives reflect and fold into each other. Late in his script, Gaiman describes "probably the key scene in the dream" as follows:

> Bottom, with ass's head, now twined with flowers, and looking less like
> an artificial thing than it did before, is lying with his head in Titania's lap.
> She is stroking his hair and snout, gazing lovingly at him. To the side the
> fairies stand — young actors, and androgynously pretty. While they're
> still on the grassy stage, it's now as if some subtle glamour has come over
> them — possibly because they're now acting with Puck, and all of them
> look a little more like the real thing than they did before. (Script 23)

The description of this panel on page 18 is accurate. In fact, however, glamour has broken out earlier in Gaiman's script and Vess's art, before a supernatural presence could have caused it. On page 4, as the young actors begin to put on dresses and wigs, they are unquestionably male ("Condell will be Titania, but he currently looks like a short-haired boy pulling on a dress"), but then they don the costume, turn away, and are transformed when we next see them ("Condell has turned his back to us, his wig flowing, looking a lot more female than he did before") (Script 6). Somewhat later, in the first panel of page 10, we are startled to see the actor Puck entwined very physically with a convincingly female fairy. We *know* that the fairy actually must be a boy actor, but what we see of her face and body contradicts our certainty. Gaiman's directions emphasize this contradiction. His directions identify the figure as "the actor playing the fairy" but add, "I imagine the fairy as a female, and the way I tend to imagine this scene is as a fairly erotic one — as a pick up, and a flirtation" (Script 13). And so it is. Offstage, the real sex of an actor playing a female role reappears when he is shaken by

Fig. 2: Writer: Neil Gaiman Artist: Charles Vess "A Midsummer Night's Dream"
Collected in *The Sandman: Dream Country* [©1995 DC Comics]

noticing the non-human audience and thus falls out of character (AMND 9). [*Fig. 3*] Onstage he becomes what the play and the audience need him to be.

Besides costumes and makeup, "glamour" tends to transform the actual masks the actors wear.[7] The prop ass's head is an inert, "artificial" object on page 13 only until it is donned. At that moment, the mouth begins to show expression, and the eyes on its face no longer belong to the man wearing it; they are in the wrong place and of the wrong size to be anything other than the donkey eyes of Bottom-the-transformed.

Note also that, although Puck and the fairy are seated on a bench that reasonably could have come from one of the wagons of the touring actors, they are not shown against the painted backdrop. There is no background, and the panel has no borders. Vess creates a new, distinct space for moments when the play becomes real.

Such moments, in which an artificially constructed thing comes to life, are the core of AMND. Gaiman knows, as his frequent reminders to Vess show, that the female characters in the play are actually boys. However, Gaiman realizes that the actors will be transformed before the audience realizes what is happening, in the same way that props come alive and action escapes the limits of the stage. Or, to put it another way, people in the audience somehow will not notice that *they* are creating the magic called art. It is hard to imagine any artistic medium better than comics for demonstrating this transformation. If seeing is believing, then we accept that what we see is true. Comics thus show us one truth after another, panel by panel, sometimes presenting alternative, even contradictory truths next to each other. The reader puts them together and decides what to believe. According to Scott McCloud's *Understanding Comics*, the essential quality of comics is this ability to involve an audience in relating separate panels into a coherent, significant whole (65 ff.). In "A Midsummer Night's Dream," incompatible realities merge, different truths overlap, long-established categories redefine themselves according to momentary desires. We see this happening in Vess's art. We even participate in the process. And so Vess's playing with reality effectively presents the major concern of AMND: How is it that we find ourselves telling stories — and why do we bother?

AMND shows that using the imagination this way is natural, satisfying, and necessary.

It is, first of all, natural for people to involve themselves in the process of storytelling. Some people who consider themselves realists would object that anything that plays with facts can be ignored. Gaiman and Vess's AMND shows that they are wrong. Toward the end of the production of *AMND*, supposedly hardheaded realist Theseus (played, ironically, by Shakespeare himself) compares madmen, lovers, and poets:

> I never may believe these antique fables, nor these fairy toys. Lovers and madmen have such seething brains … The lunatic, the lover, and the poet are of imagination all compact. One sees more devils than vast hell can hold. That is the madman. The lover, all as frantic, sees Helen's beauty in

Fig. 3: Writer: Neil Gaiman Artist: Charles Vess "A Midsummer Night's Dream"
Collected in *The Sandman: Dream Country* [©1995 DC Comics]

> a brow of Egypt. The poet's eye, in a fine frenzy rolling, doth glance from
> heaven to earth, from earth to heaven. And, as imagination bodies forth
> the forms of things unknown ... The poet's pen turns them to shapes,
> and gives to airy nothing a local habitation and a name (AMND 20).

His comparison is scarcely to the advantage of artists, since it is unclear whether they control the creative process or are overpowered by it. When Hippolyta later dismisses the presentation of *Pyramus and Thisbe* as "the silliest stuff that I ever heard," Theseus further damns storytelling with faint praise: "The best in this kind are but shadows; and the worst are no worse if imagination amend them" (AMND 21). But this does not mean that Theseus shuns poets' productions. Remember: He is sneering at unrealistic storytelling while voluntarily watching a good play. He appears to be a regular enough theatergoer to tell bad from good drama, even if he doesn't know what to think of the latter.

Moreover, Shakespeare's play shows the importance most people do place on the forms imagination gives to airy nothings. Bottom is just a silly bumpkin; still, as Gaiman notes, he also is a meaningful, tragic figure at the moment he awakens from his enchantment and recognizes that he has become only himself again. Shakespeare himself, as Gaiman pictures him, has chosen to be enchanted by his art. He eagerly made his bargain with the Sandman and will pay more attention to the stories he is telling in his plays than to the people around him. His eight-year-old son, Hamnet sadly recognizes the truth of a family joke: that Shakespeare would react to the death if his own son by writing a play: *Hamnet* (AMND 13).

Hamnet's small joke (and the fact that he can joke about his own death) illustrates the second reason we are drawn to storytelling and other art: the satisfaction of apprehending something new. Readers of AMND understand that Hamnet Shakespeare *will* die in a few years and that in reaction William Shakespeare *will* write *Hamlet*. This insight into Shakespeare's obsessed creative thinking is shocking but also somehow satisfying; we feel we have learned something important enough to outweigh our sympathy with the turmoil Hamnet feels and his father avoids. We somehow are able to find pleasure in contemplating even unpleasant subjects when they have been transformed into art. And this satisfaction is not lessened for being discovered in a comics story.[8]

The fact that we naturally enjoy stories, even without appalling subjects, suggests how necessary art is in a frequently appalling world. The enduring, unresolvable paradox Gaiman and Vess present in "A Midsummer Night's Dream" is that stories simultaneously are about and not about how we live in this world. Hardheaded realists, as Theseus imagines himself to be, distrust imagination when it asks to be taken seriously while going beyond familiar, distinct, particular reality. Such "realists" nevertheless attend plays because they sense that real objects don't last and don't reveal their meaning. Consequently, humans feel the need to generalize beyond immediate, individual experience, and they are also aware (however dimly and unwillingly) that artists are not simply lying when they go a step farther to create a fictional reality on the other side of the generalizations. In the issue of *The Sandman* before AMND, an inquiring cat listens to one of the Sandman's creatures explaining the different levels of abstraction and their significance: "Wisdom is no *part of dreams* ..., though dreams are a part of the sum of each life's experiences, which is the *only* wisdom that matters. But *Revelation? That* is the province of dream" ("A Dream of a Thousand Cats" 11). In other words, generalizing gives some limited understanding (wisdom), but one must recreate anew to achieve fuller awareness (revelation). Gaining understanding of what reality *means* comes only from dreams and the art that uses them.

Whatever the Sandman's overall motives (and they are complicated enough to need the entire seventy-five issue run of the magazine to reveal themselves) he recognizes the importance and at least part of the function of art. At least, he knows that art lasts longer than life, even if he isn't certain why that matters. Before the play, when Auberon says that the fairies were surprised to be invited because they supposed they "were quit of this plane forever," the Sandman replies "Is anything forever?" (AMND 6). Puck impolitely but accurately reminds him that he (and the other Endless) will endure "until the death of time itself" (AMND 6). In fact, the Sandman says much the same thing to Auberon and Titania near the end of the play to explain that he had this play written so that mortals will remember the faerie at least "until this age is gone" (AMND 21). Humans are terribly disturbed at how little life they have. During the play's intermission, Shakespeare is pleased at how well the performance is going and how well the play is working. "Not even Kit Marlowe will be able to gainsay that," he says (AMND 16). He is shocked at the Sandman's news that Marlowe has been killed: "He's standing there, on his own, hurt beyond measure, trying to pull himself together" (Script 21). The Sandman didn't realize how Shakespeare would react. Gaiman's directions indicate that "He's merely passing on a morsel of inconsequential gossip; after all, humans die all over the place, all the time, don't they?" (Script 21).

Awareness of their own impermanence ought, theoretically, to make humans not only hungry for something more than this temporary reality but also more careful of the people around them whom they have a temporary chance to care about. We have already seen that it does not, that Shakespeare's intense concentration on enduring human stories is accompanied by callousness toward his own son. Again, following his shock at Marlowe's death, Shakespeare becomes engrossed in the performance of the rest of the play. When Hamnet approaches his father to share the information that during the interlude Titania has been inviting him to leave this reality and go with the faerie, Shakespeare has no time for him. "Not now, child. I must see this," he says, staring at the stage (AMND 17).

Shakespeare is much to blame for ignoring Hamnet, especially since the readers are free to surmise that the boy's death a few years later is the result of his estrangement from his father and the temptation Titania offered of a happier world. Still, we cannot despise the man. For one thing, as Gaiman must be aware, we all have been conditioned to accept Shakespeare as the writer who speaks most enduringly for the greatest variety of human experience. For another, in AMND Gaiman is careful to make Shakespeare more uncertain than overbearing, just beginning to grasp the significance of his access to the great stories. We are encouraged to sympathize with him, even to identify with him. In fact, at the end of the play when Hamnet stares at his father from backstage, "staring at *us* [emphasis added] with longing, with love"(Script 26), Vess shows the boy gazing straight at the reader (AMND 20).

Our reaction to Gaiman's Shakespeare may also be conditioned by other Sandman stories published just before AMND. Two issues before, *The Sandman* had contained Gaiman's "Calliope," in which author Richard Madoc exploits one of the muses in order to get ideas for his second novel. The opening pages of that story encourage sympathy for Rick — he is, after all, a young man under a lot of pressure to live up to his reputation as a storyteller. But when he buys Calliope from an older writer and rapes her before sitting down to write, we realize that he cares only about himself and his fame, not the substance of his stories ("Calliope" 8). Eventually, the Sandman coldly judges the best-selling media star and appropriately punishes him with a torrent of ideas that cannot be developed fully into significant stories, a demonstration of what Rick was already doing in his career (19-21). On the other hand, the next issue of *The Sandman*, immediately before the one containing AMND, featured "A Dream of a Thousand Cats" in which cats realize that stories not only reflect but shape reality: Just as humans once chose to believe that they were superior to cats, if enough cats harmonize their dreams *they* can become dominant. In the context of these two stories, AMND presents Shakespeare as a relatively benign mortal dreamer. He does not write plays to accumulate fame and glory. Of course he wants recognition, especially from a fellow playwright like Marlowe, but his primary concern is with effectively telling one of the great stories. Even if he can be faulted for using people as means to that end, Shakespeare's goal is to bring the great stories to human awareness. He does not think of transforming the world, but he does cherish his ability to make his fellows more aware of themselves.

In this also, Shakespeare is someone with whom readers can sympathize, even identify. So is the Sandman. We may already be inclined to identify with the Sandman because he is, in McCloud's terms, an iconic character (42), whose depiction is stylized/nonspecific enough to make him a vessel for our personalities. Besides that, with his black costume, stern expression, and ominous speeches, he's breathtakingly *cool*. On the other hand, Gaiman shows enough of the Sandman's inhuman callousness to make him unsympathetic, and his directions to Vess also emphasize the character's distance from the reader (Script 1).

And yet, beyond these reactions, AMND shows the Sandman in the same familiar human predicament as Shakespeare. He may be the lord of dreams, but that does not mean he is in control of the process. Rather, he is also groping for understanding, trying to see beyond his personal limits in the only way an individual consciousness can: imagination; art. Following Bottom's fumbling attempt to grasp the content of his enchantment ("Methought I was … there is no *man* [Gaiman's emphasis] can tell what" [AMND 19]), the Sandman is driven to mediate:

> I wonder, Titania. I wonder if I have done right. And I wonder why I
> wonder. Will is a willing vehicle for the great stories. Through him they
> will live for an age of man; and his words will echo down through time. It
> is what he wanted.
>
> But he did not understand the price. Mortals never do. They only see
> the prize, their hearts desire, their dream ... But the price of getting what
> you want is getting what you once wanted.
>
> And had I told him? Had he understood? What then? It would have
> made no difference. Have I done right, Titania? Have I done right?
> (AMND 19)

He is serious, moreso than he realizes, since Gaiman's directions explain that "he's
asking her a question, trying to solve the problem of whether it's right to have ruined
Shakespeare's life, even though he doesn't know that's what he's done" (Script 25). Our first
impression of the Sandman, towering over Shakespeare (AMND 2), is of distant superiority.
He is vastly more powerful and knowledgeable than any human. His misjudging of Shakespeare's reaction to news of Marlowe's death, however, shows how ignorant he is of what
matters to humans, and he is only beginning to understand human morality and concern for
an individual as he asks whether he himself has done "right." Despite being one of the Endless, he is starting to reveal uneasiness about his unchangeable, rigid role that he has confused with personal identity. Whether one is a natural or supernatural being, "getting what
you want" means settling for the limits of a naïve understanding. One may wind up genu-
inely focused but nevertheless narrow, frustrated and baffled at being unable to see past that
small self's boundaries. This is as true for the Sandman as it is for Shakespeare or Bottom.

Seen from a slightly different angle, of course, the Sandman resembles Titania and the
other fairies — attractive but inhuman, unpredictably dangerous because such beings oper-
ate by unknowable rules according to unfamiliar laws. In attitude, they are like their name-
sakes in Shakespeare's play who amuse themselves by manipulating human beings without
considering how people like Bottom might react. After all, why should they care? The fairies
are simply amused by the play; they do not notice how it might comment on the rightness of
their behavior. They probably would find meaningless the very notion of "rightness." Before
he began the subconscious meditations that led to his commissioning Shakespeare to write
A Midsummer Night's Dream, the Sandman would have agreed. But not now. He has begun to
care.

Titania's response to the Sandman's moral pondering is at first deeply disappointing,
since Gaiman's directions explain that she "realizes she's been asked a question, and has
no idea what. She's watching the play" (Script 25): "Hm? Oh, it is a *wonderful* play, Lord
Shaper. Most enchanting and fine" (AMND 19). Her inattention certainly demonstrates

how isolated we are, how difficult it is for us to focus on other individuals. But she *is* paying attention to the play. Her reply also demonstrates the power of art to capture our attention, and AMND at least sometimes shows how art can connect members of its audience through imaginatively shared experience. Almost certainly, an awareness of the power of art and a much vaguer awareness of his own confusion is what caused the Sandman to approach Shakespeare in the first place and to choose the themes of the two plays he needs to have written so he can begin to see himself as he is and as he might become. Even if he is lord of dreams, his wisdom obviously is incomplete, and he needs the revelation that art can provide.

The normal human condition, as Gaiman sees it, is a nervous estrangement from other humans and from ourselves. With one part of our soul, we want to escape that isolation; yet we are frightened of trying. Rather than reinforcing that fear by attacking it directly, art helps us step outside the supposed limits of ourselves so that we can better see present realities and new possibilities. When the Sandman tells Will Shakespeare that the hillside where *AMND* will be performed was a theater "before your race came to this island," the man asks a question that shows the limits of his human imagination: "Before the Normans?" "Before the humans," the Sandman replies (AMND 2). Besides putting humanity in a long, cold perspective, the Sandman's reply also suggests that any being doing what we can call "thinking" faces the same limitations of individual consciousness and seeks to escape them in the same way: by dreams, storytelling, art. As noted above, this is true even of supernatural beings. In particular, the Sandman may be starting to feel his responsibility as a father, the very thing that Shakespeare evades.[9] For imagination may be a slow liberator or an enslaver, just as Shakespeare may be both a success as a playwright and a failure as a father (AMND 13), while the Sandman may suspect that he himself may not always have done right in his dealings with mortals. And so he ponders and watches the action played around out around him. He knows that it somehow is important. Anticipating Theseus' disparaging comments (on the same page, on the opposite side of the same row of panels) Auberon objects that "this diversion, although pleasant is not true," but the Sandman replies that, "Tales and dreams are the shadow-truths that will endure when mere facts are dust and ashes, and forgot" (AMND 21).

Puck notes the same fact earlier, when he exclaims "This is magnificent — and it is true! It never happened; yet it is still true. What magic art is this?" (AMND 13). The magic *is* art. Art is the only magic suited for humans. And yet (natural, pleasurable, and necessary as it is) storytelling is done and witnessed by fallible beings. Art can provide a mere escape from pressing concerns, and it also can become an addiction that desensitizes its audience to life. Thus Shakespeare's concentration on art is as distressing as it is noble. And thus Bottom is tragic as well as laughable when he tries to express his magical experience in words: "The eye of man hath not heard, the ear of man hath not seen, man's hand is not able to taste, his tongue to conceive, nor his heart to report what my dream was" (AMND 19). Even valuing art as we do, we recognize its limitations. Shakespeare could not save Christopher Marlowe's life, but he might save his own son if he were able to turn away from the great stories long enough to look at the little boy who needs him immediately, now. And the Sandman watches and keeps his own counsel on what he is learning.

None of this is especially comfortable to reflect upon. We do not like to think that we live in a tangle of love and fear, that we try to climb past our limits through art, and that the escape may itself become a trap. Comics may be an especially apt medium for such a disconcerting subject because it naturally involves its audience in the process of creating meaningful "stories." In addition, a comics story can make a stealth attack on the complacency of readers who would not expect it to address such a serious subject. To succeed, such a story would also have to delight readers who have been bored by related platitudes, don't want to listen to abstract discussions, but might be able to look at something mortally important if it were vividly shown.

Gaiman and Vess *have* shown us.

ENDNOTES.

1. Directions and commentary are in caps in the original script; here and elsewhere, I've put them in normal type to avoid the impression of Gaiman screaming at the top of his lungs. I also have made a few minor corrections: i.e., the story gives Auberon as the name of the king of fairies, while the script calls him Oberon; I've used Auberon consistently.

2. A story is concerned with an individual in a particular set of circumstances, but a great story uses the particular to get into more universal, longer-lasting concerns. Thus a great story can have something of the power of myth by giving a shape to continuing puzzles of human experience, and it even can have the power of religion by insisting that there *are* enduring shapes beyond our transitory lives.

3. Drawing the action, Vess makes some minor but vital corrections in Gaiman's directions. The very first panel, for example, is described in the script as a panorama showing the Long Man of Wilmington on his hillside in the background and the actors moving down a road toward us (Script 2). Since the performance of *AMND* will be at the foot of a hill, Vess correctly shows the actors traveling away from us and *toward* the hill.

4. Overall coloring of Vess's work was done by Steve Oliff, in close consultation with the artist (Vess).

5. Gaiman recognizes that the performance of the play takes time, so that in the "real" world/day, light fades as the sun sinks (script 26). The effect is to make the onstage and offstage lighting schemes alike and thus further blur the distinctions between "levels" that readers might have imagined to be important.

6. As a rule, elsewhere in the story Vess actually uses overlapping panels (cf. pages 20 and 21) or borderless panels (cf. p. 18 and 21) to make it difficult to recognize where "levels" end.

7. Not always. On page 10, the onstage Puck clearly is wearing a mask because part of his

own mouth is visible through the mask's. Those glittering human teeth barely suggest the menacing grin of the real Puck, whom Gaiman describes as staring "at the stage, almost hungrily. Grinning like a werewolf eating shit from a barbed-wire fence" (Script 13). Perhaps it is the real Puck's overwhelming presence that keeps this mask from coming alive.

8. People who take comics seriously are sometimes exasperated by the name "comics," which seems to suggest shallow amusement. And yet a "serious comic" is no more an oxymoron than a "tragic play."

9. See my essay "Of Parents and Children and Dreams" elsewhere in this book.

WORKS CITED.

Bender, Hy. *The Sandman Companion*. New York: Vertigo/DC Comics, 1999.

Gaiman, Neil. "A Midsummer Night's Dream." Script. 1990.

— and Charles Vess. "A Midsummer Night's Dream." In *Dream Country*. New York: DC Comics, 1991. [Also contains "Calliope" and "A Dream of a Thousand Cats."]

McCloud, Scott. *Understanding Comics: The Invisible Art*. Northampton MA: Kitchen Sink Press: 1993.

Vess, Charles. Conversation at Fiddler's Green, Minneapolis MN, November 13, 2004.

A GAME OF YOU – YES, *YOU*

by David Bratman

✳

The *Sandman*, by Neil Gaiman and his collaborating artists, is a comic sufficiently good that it appeals even to readers like myself, who do not read many comics and know Gaiman more for his prose fiction. It has its highlights and its low points, but its finest moment to my taste is *A Game of You*. This magnificent graphic novel, volume five in the series, interweaves disasters in the primary and secondary worlds in a poignant tale of vividly realized misfit characters. Yet it was relatively unpopular among readers, and has received some sharply negative critical assessments. This is worth exploring. Let's begin by reaching *A Game of You* through the context of the four volumes of *Sandman* that preceded it.

Volume one of *Sandman* is called *Preludes & Nocturnes*, and as a unit it reads more like a fix-up novel than other volumes do. Morpheus, the Sandman, King of Dreams — he has many names — is captured in 1916 by a group of English occultists. They lock him for seventy years inside a magic circle in their basement. He finally escapes, wreaks his revenge, and goes on a quest to find the three magical objects that were taken from him on his capture, now long dispersed. He retrieves the first, his pouch of dream-dust, with little difficulty; he successfully contends with a demon for the second, his helm. The third, a ruby of power, is more difficult. It has come into the hands of a madman, John Dee, who in the chapter "24 Hours" uses its power to control the minds, torture, and finally kill the people he finds in a small-town diner, in one of the most chilling and blood-curdling stories I have ever read. Gaiman is a dark fantasist, and much of what he writes is frightening, but "24 Hours" is the only place in *Sandman* where he seems to me to cross the genre line into outright horror. Then, in one of those "If the bad guy wins, he automatically loses" plot twists we're all familiar with from Stephen R. Donaldson and others, Dee crushes the ruby when confronted by Dream, but instead of destroying Dream's power as he hopes, this act releases it, and the quest is complete.

I hope you realize by now that this is a classic "Collect the Coupons" fantasy plot, a term coined by critic Nick Lowe to describe stories like Susan Cooper's *Dark Is Rising* series in which the characters must collect a specified number of magical items before they can, in Lowe's words, "send off to the author for the ending." It helps if the magical items are McGuffins; that is, they serve no purpose except to be collected. This too is the case here, for the ruby is more useful destroyed than extant, and while the pouch and helm show up in later stories for dramatic emphasis, they're never really essential; indeed, as Dream's face is invisible under the helm, it's a good thing he takes it off whenever the action gets interesting.

What's more, when the story is over, Dream feels let down, even depressed. What does he do now? He's forgotten to have a life while wrapped up in collecting the coupons of which he's now completed the set. In a move of amazing audacity, Gaiman summons up a new character to appear to Dream and tell him this: Dream's sister, Death. Boldly referring to their own fictionality, she tells him: "You are utterly the stupidest, most self-centered, appallingest excuse for an anthropomorphic personification on this or any other plane! An infantile, adolescent, pathetic specimen! Feeling all sorry for yourself because your little game is over, and you haven't got the — the balls to go and find a new one!" ("The Sound of Her Wings" in both *Preludes & Nocturnes* and *The Doll's House*).

It's hard to count the number of ways Gaiman violates the rules of good writing in this volume. It's episodic, it shifts between story genres, it's got a hack fantasy plot, plus the author's superego in the form of a character to literally whack the protagonist in the head, remind him that he's only an anthropomorphic personification, and get him moving again. But there is no rule of writing that a sufficiently good author cannot violate and make a good story out of. As in his novel *American Gods*, which has similar surface problems, Gaiman is here a sufficiently good author. His pacing and imagination are fine; and in particular, the characters in the individual quests are so well drawn that the quests themselves are secondary to our getting to know these people, many of whom never appear again. Dream's depression is not just an authorial indulgence in the form of an implicit confession that he's stuck after finishing the plotline; it's an honest psychological depiction of how anyone might feel on losing a long-held sense of purpose.

It's a fine story, but what really sold me on *Sandman* was volume two, *The Doll's House*. This is a full-length, more tightly constructed story of considerable complexity. It's a six-chapter tale packed into a volume with two short stories unrelated to it except thematically. One of the short stories is what will prove to be the backstory to volume 4, told in the form of an African legend; the other, "Men of Good Fortune," is to my taste the best single issue of *Sandman*: starting in the 14th century, a man who does not die meets Dream in the same tavern once every hundred years, and tells him what fortune the intervening century has brought to him. It's a tale with richly mythic overtones.

The story of *The Doll's House* itself is so intricate that it would be pointless to summarize it: I'd spoil the story for anyone who hasn't read it, while still leaving them confused. I just want to mention a few points, and then return later to some parallels with *A Game of You*. *The Doll's House* is a story drenched in dreams: The characters' dreams, both their sleeping thoughts and their hopes and fears, permeate it. But it is not drenched in Dream, the character. He lurks in the background here, acting twice, decisively; but otherwise his presence merely lets the reader know that he's watching this intensely human, intensely mortal story, so that his interventions do not become an arbitrary *deus ex machina*, but flow from the plot. This is precisely where most authors would fall down, so not doing so becomes a masterly achievement of Gaiman's.

Two things about *The Doll's House* have proved controversial. One is that one of the characters is G.K. Chesterton. He calls himself merely Gilbert, but anyone who's seen a picture of the man will recognize him. Well, of course he's not the real G.K. Chesterton, because what would the real G.K. Chesterton be doing living as a recluse on the top floor of a boarding house in Florida in the 1980s, and fighting off a gang of muggers with a walking stick? At the end of the story we find out who, or what, he really is; but I would say that the fact that something is obviously amiss here from the beginning is enough to obviate any criticisms that this wonderful homage is a misappropriation in a non-Christian story. Why should a clear imposter be expected to perfectly mirror his model? Nonetheless there's something about Gilbert, from the beginning, that makes it clear he's not just a nut in a costume, nor is he.

The other controversy is over chapter five, the serial killers' convention. This is Gaiman's version of what critic Roger Wilmut, in discussing *Monty Python's Flying Circus*, called a format sketch. Monty Python would take a strongly recognizable format and empty out the content, replacing it with something ludicrous: so they'd have a talk show with stuffed animals as guests, or a sitcom starring Attila the Hun (Wilmut 198). Gaiman has a darker mind, so he takes the format of a comics or science-fiction convention and fills it up with serial killers. They have a hotel, name badges, panel discussions, a film program, a nervous chairman, a guest of honor, and even a dance. Except that they're all serial killers, each with a bizarre *modus operandi*. Is this too implausible to be credible? Yes it is, and the sheer ludicrousness of the notion is what makes pursuing it seriously black humor rather than sick: watching these sociopaths network, or failing to network, and failing to control their murderous urges despite the practical necessity of doing so. We see how pathetic they really are: fanboys worshipping a nightmare. Unlike authors like Stephen King or Bret Easton Ellis, or himself back in volume one, Gaiman neither wallows in violence nor glorifies it: he is in fact remarkably restrained in the actual violence he depicts here. I am not a reader of horror, but the only discomfort I had from reading this was the disturbing thought that I too, by attending conventions, might be more pathetic than I think: a thought worth having. By courageously goofing off with very dire material, Gaiman is in the company of a distinct category of great humorous horror writers such as John Bellairs and Joss Whedon.

Of volumes three and four of *Sandman* I have less to say. Volume three, *Dream Country*, consists of four short stories, each one distinctive and memorable, and in all of which Dream is a referent or a background mover, rather than the principal character. In one, "A Midsummer Night's Dream," William Shakespeare's company of players perform the play of that name to an audience of fairies. Why the fairies would want to see clumsy human depictions of themselves, other than for the reasons that fans hold group readings of "The Eye of Argon," is not made clear: still, this issue did win the World Fantasy Award for Best Short Story, the first story in comics format to do so.

Volume four, *Season of Mists*, brings Dream back to center stage, but without, in my opinion, the assurance shown in *Preludes & Nocturnes*. Here is where it's clarified that Dream and Death are but two of seven siblings representing abstract concepts, the Endless, six of whom get together here for a family conclave. Individually, the Endless are vivid, imaginative creations. I particularly enjoyed the sequence in volume seven, *Brief Lives*, when Dream and his aptly named sister Delirium travel by car in the waking world. I was reminded of this when reading of Shadow and Wednesday's travels in Gaiman's novel *American Gods*. But put together as a group, the Endless are tiresome petty squabblers who remind me of Roger Zelazny's Princes of Amber. This is not a good thing. Like Amber, they seem less real than their surroundings, instead of more so as they should. Depicting gods, or godlike creatures (for the Endless are not gods, but supposedly something older and deeper), one has to hold them at a distance, or they lose something of their magic, and their reality. J.R.R. Tolkien knew that in *The Lord of the Rings* when he kept Sauron offstage, and wrapped Gandalf in enigmas. Most of the time Gaiman knows it too, but here he has not kept the Endless at a sufficient distance. Nor is the plot the best-conceived. Dream has to make a hazardous visit to Hell again, for rather implausible reasons: been there, done that in volume one.

Never mind: there is much that is imaginative in *Season of Mists*, especially the hell for dead schoolboys, and it was followed by *A Game of You*, which I consider Gaiman's finest achievement in *Sandman*. This is a novel in six issues or chapters, that interestingly tracks *The*

Doll's House, reading like a superior remake of its already excellent predecessor, in the way, though not to the degree, that *The Lord of the Rings* is a remake of *The Hobbit*. It revisits the same themes and ideas with more assurance. Though it is deeper and better integrated than *The Doll's House*, *A Game of You* is not more complex: In fact the plot is relatively simple, and this discussion will make much of it clear to anyone who has not read it.

The direct plot tie between the two novels is *Game of You*'s central figure, a young woman called Barbie. She was a minor character in *Doll's House*, one of the boarders in the house where two of the chapters take place. Now divorced from her husband Ken (yes, the obvious joke was made), she is no longer crisp and natty, but is living rather grungily in a cheap, ratty apartment in New York City. The other inhabitants of the apartment building take the place of the boarders in the previous story, but this time they are better integrated into the plot. Except for Gilbert, the boarders in *Doll's House* were interesting but detachable incidental characters who could have been exchanged for other characters without affecting the story. In *A Game of You*, everyone is essential to the story and vital to the theme, and the tale is mostly self-contained around them. Perhaps Gaiman thought he didn't do the previous story's boarders justice, for most of them reappear later on in *Sandman*, and Barbie in *Game of You* is the first.

At one point in *Doll's House*, all the boarders are asleep, and all dream. What's startling is how different their dreams are. Ken, on the surface an amiable man, has cold, mechanical dreams of money and prostitutes: he's like a development of the character Mark from "24 Hours." Barbie's dream is a girl's castle-building fantasy, in C.S. Lewis's term: She's Princess Barbara on a dangerous quest with a faithful fuzzy animal companion through a — let's face it — hack fantasy realm. *A Game of You* is about what happens when Barbie's fantasy realm starts to impinge on the waking world, and the waking world on it. Like some other stories in *Sandman*, but more so than most, it's a meta-fantasy. Other characters have their own dreams, but the important thing in *Game of You* is their relationship with Barbie's dream, which becomes literal — in the manner of Charles Williams or contemporary indigenous fantasy — when the dream begins to invade both the other characters' dreams and Barbie's waking life. Led by a mysterious witch-woman whom we find is living among them, three women from the apartment building travel into Barbie's dream to learn what is threatening her and them. This in turn puts both them and the waking world in danger. "You have been foolish and unconsidered in your actions," Dream tells Thessaly, the witch-woman, near the end. "You will hardly survive another century if you continue in this manner of behavior, lady" (170). The spell that enables her to travel causes a storm to rise in New York. Gaiman likens this storm to the tornado in *The Wizard of Oz*, a story referenced several times in *A Game of You* (Bender 116), but it reminds me more of the great English storm of 1987 so uncannily predicted by Tolkien in his unfinished novel of the 1940s, *The Notion Club Papers*.

And where has Dream himself been during all this? Even more than in *Doll's House*, he is watching, waiting in the background, and this time he takes no real initiative. This is deliberate, and reflects Gaiman's view of the role of the Endless. "As personifications of things," he says, "they're not causative. They're barely reactive" (Bender 33). In the first four and a half of *A Game of You*'s six chapters, Dream appears on only four pages. *Doll's House* had been an important event to Dream, on the cosmic scale: it was only the characters who didn't realize the significance of their story. *A Game of You* is exactly the opposite. For all the pain that the troubles of Barbie's dream-land cause, for all the concern the characters have for themselves, it's a minor event to the indifferent universe. "The skerries are distant islets in the shoals of dream," says Dream. "They live, they die. They come and go. Why should I do anything about it?" (27) At the end, he must uncreate Barbie's dream-land — rather in the manner of Aslan uncreating Narnia in C.S. Lewis's *The Last Battle* (Bender 122) (and Barbie's entrance to the Land, through curtains, is rather like the overcoats in Lewis's *The Lion, the Witch and the Wardrobe*). He also must grant her a boon, by the terms of a contract rather arbitrarily brought up, but the *deus ex machina* aspect of this is not emphasized. It is Barbie's choice of boon, a recognition that her dream was an innocent childhood fantasy that has ended and should not be revived even if it can be, that is emphasized here.

But although Barbie is the central figure in this story, she's not the most interesting, nor the most important. Far more interesting are three other residents of her apartment building whom I haven't even mentioned yet: Foxglove and Hazel, a lesbian couple who accompany Thessaly on the journey into Barbie's dream-land, and Wanda, who does not. Wanda is Barbie's closest friend, and a pre-op transsexual who has, we learn, stayed pre-op because she's afraid of surgery (55; Bender 124). And it is with Hazel and Wanda, in particular, and with Maisie, an old black homeless woman whom Wanda rescues from the storm brought on by Thessaly's imprudent spellcasting, that the really interesting discussion of *Game of You* begins.

Each volume of the collected *Sandman* has an introduction by a writer of note, and most of these introductions are, as you might guess, highly complimentary. Harlan Ellison, who introduces *Season of Mists*, is incapable of praising, or for that matter condemning, in any tone short of wild exaggeration. He hails Gaiman as a genius of literary allusion because he's capable of quoting the best-known line from *Paradise Lost*, "Better to reign in hell, than serve in heav'n" (Ellison 9, 11). This is embarrassing, or should be. You don't even need to have read Milton's poem to know that line — I haven't read it, though I certainly tried — and if Gaiman is a literary genius, this is hardly proof of it.

But you get the point: much praise of Gaiman. Which makes Samuel R. Delany's introduction to *A Game of You* stand out, because he's less than totally enthusiastic about the story he's been asked to introduce. Delany, a noted science-fiction writer and critic, develops a ponderous theory that the points of characterization he finds implausible in the story can be explained away by the fact that it's a fantasy. This is either disingenuous or an exquisite insult. Delany is not of the school of hard-technology science-fiction writers who consider writing fantasy to be like playing tennis with the net down, but he should know that "it's a fantasy" is no excuse for bad writing in the aspects of a story that aren't meant to be fantastic. If a fantasy has characters who act in implausible ways for the sake of the plot, or who can walk physically impossible distances every day on their quest, it's no defense to say something like, "Don't expect realism in a story with elves and magic in it." But this is the defense that Delany offers for Gaiman.

So what does Delany consider unrealistic? He's skeptical of "Hazel's ignorance of the mechanics of female reproduction" (9). Hazel, after all, lives in New York, not in the boonies. But, alas, Mr. Delany, ignorance is everywhere; these things really happen (Bender 122); and Gaiman is careful throughout to depict Hazel as much more naïve and inexperienced than her tough butch appearance might suggest. Appearances can be deceiving.

Delany is also disturbed by the deaths of Wanda and Maisie, who are killed in the collapse of the apartment building in the storm, as they protect the comatose body of Barbie who is walking in the dream-land. By having Maisie die, Delany points out, he has offed "the single black character in the tale" (9). Delany is himself black, but what is he suggesting here? That Gaiman has not met his quota for black characters? I wasn't aware there was one. That Maisie should be excused from dying because she's black? That Gaiman has a "thing" for killing black characters? That's a dangerous charge to imply from a single example.

Delany mentions that these deaths "drew a whole host of very concerned ideological criticism" (9) when the issue was first published. I have not gone looking for these; if I read all the criticism I wouldn't have time to read the comics. But one of these did come to my attention, and reading this deeply wrongheaded complaint is what moved me to write this paper. The comment came from Rachel Pollack, a fantasy and comics writer of some note, and once a Mythopoeic Fantasy Award finalist. Pollack is herself a transsexual, so she identifies closely with Wanda, whose fate disturbed her greatly. Pollack writes that there are two things she disliked about *A Game of You*. Actually, I count three in her statement.

One is, that Wanda is the only major character who dies. When you see a story that seems sympathetic to a minority character and then that character is the only one that dies, you have a clue that the writer cannot really accept the minority figure as a person, as a reality. (All quotes by Pollack are from Tuinstra.)

Let's not quibble that Pollack morphs from saying "the only *major character* who dies" in her first sentence to "the *only one* that dies" in the second. Instead, let's quibble over the meaning of "major character." I did a little page count on *A Game of You*. If you can measure a character's importance to a story by the number of pages on which that character appears or speaks offstage, then Wanda is on 48, or 30%, of the story's 159 pages. Thessaly, Hazel, and Foxglove almost exactly match her, and only Barbie exceeds them (she's the only character to appear on more than half the pages, and on a number of them she's comatose). If these are the only major characters, I think it's dangerous to generalize about the death of one in only five, especially as the other four are nearly trapped in the Dreaming forever, and Barbie is uninjured in the building collapse probably only because Dream promises to return her home safe and sound.

But what if there are more major characters? Who, then, are the next most important characters after Wanda and the other three? Answer: Wilkinson and Luz, two of Barbie's four talking-animal companions in her fantasy land, all four of whom are killed brutally or tragically. There isn't much of a lobby of talking animals who are fantasy critics, or we might have heard more criticism of those deaths. There are fourteen characters who appear on six or more pages of *A Game of You*, including Dream himself, and of those fourteen, seven — exactly half — are killed. (The seven survivors are Barbie, the three women, Dream, the Cuckoo, and Aunt Dora.) Gaiman is sparing nobody. The victims are the four talking animals, Wanda, Maisie – and George.

Let's consider George for a moment. He is another resident of the apartment building, a scowling, unsociable fellow who turns out to be the only real villain of the piece. The Cuckoo whom he serves, the apparent villain of the dream-land, turns out to be something more complex than a villain, and Barbie reluctantly makes the wise choice and lets her go. But George smiles as he steals innocent bystanders' dreams. He has no redeeming characteristics, and he is killed without compunction by Thessaly. He is also, save for a few tiny walk-ons, the only human male in the entire story. Had *A Game of You* been written by a woman, I think we'd hear some criticism of his character and death from a certain segment of male opinion. Gaiman has no interest in sparing characters of his own demographic, or any other.

Maisie, like most of us, is mixed. She's an obnoxious panhandler, her hygiene is terrible, she hates dogs – I'd consider that a plus, but most people wouldn't – but she has a good heart. She is immediately accepting of Wanda's transsexuality. She had a transsexual grandchild herself. "Just because someone's different don't make 'em bad" (145), she says.

And Wanda, I would say, is the most human, the most sympathetic, and the most deeply understood character in the entire story. Barbie is the leading figure, but in just as real a sense the story is about Wanda. Barbie's exploration of how her childhood fantasies fueled her dream-land might seem perhaps a little sterile and a little too specific to her, but Wanda's issues over her gender identity strike a deep chord of understanding even with those of us who don't have that problem. Possibly more than with some of those who do.

And that is why Wanda dies: not because, as Pollack says, the death of a character is "a clue that the writer cannot really accept [that] figure as a person, as a reality," but because he accepts her very well. Wanda is, Gaiman says, "the only character who was doing noble and valiant and brave and good things," and for that reason "she was the only person whose death made the story a tragedy" (Tuinstra). Think about that for a minute. I believe we have a profound variance of view of the purpose of fiction here. On the one hand, a soft-hearted view that to kill a character is to mark that person as expendable, and by implication to call expendable real people who share that person's characteristics. On the other, a hard-headed view that realizes that *it isn't tragedy unless it hurts*. In this view, to kill off a character is the op-

Fig. 1: Writer: Neil Gaiman Artist: Shawn McManus "Beginning to See the Light"
Collected in *The Sandman: A Game of You* [©1993 DC Comics]

posite of saying that character is expendable: It's because that character isn't expendable that you do it.

This is the "Cold Equations" dilemma, after a science-fiction story of that title about a girl stowaway who has to be ejected from a small spaceship to keep it from being overweight and crashing. Critics of the story have claimed it depicts the girl as expendable; but in fact the story specifies that if the stowaway had been a big tough man, the pilot would have ejected him without a second thought (Godwin 546). It's because she's innocent, and a girl, that the pilot hesitates; it's because she's innocent, and a girl, that the story is the moving tragedy that it is. If there's sexism here, it's not in treating women as more expendable than men, but in treating them as less so. Why do some readers have such difficulty recognizing tragedy? Does anyone come out of *Romeo and Juliet* thinking, "Those kids were sure expendable"?

Lack of understanding of tragedy is a problem often encountered by writers of cult fiction, whose fans sometimes love the story not wisely but too well, treating the characters as their own friends, and being not grieved but offended when one dies: Certainly criticism of that sort came to Joss Whedon when he wrote the death of Tara in the TV show *Buffy the Vampire Slayer*. But if Whedon made a mistake, it was in not signaling clearly enough that Tara's death was a tragedy and not a sign of expendability. Why that was not signaled is too complex to get into here. But Gaiman does not make that mistake, and the clarity of his thinking appears in his handling of the issue of whether Wanda is really a woman.

Pollack is critical of Gaiman for what she perceives as waffling over this. But it's being realistic: Doubt will pursue transsexuals, especially if they're pre-op as Wanda is. It isn't Wanda who "doesn't really know who she is" as Delany claims (10), it's the world that won't accept Wanda's certainty. This is realistic even though it's expressed in terms of fantasy. After Thessaly takes Hazel and Foxglove into the Dreaming by walking along the moon's road, George explains to Wanda that men aren't allowed on that road. "Gender," he says, "isn't something you can pick and choose as, uh, far as gods are concerned." Wanda is having none of it: "I've had electrolysis, I'm taking hormones. All that's left is just a little lump of flesh; but all that doesn't matter ... inside I'm a woman ... I know what I am" (113). [*Fig. 1*] Delany, who also weighs in on this, is as annoyed as Wanda is that an arbitrary fantasy trope is enforcing conventional sexual ideology (8-9), but really, it'd be odder if it didn't.

Pollack claims that George's statement never gets answered. But we have Wanda's answer, and we get the author's answer at the very end, in perhaps the most moving scene in the entire *Sandman* saga. Barbie — who'd already been the only non-family mourner at Maisie's funeral — travels all the way out to Kansas for Wanda's, braving what she knows is the severe disapproval of Wanda's family. Gaiman nicely modulates the character of Wanda's Aunt Dora, who has a kindly side despite her deep-seated prejudice, distinguishing her from Wanda's totally censorious mother, who refuses even to greet Barbie politely. They have cut Wanda's hair, which she was so proud of, dressed her in a man's suit, and buried her under the birth name that she despised: Alvin. This is tragedy for you. Wanda's self-identity has been erased,

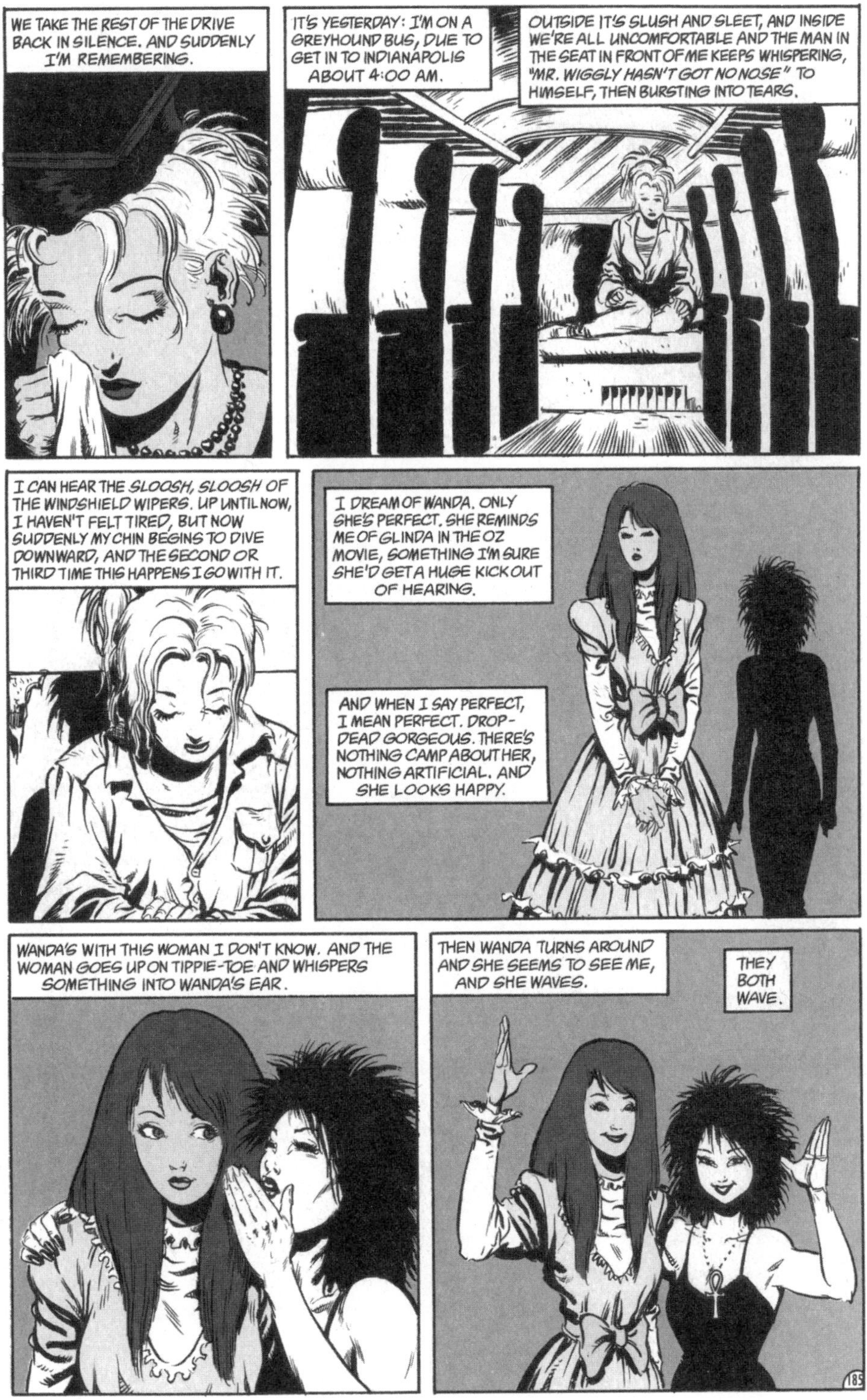
WE TAKE THE REST OF THE DRIVE BACK IN SILENCE. AND SUDDENLY I'M REMEMBERING.
IT'S YESTERDAY: I'M ON A GREYHOUND BUS, DUE TO GET IN TO INDIANAPOLIS ABOUT 4:00 AM.
OUTSIDE IT'S SLUSH AND SLEET, AND INSIDE WE'RE ALL UNCOMFORTABLE AND THE MAN IN THE SEAT IN FRONT OF ME KEEPS WHISPERING, "MR. WIGGLY HASN'T GOT NO NOSE" TO HIMSELF, THEN BURSTING INTO TEARS.
I CAN HEAR THE SLOOSH, SLOOSH OF THE WINDSHIELD WIPERS. UP UNTIL NOW, I HAVEN'T FELT TIRED, BUT NOW SUDDENLY MY CHIN BEGINS TO DIVE DOWNWARD, AND THE SECOND OR THIRD TIME THIS HAPPENS I GO WITH IT.
I DREAM OF WANDA. ONLY SHE'S PERFECT. SHE REMINDS ME OF GLINDA IN THE OZ MOVIE, SOMETHING I'M SURE SHE'D GET A HUGE KICK OUT OF HEARING.
AND WHEN I SAY PERFECT, I MEAN PERFECT. DROP-DEAD GORGEOUS. THERE'S NOTHING CAMP ABOUT HER, NOTHING ARTIFICIAL. AND SHE LOOKS HAPPY.
WANDA'S WITH THIS WOMAN I DON'T KNOW. AND THE WOMAN GOES UP ON TIPPIE-TOE AND WHISPERS SOMETHING INTO WANDA'S EAR.
THEN WANDA TURNS AROUND AND SHE SEEMS TO SEE ME, AND SHE WAVES.
THEY BOTH WAVE.
185

Fig. 2: Writer: Neil Gaiman Artist: Shawn McManus "'I Woke Up and I was Crying.'" Collected in *The Sandman: A Game of You* [©1993 DC Comics]

at the clear and expressed insistence of her family.

But it is a tragedy with defiance. For Barbie, lingering at the grave after the service, takes a tube of Wanda's favorite lipstick, crosses out the hated name Alvin on the tombstone, and writes "Wanda" over it, giving her back, as much as she is able to, her own self-identity. "Hey, no problem," says Barbie. "Least I could do" (183).

And it is a tragedy with hope. For on the very last pages Barbie has a dream of Wanda. In the dream, "she's perfect ... Drop-dead gorgeous. There's nothing camp about her, nothing artificial. And she looks happy" (185). [*Fig. 2*] Pollack, alas, misunderstands this crucial image. This is her third criticism: the dream, she says, shows that "[transsexual] women can only exist ... in a fantasy world in the writer's head." But this dream is not just in Barbie's head. Wanda is with another woman whom Barbie doesn't know and who is not identified. But the readers of *Sandman* recognize her: She's Death. And we know from our previous encounters with Death that she really does meet with people's spirits: That person is really there. Death "whispers something into Wanda's ear. Then Wanda turns around," Barbie tells us, "and she seems to see me, and she waves" (185). She sees her, all right. This is the real Wanda at last, the last gift of a friendship that began on the first pages of *A Game of You*.

Another transsexual writer, Caitlín R. Kiernan, calls Wanda "the most positive transsexual character I've ever encountered ... someone I actually identified with, above and beyond the issue of being [transsexual]" (Tuinstra). I am a pure vanilla white heterosexual birth male, but I can identify with Wanda too, so I think Kiernan is right. The funeral and dream, placed at the very end, keep Wanda from being forgotten about after her death, as Delany fears would happen to her, as happens to characters who are killed because they *are* expendable. The ending keeps Wanda as a central character, and a deeply realized tragic one. Anyone can identify with Wanda, transsexual or no: grieve at her tragedy, share in the defiance and hope. The fastidious critics have missed the point. Neil Gaiman's gift for characterization, which saved *Preludes & Nocturnes* from being routine, has come through again. Both here, and in the other volumes of *Sandman*, he has created characters as real as ourselves, who could be ourselves: me and you. And that is why I titled this paper "A Game of You — Yes, *You*."

WORKS CITED.

Bender, Hy. *The Sandman Companion*. New York: Vertigo, 1999.

Delany, Samuel R. "Skerries of the Dream." Preface. *The Sandman: A Game of You*, by Neil
    Gaiman et al. New York: DC Comics, 1993. 6-13.

Ellison, Harlan. Introduction. *The Sandman: Season of Mists*, by Neil Gaiman et al. New York:
    DC Comics, 1992. 7-11.

Gaiman, Neil, et al. *The Sandman*. 10 v. New York: DC Comics, various compilation dates.

Godwin, Tom. "The Cold Equations." *The Science Fiction Hall of Fame*, ed. Robert Silverberg.
    New York: Avon, 1971. 543-69.

Lowe, Nick. "The Well-Tempered Plot Device." *Ansible* 46, July 1986. Also at http://www.

ansible.co.uk/Ansible/plotdev.html

Tuinstra, Richard. "The Life and Death of Wanda." http://www.woxberg.net/gaiman/litera-
ture/wanda.html

Wilmut, Roger. *From Fringe to Flying Circus*. London: Methuen, 1980.

⚜⚜⚜

THE KING IS DEAD, LONG LIVE THE KING: ORIENTALISM, *THE SANDMAN*, AND HUMANITY

by Renata Sancken

✦

Neil Gaiman's *Sandman* series excelled in thwarting the expectations of readers, always giving readers a new twist or surprise. For example, Gaiman is fond of telling stories about the letters he received after *Sandman* #7, asking when Dream's "older brother" Death would appear. Readers thought they knew who could fill such an important role, but they were wrong. And, in his understated way, Gaiman enjoyed demonstrating how foolish it is to rely on preconceptions. *The Sandman*'s manipulation of Orientalist conventions might not be as startling as the introduction of Dream's elder *sister*, but it is ultimately as necessary to telling some of *Sandman*'s stories as Death herself. "Soft Places" and "Ramadan," two stories in the *Fables and Reflections Sandman* collection, both use traditional Orientalist storytelling elements while actually subtly creating works that show not the West dominating and defining the East as readers expect, but instead emphasize *Sandman's* overarching themes of change and of the power of storytelling in defining and uniting humanity. In Mikal Gilmore's introduction to *The Wake*, he wrote:

> With *Sandman*, Gaiman aimed to use a comics-based mythos to expand on, interact with, and *deepen* classical legends of mythology and popular history. On one hand, this approach might seem like merely another clever postmodern ruse, taking old Greek and Norse myths, European and Asian and Islamic folk-tales, plus scenarios from Dante, Blake, Milton, and Dore, and mixing them with 20th-century comics and horror elements ... At the same time, it was as if you had discovered a timeless trove of fascinating lost legends and mysteries: missing vellums that revealed how so many different peoples shared so many similar patterns of fable and providence in their disparate histories of storytelling.

This is what Gaiman does with both "Ramadan" and "Soft Places," using Orientalist storytelling styles and histories to reveal the similar patterns shared by all people, including the acceptance of change. Edward Said's groundbreaking *Orientalism* describes the Orient as the polar opposite of the Occident, something that exists simply to be everything the West is not. The Orient is "almost a European invention, ... place of romance, exotic beings, haunting memories and landscapes, remarkable experiences" (1).

At first glance, the Baghdad of "Ramadan" would certainly seem to fulfill these criteria. Haroun al Raschid's kingdom is a place of romance (and lust); it is full of beautiful women, "adept at the arts of pleasure" (*Fables and Reflections* 229) and beautiful boys as well. Haroun's queen is beautiful and beguiling, promising to Haroun that she "can smooth away the darkness in your soul, beneath [her] thighs" (*Fables and Reflections* 234). Beyond that, the palace is simply a beautiful building. Exotic beings abound as well: Magicians, enchanters, and other marvels fill Haroun's palace, which is, after all, "the palace of Wonders," in "the days of wonders" (*Fables and Reflections* 230-1). His palace also contains eggs of exotic creatures, from the egg of the Rukh, "the bird that nests on mountaintops and carries off bull elephants to feed its young," (*Fables and Reflections* 240) to the Other Egg of the Phoenix. The market, too, abounds with wonders: colorful birds, a veiled woman accompanying a gorilla, a beautiful slave girl "of the most exotic kind" (*Fables and Reflections* 251). Then there are the "nine thousand and nine ifrits, djinn, and demons" (*Fables and Reflections* 242) that Haroun uses to summon Dream. Finally, there is Dream himself, who appears in "Ramadan" looking more magnificent than ever before. P. Craig Russell explained, "The Sandman had to be dressed mostly in black to stay in character, but he had to look opulent and kinglike to fit the story" (Bender 157). Dream's first appearance in the story, with his long, beautifully patterned robe flowing beneath him as he floats up to Haroun, certainly makes him seem an exotic being.

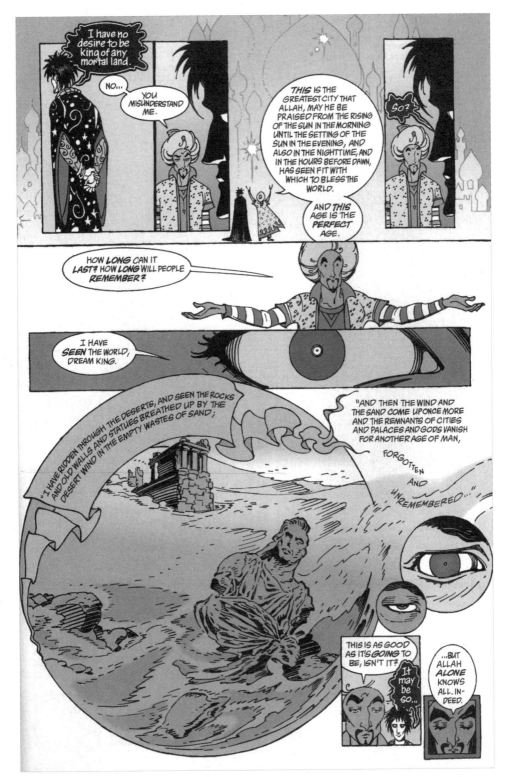

Fig. 1: Writer: Neil Gaiman Artist: P. Craig Russell "Ramadan"
Collected in *The Sandman: Fables and Reflections* [©1993 DC Comics]

P. Craig Russell's artwork certainly creates "haunting landscapes," and not just outside the palace's walls. As far as remarkable experiences go, one need not look much further than a flying carpet ride above this beautiful city. The city looks extraordinarily different from any other, just as was certainly intended.

Even the lettering, which Todd Klein described as "curved and curly, elaborated and ornate" (Bender 157) exoticizes the city and the story being told, setting "Ramadan" apart from other *Sandman* stories just as Dream's distinctive white-on-black lettering sets him apart from other characters throughout the series. So does this make "Ramadan" a comic that uses what Said calls a "Western style for dominating, restructuring, and having authority over the Orient" (88)? The answer is in Haroun himself. Despite his exotic surroundings, meant to mimic the *Arabian Nights*, Haroun is a real human character who is able to define himself and his city.

Haroun recognizes both the perfection his city has attained and the ephemeral nature of the perfection. [*Fig. 1*] For this reason he summons Dream, giving him Baghdad as a gift, in return for which Dream will ensure that "as long as mankind lasts … our world is not forgotten" (*Fables and Reflections* 255). Haroun makes the choice to sacrifice the present glory of his city (after his meeting with Dream, he abandons his once-flying carpet behind on the street) in exchange for the eternal glory of "the Other Baghdad," which, we see, lives along with "the Other Egg of the Phoenix" in the dreams of a young boy in war-torn contemporary Baghdad. [*Fig. 2*] Haroun's ability to accept and confront change very definitely set him apart from the "irrational, depraved, childlike" Oriental (Said 40).

In his preoccupation with change, Haroun himself also demonstrates that the Other, when simply defined as an Easterner, is not so different from the ordinary (whatever "ordinary" means to you). Haroun is a legendary king of a legendary city. His palace is full of exotic and sexualized women (and men). As a further demonstration of his power, he is able to summon the King of Dreams, even if his methods for doing such aren't pleasing to Morpheus himself. Yet Haroun's ultimate concern is making sure that his city will be remembered as it is, at the peak of its glory.

The desire to be remembered, along with the things one loves, seems to be a fundamental human desire. And if the Other Baghdad is exotic and "other," it is because it was defined that way by those who loved it, not because otherness was forced upon it by dominant Westerners.

Hy Bender points out a number of motifs common to all the stories in *Fables and Reflections*: storytelling, the personality of places, the Fates, and the conflict between personal dreams and other values (139-40). However, "Ramadan" and "Soft Places," while sharing many of those motifs, also share the theme of change and the use of Orientalist conventions to confront the diversely uniform nature of humanity. In "Soft Places," Marco Polo, whose tales of China are legendary (if sometimes historically dubious), stumbles into the "soft places" where time blurs, and encounters an older version of his friend Rustichello, Gilbert

Fig. 2: Writer: Neil Gaiman Artist: P. Craig Russell "Ramadan"
Collected in *The Sandman: Fables and Reflections* [©1993 DC Comics]

(also known as Fiddler's Green), and an exhausted Morpheus. Marco's stories are nothing if not Orientalist, as defined by Said, which is to be expected. Said describes the way "the Orient, and in particular the Near Orient, became known in the West as its great complementary opposite since antiquity," through the Bible, travelers like Marco Polo, fabulists, conquering movements, and militant pilgrims (58). Consequently, such tales fall into " a restricted number of typical encapsulations: the journey, the history, the fable, the stereotype, the polemical confrontation" (58). But if Marco's tales define the Orient in his own terms, not those of Khan or other Easterners, he is still part of a larger tale. Marco is defined by the story he is now a part of, where his future cellmate tells him about things that he has not yet experienced and where Gilbert talks of times and places Marco has not and will never experience. The frame of the story itself humanizes Marco, who has himself become exoticized in his own way over time. Though he is now associated with his travels and the distant mystery of the time and place he inhabited, in "Soft Places" he is not a dominant, conquering European but a lost, confused traveler, dependent upon the mercy of Dream to get home.

While Marco's encounters with Gilbert and Morpheus are important, and certainly characterize the interplay between popular history and comics characters, the interactions between Marco and Rustichello seems more key in their depiction of common human themes. Even though Marco describes China in exoticized terms, particularly as shown in the illustrations of his narration, he still speaks of Kublai Khan as a human being, one whom Marco seems to respect, despite the fact that he is "a heathen and an idolater" (*Fables and Reflections* 136). It is worth noting, however, that what Marco comments upon most favorably the fact that he "looked favorably upon the Christian faith"(*Fables and Reflections* 136). Marco appreciates the tolerance of Khan, while at the same time exoticizing him, describing the miracles his "idolater priests" can accomplish (*Fables and Reflections* 136). When Marco tells the story of Pope Gregory, pointing out that he had no miracle workers, Gilbert interjects to tell of Saint Joseph of Copertino, a Franciscan monk with an "IQ of sixty" who "can honestly fly" (*Fables and Reflections* 137). Joseph seems like the perfect man for Gilbert to introduce into the conversation—a European, not too bright, but with a magical ability. Here is a man who does not fit neatly into the Oriental/Occidental divide—if Western readers expect the Oriental to serve only to provide definition to the "rational, virtuous, mature, 'normal'" European (Said 40), Joseph might well be considered more of an Other than Haroun al Raschid, and yet he is a European Christian monk. Gilbert himself seems not quite a complete Westerner, since he dresses and acts like a British gentleman, but isn't actually a human being. Too, his familiarity with the Dreaming and unusual occurrences make him not quite "normal." What might be expected to separate these characters is less important than what they share. The unique array of characters in and alluded to in "Soft Places" may have different backgrounds, but they are all, it would seem, able to appreciate the power of a good story.

In these stories, what Orientalism really comes down to is one person's power to define another person (or place). Thus, Marco and Rustichello have something else in common with Haroun al Raschid — an appreciation for cities, and an acceptance of the ephemeral nature of memory. Rustichello states that Marco's genius was "being able to *describe* cities. Not just the land, or the trade, but the *soul* of the city. What made it *uniquely* itself ..." (*Fables and Reflections* 137). Rustichello then claims he is "writing it all down for [Marco]. So it'll be remembered" (137). Marco and Rustichello understand that, if the story is not written, it will be forgotten, as will the cities themselves. More importantly, the stories and the cities would change. This is just as Haroun understood that his city could change from what he considers to be its perfect state if he did not take steps to prevent it from happening. All three understand that stories and dreams have the power to keep something alive. The person who tells the stories has the power to define the story.

Haroun's Baghdad is, in a way, the opposite of the malleable soft places. He wants his city to be permanently defined, locked into one true Baghdad of memory and dream, while the city of the waking world ages and changes. In the soft places, the waking world, and the dreaming world, the mundane and the fantastic, the ancient, the modern, and the future all blur together. Haroun is almost acting in the role of the Orientalist Westerner by defining his city and trying to preserve it on his terms. What sets him apart is that he is actually from the East. In Orientalist writings, "what gave the Oriental's world its intelligibility and identity was not the result of his own efforts but rather the whole complex series of knowledgeable manipulation by which the Orient was identified by the West" (Said 40). "Knowledgeable manipulation" certainly plays a part in the definition (and continued definition) of Baghdad, but it is Haroun who bargains with Dream and reifies his city's identity, not an outside Westerner. Haroun has power enough to summon the King of Dreams and bargain with him, and he makes the decision to convert his Baghdad into the Other Baghdad, just so that the city will continue to exist as he believes it should, in all its perfectly fulfilled glory.

This idea of permanently defining boundaries also comes up in "Soft Places." It is the complaint Gilbert has with Marco, as well as with "Hwen T'sang, Ibn Battuta, the lot of you. The explorers, and the ones who came after you, who froze the world into rigid patterns" (Gaiman 140). The soft places—the Desert of Lop, the "few thousand square miles of central Australia, a couple of Pacific islands, a field in Ireland," and the "occasional mountain in Arizona" (Gaiman 141)—have not yet been defined by anyone, and can take on multiple identities of time. Interestingly, the soft places Gilbert names are geographically diverse, not limited to East or West. These places are as Westerners viewed the Orient, blank slates to be defined by whoever can claim knowledge of them and describe them. This idea of geographic fluidity, that something is not permanent until it has been mapped and defined, would seem colonialist. However, Gilbert seems to oppose this geographical reification, enjoying the wonders provided by these undefined places and times.

For that matter, Gilbert is himself a place without firm boundaries — who could map a sailor's paradise that exists in the Dreaming? Gilbert's character is also, ultimately, another symbol of change and choice. In *The Wake*, when Daniel attempts to bring Gilbert back from the dead, Gilbert refuses, saying, "I understand *perfectly* what you are offering. I am, however, *declining* it. With thanks" (34). The reason, Gilbert explains, is that if Daniel brings him back to life, his "death will have no *meaning*" (*The Wake* 34). Gilbert is unwilling to give Daniel the power to define his death, and Daniel agrees to leave the decision in Gilbert's hands. Sometimes, difficult as this is for Westerners to imagine, what one preserves is less important than what one gives up — or of the choice of selflessness, surely an "Eastern" concept. Still, Western readers can sympathize and almost accept Gilbert's choice.

Dream himself obliquely acknowledges the theme of superficial differences masking basic similarities when Marco asks him if he always looks so pale. Dream responds, "That depends on who's watching," making reference to what *Sandman* readers already know — there are as many Dreams as there are dreamers, with Dream having appeared in a variety of ethnicities. The Dream King is defined by dreamers. Within an Orientalist framework, this reaffirms his role as the Other, not as a European. And yet he is still, after all, the Dream King, and does have power to define reality within the realm of dreams. This is *Sandman*, after all, and nothing is uncomplicated.

In a way, Dream himself, along with the other Endless, is the ultimate Other. The contrast becomes not East and West, but Dream and humanity. In *The Wake*, Matthew questions Lucien about Morpheus's death, and Lucien replies, "Charitably ... I think ... sometimes, perhaps, one must change or die. And, in the end, there were, perhaps, limits to how much he could let himself change" (59). Lucien identifies the separation between Morpheus and humanity. Humans change because we must. Haroun and Marco both recognize that time and change will take their tolls on the cities they have cared about. Frank McConnell, in his introduction to *The Kindly Ones,* points out that Dream's imprisonment has taught him "that he is not only a transcendent projection of human consciousness, but that he is, after all, dependent upon human consciousness for his existence." Ultimately, as Lucien hesitantly admits, Dream recognizes this on some level, and makes the choice to *not* change, but to be merciful, to keep his word to his son, and to die.

Orientalism, according to Edward Said, "was ultimately a political vision of reality whose structure promoted the difference between the familiar (Europe, the West, 'us') and the strange (the Orient, the East, 'them')" (43). With a little work, this analysis could apply to *Sandman*: *Sandman* displays the supposed difference between the waking world and the dreaming world but also shows how terribly thin the line between the two is. In the ever-shrinking postcolonial world, the distance between East and West is not far. The distance between the dreamer and the dream is even smaller. If everyone tells the same stories, has the same dreams, who is the "them?"

While the use of Orientalism in *Sandman* is more apparent in stories like "Soft Places" and "Ramadan," which use stories that are actually from the East, or that take place in the East, the greater ideas of Orientalism are present throughout the full run of *Sandman*. "Us versus them," or rather, "Us defines them," is Orientalism in a nutshell. When the definition is broadened to include any subjective definition, including the ability to recognize when you are letting someone or something else define you, and to change your situation, it becomes a theme clearly present throughout *Sandman*. Change is what both Mad Hettie and Delirium want, what Dream wishes to avoid, and what ordinary mortal dreamers cannot avoid. Like Haroun or Marco Polo, humans can and do try to confront change with storytelling, but ultimately there are not many things we can do in the face of a changing world except to set objects out of the flux of time by using our imaginations. *Sandman* points out that this is a problem shared by all of humanity.

WORKS CITED.

Bender, Hy. *The Sandman Companion.* New York: Vertigo Books, 1999.

Gaiman, Neil, et al. *Fables and Reflections.* New York: DC Comics, 1993.

—. *The Kindly Ones.* New York: DC Comics, 1996.

—. *The Wake.* New York: DC Comics, 1997.

Said, Edward. *Orientalism.* New York: Vintage Books, 1979

❧ ❧ ❧

ILLUSORY ADVERSARIES?:
IMAGES OF FEMALE POWER IN
SANDMAN: THE KINDLY ONES

by K.A. Laity

✳

"It is the feeling of secret we become acquainted with when we dream, that is what makes us both enjoy and at the same time fear dreaming."
— *Hélène Cixous*

Challenging the stereotypical assumption of its time that the only successful comics were about superheroes in tights, *Sandman* (1989-1996) captivated a broad following of both male and female readers. Many of the latter were — and continue to be — drawn in by the abundance of complex female characters who provide a welcome relief from the more ubiquitous buxom vamps offered by other mainstream titles. While the comics form offers a canvas upon which all manner of tales can be told, market practices in the United States assure the continued focus on the bizarre creations of young males' fantasies. Though *Sandman* writer Neil Gaiman attempted (deliberately or coincidentally) to subvert the phallogocentric thrust of much of the medium's current discourse, images of female power remain problematic in the series, nowhere more so than in the cataclysmic story arc of *The Kindly Ones*. Although the stylized artwork of Marc Hempel produced more straightforward images of power for the female characters, they were nonetheless unable to allay completely the patriarchal code.

The profusion of well-rounded female characters in the *Sandman* series, while a statement in itself, is complicated by the portrayal of female power in characters in *The Kindly Ones*, such as Lyta Hall, Thessaly/Larissa, and of course the Furies, as something horrifying even to the women themselves. In addition, interactions and manipulations occur between humans and divinities (and those who fit neatly into neither category); these disparate levels of existence shift balances of power further yet. Using an approach colored by the theories of French feminist Hélène Cixous in *Three Steps on the Ladder of Writing*, I examined the images of female power in Gaiman's narrative — as complemented by the art of Marc Hempel, as well as by Teddy Kristiansen and others — in *The Kindly Ones* story arc, and determined that *Sandman* did not entirely escape the patriarchal grip of its muscle-bound cohorts.

The explicit storyline of *The Kindly Ones* encompasses a threat from without to the eponymous hero. The Furies act as an engine of revenge against Dream, aided by Thessaly and set in motion by the distraught Lyta Hall, who seeks recompense for the (supposed) death of her son Daniel. However, as becomes clear in the final conversation with his sister Death, Morpheus has orchestrated his own downfall, and consciously prepared its path for some time. Although he claims the decisive moment to be the killing of his son Orpheus (which occurs at the end of the earlier *Brief Lives* story arc, issues #41-49) preparations reached back much further — if not to the very beginning of the series, where we first met the Sandman while imprisoned by the magus Roderick Burgess.

Although this weaving of narratives has the effect of creating a neat circular structure to the narrative of *Sandman* as a whole, it nevertheless undercuts the power and menace of the supposed adversaries of Morpheus. The slow build-up of the Furies over thirteen issues, ends with their anticlimactic dismissal by Death in the final issue. All these female characters serve only as instruments for Dream's death-wish and creator Gaiman's narrative completion. The adversaries in the end are only pawns, and Death acts as her brother's agent to express his deepest desires. Apparent female power turns out to be merely a tool for male composition. As Hélène Cixous writes regarding the narrative process, "We always have the belief and the illusion that we are the ones writing, that we are the ones dreaming. Clearly this is not the case" (98). For Lyta, the Furies and the witch Thessaly, it certainly is not the case; although they imagine themselves composing a tale of revenge, they find themselves only steps on Dream's ladder to his own dramatic death.

In *Three Steps on the Ladder of Writing*, her thoughtful investigation of the art of writing, Cixous asserts that the by-product of creation must be destruction, that "everything is crime" (32), that the painter has to take the model's life. In creating the truth of his death, Morpheus destroys — for the second time — the life of Lyta Hall. Tired of the known worlds, fatigued by his responsibilities, he wants to move forward into nothingness. As Cixous writes, "the desire to die is the desire to know; it is not the desire to disappear, and it is not suicide, it is the desire to enjoy" (34). Dream finds the freedom and responsibilities of his world stifling and wants to shed this existence, to enjoy an end to his endless duties. To do this, however, he needs not only Lyta's child to take his place, but also her (at least *symbolic*) death. "There can't be life on both sides," Cixous reminds us (31). While Dream wishes to die, he must construct his own death powered by the life and energy of Lyta Hall and her son. The Dream King seeks the oblivion of death, but he must draw on "life, real, substantial, material life" to make it possible, which costs the mortal life of Daniel and the energy of Lyta to bring about. Morpheus seems to regret this necessity, but Cixous has anticipated the guilt of the artist, too: "We might expect him to be proud of the work but he can't be...we cannot create in a just manner" (32). Perhaps, knowing the cost of his creation, the Dream King offers Lyta an illusion of power to mitigate the eventual dissolution.

The orchestrations of the character echo the manipulations of the writer. As shown by the available script for "Calliope" (as found in the collection *Dream Country*), Gaiman exerts almost complete control over the images that accompany his storyline. His detailed instructions assure the form each image will take, just as his choice of artist determines style. Gaiman controls the narrative, the art and all design elements (like the striking covers by Dave McKean), indeed, the outcome of the final product — assuring the control is ultimately male. Despite this, however, artist Marc Hempel, who illustrates the bulk of *The Kindly Ones*, subverts the tale's overarching masculine hegemony by empowering the images of the primary female characters. This problematizes their apparent subordination to make the outcome less straightforward and to challenge the narrative authority. This schism creates tension. A particularly large gap forms between the narrative construct of Lyta Hall and her visual portrayal through Hempel's images. In this gap lies all of Lyta's true power.

We first meet Lyta in the second major arc, *A Doll's House* (#8-16), the pregnant captive — along with her deceased husband Hector, a heroic incarnation of Sandman — of the nightmares Brute and Glob, who have escaped Dream's dominion during his lengthy imprisonment. Morpheus arrives to capture and punish his minions, to send Hector to Death, and to lay claim to the child Lyta has carried for two years in the Dreaming. "You've ruined my life," Lyta tearfully informs the Dream King (#12, 23, panel 3). As he notifies her that he will come one day for the child, Lyta has already become part of the background maelstrom caused by the intrusion of reality into what had been in the Dreaming; her ineffectual retort "Over my dead body ..." is nearly lost as she fades away into the darkness of the corner (panel 7).

This sequence, penciled by Chris Bachalo, is reinterpreted in the later story arc by Hempel. Here, when Morpheus informs her that he will return for the child, Lyta is neither part of the background nor is she in tears (#59, 23, panel 5). [*Fig. 1*] Her image balances that of Mor-

Fig. 1: Writer: Neil Gaiman Artists: Marc Hempel & D'Israeli "The Kindly Ones: 3"
Collected in *The Sandman: The Kindly Ones* [©1996 DC Comics]

pheus just as her dark eyes mirror his. When she prophetically promises him "Over my dead body," it is not from the shrinking, darkened corner but from the center of the frame 24, panel 4). Shadows on her face make her visage more menacing than her seated, splay-legged posture initially conveys. Her statement becomes what is was meant to be: a threat. Yet, even in this moment of power, voices undercut her authority — presumably the voices of the Eumenides who have begun to intrude in her thoughts — who say "oh that I were a man or that I had power" (panel 6), while her image remains fierce, matching her decisive words "I know exactly what I must do" (panel 7). This close-up mirrors the starkly drawn image of Lyta in the first issue of the arc, where she promised Carla, "If anyone hurt Daniel I'd *kill* them" (#57, 7, panel 6, emphasis in the original).

The Lyta Hall of *The Kindly Ones* is at least initially a more imposing, powerful character than the lost dreamer of *A Doll's House.* She smashes through doors like a truck; she breaks bones without conscious effort (#59, 18, panel 6). But it is only in the name of motherhood; a woman's fury, it seems, is more acceptable when it is on another's behalf than for herself, especially for her child. After her husband Hector's death, her only life is Daniel. It is only when she dares to step away from his centrality (to interview for a job) that she loses him (#57, 17-24) — and, as a result, her own life for all intents and purposes. Always Lyta is manipulated from outside by the men in her life. As she confesses in her first encounter with the threefold image of herself, "I never did anything in my whole life that wasn't someone else's idea" (#61, 21, panel 3). Even joining with the Furies for vengeance turns out to be someone else's idea.

Setting off on her journey to reclaim her child and claim her vengeance, Lyta sets in motion the final chain of events leading to the finale, but she also initiates a split between the verbal Lyta and the visual one, a split which mirrors the divergence of her physical and mental identities within the storyline. The narrative Lyta wanders dazed and confused toward her inevitable fate, already stripped of any power she may have been loaned; the visual Lyta, however, coalesces into a reflection of her rage. Though ultimately impotent, her wrath gets a visible expression as she grows into a menacing figure.

A pivotal scene in *The Kindly Ones* directly echoes another image from the earlier *A Doll's House.* Lyta signals her seemingly inherent passivity by returning to the image of "a girl in a mirror" (#61, 21, panel 4). The reference is to a full page sequence of images of Lyta before her mirror, reviewing the steps of how she came to be there in that house (#12, 9, panels 1-6). The sequence reveals how she had been passive reflection of her childhood dreams, of Hector's desires, of her vanished mother's legacy. Even in her persona as a superhero she is reduced to tears as she claims that she and Hector are happy, "so very, very happy" (#12, 9, panel 6). This progression shows her apparently innate submissiveness.

The parallel episode in *The Kindly Ones* however, concludes in a strikingly different manner — with action (#63, 17, panels 1-6) [*Fig. 2*], in which Lyta breaks with this passive image. Further, the reflective images of the steps in Lyta's life actively engage her in a dialogue,

Fig. 2: Writer: Neil Gaiman Artist: Marc Hempel "The Kindly Ones: 7"
Collected in *The Sandman: The Kindly Ones* [©1996 DC Comics]

forcing her to make a conscious choice and to act upon it. Lyta's naked self-image tells her to stop her pursuit. Her child self expresses vehement disappointment in the woman she has become and vows not to become "a crazy woman" when *she* grows up (panel 4). Lyta's despairing claim that she is not crazy appears at first to be backed up by the Fury — but her superhero image proves just as troubling to Lyta. The unhelpful superhero persona is next displaced by the reflection of reality in all its dishevelment. This image claims that there is always a choice, that Lyta can abandon her journey; it is the last practical advice in the face of what they both know to be a hopeless cause (panel 6). However, Lyta has already incorporated the knowledge of her powerlessness at least on a subconscious level; she knows the time for self-reflection has passed — if it ever existed. It is in acknowledgement of this — as much as in frustration — that she cuts off the past and all future alternatives by smashing the mirror and making her choice to pursue vengeance even against an immortal (18, panel 1-3). But the fact remains that the narrative Lyta Hall is merely a pawn within the power of a larger event. She recognizes that her venture is doomed to fail and that she no longer desires its outcome, though she is not yet cognizant of its ramifications. However, the clues have been there all along, from the parting words of Morpheus in *A Doll's House* (#12, 23, panel 5) to the sudden appearance of sand in Daniel's bed in the first issue of *The Kindly Ones* (#57, 4, panels 1-4). Despite the subterfuge of kidnappers and mysteries, Dream has set out to claim his heir.

Despite her narrative impotence, the visual Lyta is allowed some expression of her rage and anger through Hempel's created images, if only in a very carefully circumscribed arena. After all, the avenging mother remains one of the few acceptable images of female fury allowed in patriarchal culture. A woman angry is an abomination even to herself, as Lyta's reflections in the mirror sequences demonstrate. Lyta is allowed her anger on behalf of her male child and her husband, and Hempel makes the most of this latitude until her eventual dissolution and return to the posture of defeated resignation, now familiar from her first appearance in *A Doll's House*. Ringed by the snakes in her hair, her face shadowed with resolve (#61, 4, panel 4) [*Fig. 3*] or completely blackened in silhouette (#63, 22, panel 8), Lyta's visage remains terrifying for a good part of the arc — only to be reduced to slumping defeat in the final issue.

Likewise the three Furies themselves, though frequently menacing visually, remain impotent and are simply dismissed by Death at the climax of the story arc. Gaiman the writer manipulates them even more than Lyta the character, having them appear in whichever permutation suits the storyline at the time — as the graces, the furies, the witches or the fates. The three-in-one female force makes its first appearance in the second issue of the series as the Hecateae, from whom Morpheus receives clues about his tools stolen during his long imprisonment in the waking world (#2, 18, panel 3). Here — penciled by Sam Kieth — the three appear cartoonish, in a style somewhat reminiscent of the old EC Comics caricatures. These images give little indication of the Furies they are capable of becoming.

Fig. 3: Writer: Neil Gaiman Artists: Marc Hempel & D'Israeli "The Kindly Ones: 5"
Collected in *The Sandman: The Kindly Ones* [©1996 DC Comics]

Even in their initial appearance in *The Kindly Ones* story arc is as the three Fates (#57, 1, panels 2, 3, 5). Their demeanor — parallel to this neutral aspect of their persona — is nonthreatening; they appear simply as maiden, mother, and crone without embellishment. Hempel draws them in a comfortable sitting room about to have tea — an image they return to at the end of the arc when the final thread is snipped. However when Lyta first encounters them in her dreams, they appear markedly different.

It is not their physical form that has changed, however. Their lines are little altered from the initial genteel scene, but their location has moved to a subterranean site, as they prepare to move toward their vengeful aspect. The scene itself — which comes immediately after Daniel's disappearance — has mutated to a dingy underground chamber, lit only by candles which reflect a sickly greenish hue upon the inhabitants of the room, now armed with a large carving knife (#58, 15, panel 1). The three are absorbed in labours over a simmering pot. Its contents include, we find out, a finger from a baby "ditch-delivered" and "birth-strangled," and they even seek to add Lyta to its contents.

Their features become increasingly menacing as the tale unfolds. The three reveal that they have no power to pursue Morpheus for Daniel's death, but that they can hound him for the death of his own son, Orpheus. Visually, their threatening images balance the glowering portrait of hate that Lyta has become. When she discovers that Daniel is not dead and tries to turn their energies to rescue, Lyta learns that she has no control over the vengefulness she has set in motion. When she implores them to save her child, the Furies wax bitter on the hate they had for the twice-dead Orpheus and increase their frightful appearance — highlighted by angry red and orange hues and complemented by bones and a knife (#67, 21, panels 2-7). Their final permutation proves so harrowing that in the end they can only be glimpsed in silhouette (#68, 18, panel 5). For much of their apocalyptic journey through the Dreaming, they remain unseen — we see only the destructive result of their passage as they kill off well-known characters. When they at last come face to face with Morpheus himself — here drawn by Teddy Kristiansen — they are still in silhouette (#64, 18, panel 1).

Yet they suffer the same futility as Lyta. The Furies say "Gods fear us. Demons fear us. We have hounded kings and angels. We have taken vengeance on worlds and universes" (#66, 16, panel 6). They lay waste much of the Dreaming —Gaiman seems to revel in the destruction of long-beloved characters like Fiddler's Green/Gilbert (#65, 16) and Mervyn Pumpkinhead (#66, 17, panels 1-3) — but they are dismissed curtly by Death as they reach their goal. "Enough!" she tells them, the metanarrative[1] elements clearly indicating a shout with the increased font and jagged-edged word balloon, "Leave us alone. This is between me and my brother" (#69, 9, panel 4). Here is the last assertion of female power; though Death, as always, has the final word, she too has been summoned forth by the machinations of her brother, who has chosen to give up his life as an immortal. She is confused as to why he demands this, asking "I just want to know *why?*" (#69, 5, panel 4, emphasis in the original). As John Donne once noted, even Death is a slave to "fate, chance, kings and desperate men."

Here she too must accede to her brother's desires.

In the end, the women are all ineffectual pawns, part of larger circumstances over which they have no real control. Dream dies but makes clear it is his choice — not their revenge — and part of the plans he has carried out over most of the series' length. As his sister notes with some pique, "Hmph. You've been making [preparations] for *ages*. You just didn't let yourself know that was what you were doing" (10, panel 1). Even the Norse god Loki — who with Puck had kidnapped Daniel and, Isis-like, had tried to burn away Daniel's humanity — realized at almost the same moment that he too had played a part in the elaborate scheme. The impersonal narrative voice reports that "the master manipulator realizes how, ultimately — how strangely, how elegantly — he too had been manipulated" (8, panel 2). The Furies are denied even this moment of self-recognition. They return to their comfortable existence by the end of the arc, apparently resigned to the eternal lack of satisfaction, noting, "And how could I *ever* be satisfied?" (23, panel 4).

The witch Larissa — called Thessaly in an earlier arc and a later series — suffers much the same fate of ultimate powerlessness. She is a centuries-old witch of incredible knowledge and power, and often ruthless in her demonstration of that authority. Unlike Lyta, she needs no surrogates to claim power. Though initially she seems to have control over events in this arc, even able to thwart the wishes of the Dream King for a time, she too finds that her scope of influence is small and that she unknowingly plays into the hands of the male manipulator of power. Nonetheless, her role is complicated by the powerful images she takes. Her initial appearance in the series, drawn by Shawn McManus, in *A Game of You* is owlish, scholarly and ironically childlike (# 32, 7, panel 2). Even the revelation of her true nature as an ancient Greek witch (able to force the corpse of her neighbor George to talk) does little to reduce this initial depiction of her (#34, 14, panel 6). Later drawings of her within that story arc frequently bring attention to her fuzzy bunny slippers, as well as the round glasses and head that echo her ties to the moon, which she calls down to travel into the land of dreams. Her assessment of the ruler of that realm is clear. She warns those who walk the moon's path with her that "the Dream King has little time for you women, and even less for my kind" (17, panel 9). While Thessaly dispatches a number of other characters with quick violence, her actions are softened by the iconic pink slippers and neotenic figure.

Her first appearance in *The Kindly Ones*, however, while maintaining the easily recognizable features — even her slippers — adds considerable menace. Behind the full-moon glasses her expression is serious, even cruel (#63, 1, panel 4). When blood is spilled — as it must be whenever Thessaly appears — she feels its sting, in contrast to her matter-of-fact approach to the removal of George's face in the earlier arc *A Game of You* (14, panel 2). The familiar bunny slippers make their appearance as iconographic signifiers, but they are downplayed by appearing only once and in shadow (#65, 19, panel 1).

Her position within the framework of the story originally seems to be one of strength. She is able to prevent the Dream King from directly reaching Lyta's physical self through her own magic. Thessaly takes a grim satisfaction in her apparent power (19, panel 6). She has thwarted his aim as he once thwarted hers in *A Game of You*. His seemingly impotent rage, demonstrated by the smashed windows as he leaves, surprises her initially, but she is quick to dismiss it, implicitly believing herself to exist securely within a realm of female power (22, panel 1-3).

But her power is as illusory as that of the other female characters. Thessaly finds that she too has been manipulated, assuring the end result (Dream's elaborate suicide) through her own actions, for by preventing his destruction of Lyta she has allowed the Furies to invade the Dreaming. After the death of Dream, Thessaly tells the newly awakened Lyta that she is now "a pawn ... who briefly became a knight ... or a queen. And you've just been taken off the board" (#69, 20, panel 4). What she doesn't tell Lyta is that they both share that fate. However, the pawn is also a scapegoat — Thessaly informs Lyta that "Lots of people are going to want to hurt you or kill you for what you've done," including Thessaly herself (panel 6, 8). In the end the powerless turn upon one another — where their only power lies. As Cixous writes, "Not dying, living after the other, 'remaining,' is also an intolerable experience" (15). Thessaly and Lyta both face this fate. Thessaly seeks to remedy it with another death; Lyta seems dead already. She has lost all that she had left — her son has now become the new Dream, first glimpsed in the second issue of this arc when Cluracan of Faerie steps off the path through the castle (#58, 7, panels 3-5). Her son, though not dead, has been lost with even greater finality.

"It's the same old story ..." the Fates tell us at the end of issue #69, "Whatever it turns into on the way, whatever it is you originally undertake to spin or knit or weave, keep it going long enough and, in the end, my lilies, it's always a winding sheet ..." (23, panel 3). The machinations of Dream lead to Death; he has "obligations" which are always uppermost in his mind (6, panel 2). What these obligations mask, though, is fear — the fear and cowardice that Cixous claims keeps most readers from climbing down into the depths of themselves, that necessitates the work of writers who have the ability to "write the power of dreams," to be the "secret criminals" and lead us into the foreign lands of imagination (20). The poet's job — any artist's — should be, accordingly to Cixous, "to venture there where we don't have the strength or the means to venture, to the edge of our abyss" (41). There is where Dream finds himself at the end of the series. But he cannot claim death for himself but must ask it of his sister. Cixous knows that "only the ones who love us can kill us" (93), so Death cannot deny her brother what he has orchestrated for so long, even as she chides him for being unable to ask for it openly.

Thus, unable to confront Death directly either through fear or perhaps, more likely in his case, embarrassment, Morpheus resorts to subterfuge and manipulation. Writer Gaiman supports this delusion by creating illusory power for the female characters just long enough to serve the aim of the primary male character — then causing that power to vanish with a word from Death. These overt manipulations are mitigated somewhat by the very genuine power and authority constructed by the drawings of Marc Hempel, who attempts to give the women a visual power that the narrative lacks; although in the final analysis, perhaps he, too, is an accomplice — the visual aspects of the threat reinforce our (mistaken) assumptions about who is in charge and who is the adversary throughout the story. Perhaps, however, we should take our power wherever we can establish it. In the end, this is merely an echo of the current society. Life under a patriarchal system never gives more than illusory power. Cosmetic changes in society merely reflect an attempt to address the feminine cry for reformation, while basic power structures remain unchanged. As Cixous writes, hope lies in the fearless pursuit of the act of writing (and drawing, I would add, for comics prove a powerful medium), in creating "the book stronger than the author: the apocalyptic text, whose brilliance upsets the scribe" (156). The illustrations of Marc Hempel change *The Kindly Ones* into such a text, and teach us that the appearance of power can help maintain the illusion of effectiveness — perhaps just long enough to accomplish a dream or two.

NOTES.

1. I refer to the terminology introduced by Gene Kanenberg Jr. to refer to the ways in which graphic elements enhance the reading of the narrative, e.g. Todd Klein's distinctive lettering styles for the seven siblings who make up the Endless, including Dream's black word balloons with white lettering.

WORKS CITED.

Cixous, Hélène. *Three Steps on the Ladder of Writing*. New York, Columbia UP, 1993.

Donne, John. "Death, be not proud (Holy Sonnet 10)." *Poets.org Poetry Exhibit*. The Academy of American Poets Homepage. Retrieved 20 Oct 2004 <http://www.poets.org/poems/poems.cfm?prmID=1916>.

Gaiman, Neil (w), Marc Hempel, et. al. (a). *The Sandman: The Kindly Ones*. Eds. Karen Berger and Bob Kahan. New York: DC Comics, 1996.

Gaiman, Neil (w), Shawn McManus, et. al. (a). *The Sandman: A Game of You*. Eds. Karen Berger and Bob Kahan. New York: DC Comics, 1993.

Gaiman, Neil (w), Kelley Jones, Charles Vess, Colleen Doran, Malcolm Jones III (a). *The Sandman: Dream Country*. Eds. Karen Berger and Michael Charles Hill. New York: DC Comics, 1991.

Gaiman, Neil (w), Mike Dringenberg, Malcolm Jones III, et. el. (a). *The Sandman: The Doll's House*. Eds. Karen Berger and KC Carlson. New York: DC Comics, 1990.

Gaiman, Neil (w), Sam Kieth, Mike Dringenberg, Malcolm Jones III (a). *The Sandman: Preludes & Nocturnes*. Eds. Karen Berger and Michael Charles Hill. New York: DC Comics, 1991.

Kannenberg, Gene, Jr. "Graphic Text, Graphic Context: Interpreting Custom Fonts and Hands in Contemporary Comics." *Illuminating Letters: Typography and Literary Interpretation*. Eds. Paul Gutjahr and Megan L. Benton Amherst: University of Massachusetts Press, 2001. 165-192.

☙☙☙

❖❖❖

PROSPERO FRAMED IN NEIL GAIMAN'S *THE WAKE*

by Joan Gordon

✳

"As you from crimes would pardoned be,
Let your indulgence set me free."

The last lines of Shakespeare's last play are a plea — Prospero, who has just set his own slave Ariel free, begs to be set free himself, from the dictatorship of his books and his magic; but it is also Shakespeare speaking through Prospero who begs to be set free. The author, who enslaves his characters in his vision, sets them free, and then seeks to be freed from the demands of his writing and his audience. This narrative catch and release program directs attention to the dynamic among characters, author, and audience formed by the frame suddenly revealed in Prospero's last speech. Suddenly, the imaginary fourth wall of the staged world dissolves and the audience acts back to the actors with its freeing applause.[1] The audience's story now frames Shakespeare's.

This essay about framing is itself framed by two moments. The first is a comment Neil Gaiman made in passing when I met him at the International Conference on the Fantastic in the Arts in 2000. "What I like about academics," he said, "is that they have no understanding of fame." The other moment was at a book signing a few months later. I had thought I might meet him for dinner afterward until I saw the long line of black-clad youth palely loitering to have their books signed. I realized that what I didn't understand was the cause of his fame, the strong bond adhering character, author, and reader that I was witnessing. I believe that a close reading of the valedictory chapter of the valedictory volume of *The Sandman* (1988-1996), "The Tempest" in *Volume X: The Wake* (1996), helps clarify that bond.[2] To understand this dynamic relationship, I am considering the frame in two ways. First, I shall examine the framing structure of the story itself: Prospero's story is framed by Shakespeare's, which is framed by the Sandman's, which is framed by the author's telling, and by the fan's reading. But this is a comic and it is told picture by picture, or frame by frame, so I want to consider those frames as well, and the gutters, or spaces, between them. Finally, then, I, also a reader, will provide another frame around the story, while Scott McCloud's analysis in *Understanding Comics: The Invisible Art* (1993) will frame my discussion of the visual frames and gutters of the comic.

In Shakespeare's play *The Tempest* (1611) Prospero, put to sea with his infant daughter in a leaky boat by his usurping brother, has now survived on a "deserted" island for 12 years, aided by the native spirit Ariel and the hapless monster Caliban, both of whom he found on the island and enslaved through his magic. Now he has engineered a shipwreck, by that same rough magic, to deposit on the island his brother and the king who had allowed the crime, not to mention an eligible suitor for his daughter. The play shows the cycle of romance, revelation, and forgiveness that unfold on the day of the shipwreck, and concludes with Prospero giving up his magic and preparing to return to his former home. Inspired in part by a 1610 shipwreck off the coast of Bermuda, Shakespeare's play has recently inspired debate about its possible exploration of colonialist themes.

Neil Gaiman uses *The Tempest* as the foundation for his final chapter of the long-running comic series, *The Sandman*. In it, he parallels the story of *The Tempest* with the story of Shakespeare's own retirement from the stage by imagining Shakespeare back in Stratford writing the play to fulfill his final obligation to the Sandman, with whom he had made a deal: "The Sandman would give him the genius to retell the 'great stories'; and in return he would give the Sandman two original plays," including a "tribute to the Dream King [The Sandman], and to the power and land of dreams" (Gaiman qtd. in Bender 225). In Gaiman's comic, Shakespeare's daughter appears, echoing and inspiring the character of Miranda in the play, and, although colonialism is briefly touched upon in the comic as two conmen burst into a Stratford pub to exhibit the mummified remains of a Native American for pennies (154-156), Gaiman's greater emphasis is upon parent-child relationships and the valedictory nature of the play.

FRAMES AND STORIES. When Prospero steps forward at the end of *The Tempest* to address his Epilogue to the audience, he breaks out of the frame of the enchanted world his author created to become an ambassador between story and world, between words and world (to paraphrase Anne Hathaway in *The Wake* [166]): an actor playing both character and author simultaneously. Certainly, this moment draws attention to the artifice of the play itself, and transforms the fiction into a metafiction. But it also transforms the author into a fictional character as well.

For Shakespeare, and for the literary critic, Prospero is a metaphor for the author weary of his literary magic and ready to retire. But for the audience in its more rapt involvement with the play, the terms of the metaphor are reversed. The shadowy author, unseen and less real, at least during the play, is a metaphor for Prospero, demonstrating how magic can be both power and burden, and softening the disappointment of the audience's return to the mundane while allowing for the continued life of the magical in that mundane life.

For Neil Gaiman, and for the literary critic, both the character of Shakespeare in *The Wake* and the ongoing character of the Sandman, or Dream, or Morpheus, or the Prince of Stories, in *The Sandman*, are vehicles for the writer of those stories, for Neil Gaiman. Looking at the characters in that way can stimulate some useful speculation. Gaiman as Shakespeare: the father who missed much of his children's growing up, the husband seduced away by the more glamorous life of a successful writer, the man for whom words are more real than the world. When Gaiman has Dream ask Will, "Do you see yourself reflected in your tale?", Shakespeare replies, "I would be a fool if I denied it. I am Prosper, certainly" (175) [*Fig. 1*], and Ariel, and Caliban, and Antonio, and Gonzalo, and Trinculo, and Stephano as well, he adds (176). We would, then, be fools not to see Gaiman reflected in his character of Shakespeare. As Gaiman says,

> Shakespeare's plays were written by a person — and, for that matter, by a writer. I'm by no means as talented as Shakespeare, but you know what? I can write about people. And I can portray the process of writing, because I've been there. So it didn't scare me to do stories about Shakespeare, nor strike me as some sort of hubris, because my whole approach to him was, "This is a man. This is a writer." (Bender 226)

Gaiman uses Shakespeare as a vehicle for his own experience of writing, but he does not stop there, any more than Will stopped in seeing Prospero as his vehicle.

We would, of course, see Gaiman reflected in the Prince of Stories also, and with no more hubris than in his use of Shakespeare, though the parallels are less direct. Near the end of *The Wake*, Dream takes Shakespeare to his realm and tells Will why he chose to use Shakespeare as his own vehicle for transmitting dreams to the waking world in story. He says, "I am ... in my fashion ... an island ... [...] I am not a man. And I do not change [...] I am Prince of

Fig. 1: Writer Neil Gaiman Artist: Charles Vess "The Tempest"
Collected in *The Sandman: The Wake* [©1997 DC Comics]

stories, Will; but I have no story of my own. Nor shall I ever" (182). Dream's direct claim is that Shakespeare makes a redemptive story about someone like Dream — an isolated and en-isled magician who controls the wills of others, but can, in the play at least, rejoin society — because Dream himself has no story, cannot change, and is utterly isolated. This suggests that any writer, any "Prince of Story," is isolated, empty, and changeless, living only vicariously through his writing, accusations Ben Jonson makes of Shakespeare in *The Wake*: "I've lived life to the full. What've *you* done, Will?" (159).

Shakespeare answers Jonson in Gaiman's story, "I've lived as much *life* as you, Ben ... All one needs to understand people is to be a *person*. And I *have* that honor" (159). So we must look at the mythic Dream's claim to changelessness and realize that it is false, even though Dream is not a person: After all, Dream dies — his death is the subject of *The Wake*. Death is ultimate change, but anyone following the ten volumes of *The Sandman* has seen Dream change, and has seen him connect with others, and has been reading his story. Indirectly, then, when Gaiman uses Dream as a vehicle for himself as writer, it is to remind himself and his audience of the humanity of the author at the same time as it reminds us of the writer's power to create worlds and control audiences with words.

I have called Prospero an ambassador between words and world but have considered only one direction of the envoy. I wish now to switch my allegiance and look from the world back to the words, from the audience rather than the stage. The audience watching Shakespeare's play involves itself in the lives of the characters first of all: only in retrospect or in a distanced viewing does an audience analyze metaphor, for instance. However sophisticated we are, we all relish the experience of falling into the world of the words, and the most gripping plays invite that identification, even if an epilogue at the end releases us to our own world and to our own analysis. *The Tempest*, whatever its magic and masque, invites us to identify as parents and children, and all of us have been one, many of us both. Prospero and Alonso are parents, Gonzalo fatherly; Miranda, Ferdinand, Caliban, and Ariel are their children. Whatever our status in society, whatever the age in which we live, whatever our experience or education, we look at the stage and see parents and children and forge that identification. We may find Prospero protective or controlling, for example, depending upon our own inclinations and experiences. We might identify with his desire to protect his child, his fear of losing her to the wrong mate, his struggle to balance the dynamics among his children, his varying feelings for the different children. We might identify with the favored and sheltered Miranda, the rejected and difficult Caliban, the flighty and attractive Ariel.

That identification is sealed, rather than broken, by Prospero's breaking of the frame, because he speaks to us as father to child, when he asks to be set free from the audience's claim on his existence. The aging parent can no longer manage, the maturing child can no longer obey; without release from the bonds childhood enforces on the family, anyone's "project fails/Which was to please" and the "ending is despair." The end of the play — of the world within this play, of the relationship between author and audience in any play — necessitates a similar release, the parent from the obligation to control the world, the child to the responsibility of controlling it.

There is no question that the readers of *The Sandman* identify with its characters.

At Gaiman's readings, the audience is filled with young women dressed like the character Death, young men dressed like Dream. Nor is there much question that his readers identify Gaiman himself with Dream. Gaiman doesn't particularly discourage this identification in that he himself is always dressed in black, although he claims the practicality of the fashion statement: "It's a sensible color, it goes with anything black" (Bender 10). That strong identification with characters and author explains much of Gaiman's huge fan following. As in Gaiman's source in *The Wake*, there is a lively dynamic among characters, author, and audience, and, if one considers all ten volumes of *The Sandman* and its association with the Goth movement, there is a rich variety of reasons for that lively dynamic and strong identification. Here, however, I will focus upon that dynamic as it operates in this final chapter of *The Sandman*.

Gaiman's audience, I believe, sees him first as a personification of Dream at his most mythic and abstract: "an island ... not a man," changeless and storyless. Hence, the long lines after his readings for brief word and a signature, acts of worship more than interaction. The critic Ronald Takaki says of Prospero: "A personification of civilized man, Prospero identified himself as mind rather than body. His epistemology was reliant on ... the linear knowledge of books rather than the polymorphous knowledge of experience" (150). This description also fits Ben Jonson's idea of Shakespeare, Dream's idea of himself, and, to some extent, Gaiman's audience's idea of him. While it seems true on occasion, as the writer goes from signing to signing, that his life is isolated, empty, and changeless, and while that mythic view is emotionally satisfying to his audience at first, they must also realize that he is, indeed, a man, not an island. Hence, the lively interest in his online journal and the many humanizing interviews. And, seeing him as a man, then, they would become receptive as well to engaging his characters, and through them, him, in the father-child relationship established in *The Wake's* final chapter, that between Shakespeare and his daughter Judith.

Judith says to her father, "*Why* did you have to go to London? *Why* make up the plays? ... I would have given the *world* to have had you here — when I truly *was* a little girl" (164). This longing must seem especially poignant in our present age of broken families, of families in which both parents must work, and often for long hours. Judith asks Shakespeare, "Did you not *think*? Did you not *care*?" And Shakespeare, a man of words unlike many of the readers' parents, can answer movingly, "I ... followed a dream. I did as I saw best, at the time. Not much longer, Judith. Not *too* long, now" (164). More movingly, he can write *The Tempest*, about a father who is always present, who can say, "I have done nothing but in care of thee" (I:2; 13). When Miranda says, "what trouble/ Was I then to you!" Prospero replies, "O, a cherubin/ Thou wast that did preserve me" (I:2; 23). If Gaiman's readers identify with Miranda and with Judith, they must see Prospero and Shakespeare as fathers, one ever-present, one struggling to make up for absence, both comforting.

The chain of correspondences leads beyond these characters to the character of Dream, who is both present to Shakespeare in his dreams and as he writes most of his plays, and absent from him as he struggles for the final words of his final play: "You *left* me the epilogue to write, my pale friend. And to write it with no magic but mine own words" (183). And beyond that, the chain of correspondences leads to the author — absent as an abstract, intellectual, and mythic creator of stories, yet present as the man who talks about his Halloween preparations and writer's blocks, for instance, in the online journal and interviews.[3] This is the paradoxical nature of the two roles explored in *The Wake*, of the father and of the writer.

That paradoxical role is made clearer by the implied frame that the audience provides for *The Sandman*. Just as Prospero's Epilogue draws the play's audience into the play in a dynamic relationship — its indulgence will "set me free" — the thematic emphasis on parent-child relationships extended beyond Prospero and Miranda to Shakespeare and Judith, and to Shakespeare and Dream, draws Gaiman's readership further into a dynamic relationship. The imagined fourth wall of the play is dissolved by Prospero's Epilogue to the audience. The imagined fourth wall of *The Wake* is dissolved not only thematically, not only by Gaiman's repetition of the Epilogue's final plea for release, but by the already established relationship of readers to audience in *The Sandman* series. Many of Gaiman's readers go to his readings, and have a brief moment of personal contact in the signings afterwards. They read his online journal and e-mail comments with the expectation of some reply; they read and conduct interviews with him; and they attend conventions at which Gaiman mingles with his fans. This accessibility speaks back to *The Wake*, cementing the bond among characters, author, and audience.

FRAMES AND GUTTERS.

It is particularly appropriate that the dissolution of walls occurs in the comics medium. Just as the stage erects literal walls, comics put walls between pictures. And, just as plays use actors to dissolve some of the barriers, comics use artists to dissolve the walls between the pictures. Charles Vess is the artist for "The Tempest," but, as important as his work is for this issue of *The Sandman*, and as beautiful, Gaiman himself determined the layout of the pages, the arrangement of frames and gutters on the pages. According to Hy Bender, who incorporated extended interviews with Gaiman in his very helpful *The Sandman Companion* (1999), "Gaiman wrote very detailed scripts that described the arrangement of the panels on each page, the imagery in each panel, and subtleties such as the mood he was striving for" (7). In this essay on framing, I am most concerned with "the arrangement of the panels on each page," with the frames and gutters, so it is helpful to my argument to know that the author of this particular comic has determined how those frames and gutters are to be deployed.

The frames, are of course, the borders of individual boxed panels of a comic; the gutters are the spaces between them. These terms derive almost entirely from Scott McCloud's *Un-*

derstanding Comics. In chapter three, "Blood in the Gutter," McCloud discusses closure: "Comics panels *fracture* both *time* and *space*, offering a *jagged, staccato rhythm* of *disjointed moments*. But closure allows us to *connect* these moments and *mentally construct a continuous, unified reality*" (67). The more abstract the transitions between the panels, the more work the reader does: "Every act committed to paper by the comics artist is *aided* and *abetted* by a *silent* accomplice. An *equal partner in crime* known as *the reader*" (68).

McCloud goes on to name six kinds of transitions between panels, in ascending order of abstraction, requiring an ascending level of participation from the reader to provide the "continuous, unified reality" of closure: moment-to-moment, action-to-action, subject-to-subject, scene-to-scene, aspect-to-aspect, and non-sequitur. Moment-to-moment transitions show only the smallest increments in time between frames; action-to-action transitions go from one action to the next; subject-to-subject transitions actually move from one subject, or even storyline, to another; scene-to-scene transitions move in space to a different scene perhaps occurring at the same time; aspect-to-aspect transitions are the equivalent of changing viewpoints to show different aspects of a single scene; and non-sequiturs move between unrelated things (74). McCloud analyzes a number of American comics and discovers that, except for some experimental comics, they have a consistent emphasis on action-to-action transitions, about sixty-five percent of the story, with about twenty percent of the remaining subject-to-subject, and fifteen percent scene-to-scene (76-77). In Japanese comics, although action-to-action transitions still dominate, they do so to a lesser degree. "In fact, *subject-to-subject* transitions account for nearly as many as action," with moment-to-moment and aspect-to-aspect transitions appearing as well, two kinds of transition rarely seen in Western comics (78-79). McCloud offers several reasons for this difference: the greater length of Japanese comics, the "*rich tradition of cyclical and labyrinthine* works of art" in the East (81), a greater awareness of fragmentation and intervals in art, and so on (see 82-83). The end result of these differences, however, is that Japanese comics require more closure, more participation by the reader

I attempted an analysis of "The Tempest" in the light of McCloud's ideas and found that the transitions more closely resembled those of Japanese comics than those of American ones: That is, although action-to-action transitions dominated, with about fifty-five percent of the total, there were also about twenty-five percent subject-to-subject transitions and twenty percent aspect-to-aspect transitions, with perhaps five percent moment-to-moment transitions. The imbrication of the story of *The Tempest* with Shakespeare's story and with the Sandman's meant that subject-to-subject transitions became vital, and the switching of viewpoints that enriches the comic was illustrated by aspect-to-aspect transitions. Neil Gaiman is himself interested in the Japanese anime scene and has used Japanese folk-tales in some of his work, so such a similarity is not surprising.[4] Artistically, the effect is to involve the readers more thoroughly in the experience of the work, since Gaiman's handling of transitions demands a higher degree of closure from his readers, so they become his "equal partners in crime."

The transitions of two consecutive, visually rather conservative pages from "The Tempest," pages 172 and 173, show how Gaiman's transitions work. Page 172 begins with a broad panel showing Shakespeare at the doorway to the kitchen about to read to his wife, who stands in the foreground preparing to pluck a goose for dinner. In the next three frames, directly below, the view focuses more tightly on Shakespeare, now next to his wife and looming above her, as he describes a scene from *The Tempest* and begins to read it to her while she plucks the goose. At the bottom of the page, a final broad panel zooms in on the face of Anne Hathaway while Shakespeare continues the reading. [*Fig. 2*] The first transition, from Shakespeare at the doorway to Shakespeare next to his wife, is an action-to-action transition; the next three panels, in which Shakespeare makes gestures as he reads and the feathers fly around his wife, are moment-to-moment transitions. The final transition, to the close-up on Anne Hathaway, is an aspect-to-aspect transition. The first two transitions require relatively little closure, but the last panel requires a relatively high level of closure, as the reader switches viewpoint, concentrating on the wife listening rather than on the husband declaiming. Indeed, the reader becomes the listener, looking back to the words from the world, enhancing the dynamic relationship among reader, story, and author.

On the next page, the top half of the page has three panels. In the first panel, the view shifts back to a close-up of Shakespeare, as he recites the next lines of the speech he is has written (his eyes are shut, he does not look at the page in his hands). The next panel, drawn without a border, is of Prospero continuing the next line of the speech — a very famous line: "we are such stuff as dreams are made on, and our little life is rounded with a sleep" — and the final panel returns to Shakespeare commenting on the line. Here the movement is moment-to-moment in terms of the lines of the speech, but subject-to-subject as it switches from Shakespeare to his character and back again. Thus, while the words may require very little closure, the pictures accompanying them require more; further, though the words occur moment-to-moment, they move us from the author reading what he has written, to the character personifying those lines, to the author commenting on what he has written. Again, the dynamic among character, author, and reader is invoked.

The three bottom panels on this page switch between a close-up of Anne ignoring the speech's poesy to link it, instead, to more mundane matters — "I am *pleased* you mentioned *wood-chopping*" — to a mid-range view of Shakespeare and Anne, to a close-up of Shakespeare. [*Fig. 3*] All the transitions are aspect-to-aspect, requiring more closure from the reader, and the content draws attention to the difference between the world of story that Shakespeare had been absorbed in and the world of mundane activity in which Anne was immersed. On both pages, then, the requirement of greater closure from the reader accompanies content that emphasizes the role of the audience in experiencing the story. By Gaiman's choice of transitions, then, he has further cemented the bond among characters, author, and audience.

Fig. 2: Writer Neil Gaiman Artist: Charles Vess "The Tempest"
Collected in *The Sandman: The Wake* [©1997 DC Comics]

Fig. 3: Writer Neil Gaiman Artist: Charles Vess "The Tempest"
Collected in *The Sandman: The Wake* [©1997 DC Comics]

McCloud also discusses the significance of panel shapes and borders, and of the gaps between the panels, the gutters. Applying that discussion to "The Tempest" brings similar conclusions about the heavy involvement of the reader in the world of the words. McCloud says that "each panel of a comic shows a *single moment in time*. And *between* those frozen moments — between the panels — our minds fill in the *intervening moments*, creating the illusion of *time and motion*" (94). Regularly spaced panels, marching from left to right across the page, and from top to bottom, in chronological order, with small but regular spaces between panels, would provide a very predictable sense of time and motion, and require relatively little closure from the reader. Seldom does "The Tempest" employ such a regular arrangement of the panels on the page.

Borderless panels are pictures without the line around them and bleeds are pictures which "run off the edge of the page" (103), and both create "a timeless quality" (102), according to McCloud. "The Tempest" uses panels straightforwardly on only three pages of the 38-page issue, including page 172 discussed above. On the rest of the pages we find both borderless panels (as is the panel of Prospero mentioned above on page 173) and bleeds, appropriate for a story concerning the Sandman, who is referred to throughout the series as one of the Timeless Ones. Thus, the series of panels at the top of page 173 simultaneously provides moment-to-moment transitions in terms of words, subject-to-subject transitions in terms of words, and a movement between bordered and borderless panels. In terms unique to the comics format, Gaiman sets up a constantly changing dynamic.

Eleven pages have at least one silent panel, without any words, and one page contains a completely blank panel — these too produce a sense of timelessness, according to McCloud. Bleeds and borderless panels might be inferred from McCloud's logic to require no closure since they eliminate the spaces between panels, but the opposite occurs, as the suspension of "time and motion" invites a meditative response from the reader. McCloud identifies these techniques as also being typical of Japanese rather than American comics. Here again, Gaiman draws in the audience to participate in the experience of his story.

Many pages appear to be layered, with several panels "on top of" a larger panel or a full-page illustration. Just as a metaphor invites the reader to see two things at once and to make comparisons between them, this layering invites the reader to consider the relationships between foreground and background. For example, the second page of "The Tempest" (147) has two panels showing Shakespeare at his desk, with the second panning back to reveal his daughter Judith. These appear to be placed on top of a full-page bleed showing a ship in the midst of a great storm. In script, the larger scene is captioned with the first lines of Shakespeare's play *The Tempest*. The layering technique invites us to begin making parallels between two stories, of Shakespeare's life and of his play: When Judith says, in the second of the two panels, "There is a storm brewing" and her father replies, "There *would* be a storm," it only confirms the link already forged in the reader's partnership in providing closure. The movement between script and block printing represents the movement between Shakespeare's writing and Gaiman's, so the metaphorical link between the two authors is economically rendered.

This page is also very beautiful, as is the magnificent illustration that takes up the opposite page, showing an otherworldly figure looming over a table upon which sits a hilltop village surrounded by trees, all surrounded by foliage and water. This mysterious and wordless illustration invites the reader to consider a very fluid relationship between interior and exterior narrative: It does not set a scene or offer information but it certainly invokes a mood and invites the reader's interpretation. McCloud says, "A good rule of thumb is that if readers are particularly *aware* of the art in a given story — then closure is probably not happening without some *effort*" (91). This illustration is a fine example of that statement, and there are about a half a dozen more such pages in "The Tempest." For instance, page 157 layers three realistically rendered scenes of Shakespeare at work, from three different angles of vision, over a more impressionistic picture of Prospero and Miranda drawn as if Prospero watches over not only his daughter but Shakespeare and his world. Page 178 uses elongated panels and elongated renderings of mythic characters from the realm of Dream, all in grayed pastels to render a dream sequence. Indeed, every panel, and every page draws attention to its artistic nature, through the colors, the varying styles of rendering, the shifting angles of view, and so on.

FRAMING THE DYNAMIC. An examination of the medium of "The Tempest's" story, of its frames and gutters, reveals how active the role of its reader must be, just as an examination of the narrative of the comic, its framing devices, reveals the reader's intellectual and emotional participation. In *The Tempest,* when Prospero steps out of the play, breaking that fourth wall of the stage, and asks the audience to release him by its applause, he does something more radical than requiring the audience's intellectual and emotional participation; he actually asks the audience to act upon the narrative. Within Gaiman's comic, such a radical invitation is only implied: the subject of this issue, in common with the other five issues which comprise *The Wake,* is a valedictory not only from Dream, who has died, but from the author, who is thus ending his series of *The Sandman.*[5] By using *The Tempest* as the foundation for the final chapter, Gaiman simultaneously invokes the character's and the author's requests for release.

Beyond the story, the world of words, here in the world itself, Gaiman's audience acts upon the narrative through its active relationship with the author. Consider the long lines at signings, the fans dressed like characters from *The Sandman,* the online journal and the e-mail contact, the interviews and conventions — Gaiman's accessibility and fame. His fame provides another frame around the story. It is part of the dynamic relationship among author, work, and reader made possible by the fan culture surrounding this comic.[6] This culture encourages a concrete, even familial relationship between author and fan with the story serving as the bond that links them. The relationship is both actual and abstract, a paradoxical presence and absence, an intimacy that allows the author to acknowledge that his audience is "an equal partner in crime" by begging,

As you from crimes would pardoned be,
Let your indulgence set me free.

ENDNOTES.

1. I am grateful to Madeline Scheckter for this observation.
2. In an effort to avoid confusion, I use quotes for Gaiman's "The Tempest" and italics for Shakespeare's *The Tempest*.
3. A great many Internet sites are devoted to the life and works of Neil Gaiman. His own official page is www.neilgaiman,com and it has his online journal, as well as input from friends and fans who write to him, essays on and about Gaiman, and an interview. Other useful sites include "The Dreaming" at www.holycow.com/dreaming, "Sandman, Neil Gaiman Links" at www.mayhem.com/~anne/sandman.html, and "Gaiman Archive" at www.waxberg.net/gaiman/. It is fairly easy to meet Gaiman and his audience online, reminding one that the Internet is itself a fine example of a relationship of paradoxical presence and absence.
4. Two notable examples of Gaiman's association with Japanese anime are his 1998 collaboration with the great Japanese director of anime Hayao Miyazaki in *Princess Mononoke* and his later collaboration with Yoshitaka Amano in the gorgeously illustrated short novel, *The Sandman: The Dream Hunters* (1999), a retelling of a Japanese tale about the Fox Wife. Amano is most famous for his illustrations for Kideyuki Kikuchi's 1983 fantasy book, *Vampire Hunter D*, later made into an extremely successful anime (2000).
5. Not that *The Wake* was the last word. In addition to *The Dream Hunters*, cited in the endnote above, are *Endless Nights* and *Midnight Theatre* (2003), for instance.
6. The influence of fandom on the literature it celebrates is the subject of several book-length studies, including *Science Fiction Fandom*, ed. Joe Sanders (Westport CT: Greenwood, 1994).

WORKS CITED.

Bender, Hy. *The Sandman Companion*. New York: Vertigo, 1999.

Gaiman, Neil. *The Sandman: Volume X: The Wake*. Ill. Michael Zulli, Jon J. Muth, and Charles Vess. (*The Sandman*, issue 75, 1996.) Intro. Mikal Gilmore. New York: Vertigo, 1997.

McCloud, Scott. *Understanding Comics: The Invisible Art.* Northampton, MA: Tundra, 1993.

Sanders, Joe, ed. *Science Fiction Fandom*. Westport Ct: Greenwood, 1994.

Shakespeare, William. *The Tempest*. 1611. New Folger Library Ed. Ed. Barbara A. Mowat and Paul Werstine. New York: Washington Square P, 1994.

Takaki, Ronald. "The 'Tempest' in the Wilderness." 1993. *William Shakespeare: The Tempest: A Case Study in Critical Controversy*. New York: Bedford/St. Martin's, 2000. 140-172.

✠✠✠

❧ ❧ ❧

LARGER
CONTEXTS

⚜⚜⚜

AETHER/ORE:
THE DREAMWORLD
DESCENDS TO EARTH

by Alan Levitan

✦

William Shakespeare plays a minor but radiant role in Neil Gaiman's grand comic-book saga, *The Sandman.* Given the nature of Gaiman's protagonist, Morpheus, this shouldn't surprise us. In *The Sandman* Morpheus is, after all, variously called King Dream, Oneiros (Greek, for "God of dreams"), Dreambearer, Dreamlord, Form Shaper, and Lord Shaper. The mythical figure of Morpheus connoted, according to Ovid and the ancient Romans, the spirit of shapes and forms seen in our sleep-dreams, though in popular imagination he is often taken for Sleep itself. With a Dreambearer as the central character of *The Sandman,* it's virtually inevitable that the dramatist who gave us *A Midsummer Night's Dream* and Prospero's line from *The Tempest* ("We are such stuff as dreams are made on") will figure with some prominence in the Dreamlord's spanning of the Aether and the Earth.

It is Morpheus who is Gaiman's "Sandman," and it follows that his attractive shape-changing sister is Death. The association of sleep, dreams, and death was a commonplace long before Hamlet's "sleep of death" haunted by dreams became a philosophical debating point in the Danish Prince's most famous soliloquy. The earliest pairing of Sleep and Death in Western literature is probably that passage in Book XVI of Homer's *Iliad* in which Zeus's mortal son, Sarpedon, is killed in battle and is carried off the field by those "swift messengers," Sleep and Death, for his burial in Lykia. In Homer, Sleep and Death are twin brothers; in *The Sandman*, Death is female — Morpheus' beautiful sister — and as capable of changing into myriad shapes, as is her brother.

Morpheus is no more a god than is — despite the idolaters — Shakespeare, immortal (in different senses) though each may be. Gaiman notes, in *The Doll's House* (the second volume of *The Sandman*), that "… Gods die when their believers are gone, but the Endless [the Dreamlord's race, the race that are not Gods] will be here when the last God has gone beyond the Realm of Death, and into non-existence." It's in this volume of *The Sandman* that Shakespeare makes his first appearance.

Morpheus is periodically lured into this mortal world over the course of centuries, for a variety of imaginative motives; he visits many continents, many time-periods. In a series of repeated appearances in England every hundred years from 1389 on (yes, Geoffrey Chaucer happens to be in the taven in which the Dreamlord comes in 1389, but they do not meet!), this Prince of the Nightkind keeps in touch with a more-than-ordinary mortal man named Hob. Hob has simply made up his mind not to die, like other men, but to live over centuries for as long as he chooses. Morpheus is quite taken with Hob's independent and lively spirit, and continues to meet him on the same spot every hundred years, the medieval tavern later becoming an Elizabethan tavern, a Restoration pub, and so on. In the episode taking place in 1389, the attentive reader learns a piece of news that will be important to the Shakespeare segment that transpires two hundred years later: Lord Shaper informs his sister, in an aside, that "a delegation of faerie came to me, last night. They are talking about abandoning this plane for ever."

By 1589, the Faerie will indeed have disappeared from the *face* of the earth, though not from its depths. In that same year, when the Dreamlord arrives on schedule to check up on what Hob has been doing for the last century, he overhears the conversation of two young men at a nearby table. One is William Shaxberd (historically, Shakespeare's name appeared in several permutations in his own lifetime), fresh from the reading of a new play by his tablemate that has gotten him quite excited; the other is Christopher (or "Kit") Marlowe, author of the play that has so taken Shaxberd's fancy. In one of Gaiman's frequent witty foreshadowings, Marlowe sports a broken leg tied in a splint, which he rests across the tabletop as the two friends drink their ale. Marlowe is a man who gets into serious scrapes; in about four years' time he will be stabbed to death in a tavern in an argument over the bill. (Gaiman expects his knowledgeable readers to relish touches like the broken leg, and they do.) You would be wrong to assume that Dreamshaper comes to this particular tavern at this particular time in order to confront a soon-to-be-famous playwright; the simultaneous presence of Morpheus and Shakspeare in this place, in this year, is wholly fortuitous. Each will make the most of it, though it was in no sense planned (except, of course, by Gaiman himself).

A SHORT BALLOON-DIGRESSION: The black-ink words in this comic book are enclosed by the conventional white oval "balloons," except for the Dream Lord's words, which appear in white letters against a black ground, within irregularly shaped and rough-edged balloons (not unlike the shapes of jagged-coastline islands) that signify his otherworldly origins. When Gaiman wishes to ensure the marked stress of a particular word in a sentence (and, later, in Shakespearean verse), he directs his letterer to **boldface** the word — precisely the sort of thing a teacher of Shakespearean drama sometimes wishes were a convention in the printing of certain lines in a play-text, to anticipate and prevent the kind of mis-stressing often encountered in students' reading aloud, which can render a line meaningless. Further, during the conversation between Shakespeare and Marlowe their sentences are printed as unmetrically lineated "normal prose" within the confines of the balloons [*Fig. 1*]:

> Well, Kit, your theme as I
> saw it is this: that for one's
> art and for one's dreams one
> may consort and bargain
> with the darkest
> pow'rs.

Attentive to the "giveaway" of that last word's contraction, we may re-align the words as follows:

> Well, Kit, your theme as *I* saw it is this:
> That for one's art and for one's dreams one may
> Consort and bargain with the darkest pow'rs.

In the middle line above, sense requires a reading of the words "one may" as a pyrrhic (a metrical foot consisting of two unstressed syllables), creating a run-on stronger than anything one is accustomed to in Shakespeare's style of the 1580's. (Perhaps only a literary-history pedant would bother to note this, though Gaiman might well wish to argue that Shakespeare was more daring in his conversational verse than on his written page in those early days.) The perhaps over-sophisticated run-on and the obscured pentameter lineation are witty, no matter what their intent, and could well delight more than Gaiman himself, since the audience for his comic books is uncommonly literate and literary. It's true that the verse

Fig. 1: Writer: Neil Gaiman Artists: Michael Zulli & Steve Parkhouse "Men of Good Fortune"
Collected in *The Sandman: The Doll's House* [©1995 DC Comics]

from Shakspeare's plays that *is* spoken much later by Gaiman's actor-figures in the comic book series *also* lacks pentameter division within its balloons, but that fact merely renders a reader's discovery of blank verse rhythms in the earlier Shakespeare-Marlowe "normal" tavern conversation all the more delicious. Neither poetic dramatist ever speaks mere prose to the other.

Morpheus overhears Shakespeare expressing admiration for *Doctor Faustus*, the play that William has just read (even conceivably *seen*, though the matter is left ambiguous). It's clear that earlier, Shakespeare had asked Marlowe to look over a fledgling script that *he* had written (*Henry VI*, Part I), but Kit finds fault with it from the start, quoting the "Hung be the heavens with black" opening lines and remarking "At least it scans, but 'bad revolting stars'?" "It's my first play," Will groans defensively, his head between his hands. "And it should be your last," Marlowe advises. (Despite current scholarly opinion, it would hardly do to have the dramatist say, at this point, the more historically accurate "It's my third play").

Gaiman's Shakespeare then launches into a paean of praise for Marlowe's new play, quoting from it by memory. William's next spoken thought, however, is what captures the attention of the Dreamshaper sitting at a nearby table: "I would give anything to have your gifts, or more than anything to give men dreams, that would live on long after I am dead. I'd bargain, like your Faustus, for that boon," prompting the Lord from the Endless Realm to ask Hob, with some interest, "Who is he?" "Acts a bit. Wrote a play," Hob answers. "Is he good?" "No, he's crap. Now, that chap there, with the broken leg, next to him. Bent as a pewter ducat [i.e., homosexual]. *He's* a good playwright." [*Fig. 2*] (Marlowe's "bent" proclivities are established earlier: as Shakespeare puts his arms around a tavern-girl's waist, Kit remarks "I'll stick with boys — my hornéd actresses.") But the Dreamlord is not to be put off. He knows where the greater talent lies, and he's intrigued by Shakespeare's willingness to bargain (his life? his soul? his fortune?) for the opportunity (not so much the writerly "gift," as we will later learn, but rather the opportunity) to write some immortal poetry and prose. Shakespeare's new "patron" will tell him, twenty-one years later, "I opened a door within you, that was all."

The Lord Shaper, in this first encounter, commissions two plays from Will — one at the start of his career, another toward its end — that speak on a very personal level to King Dream himself. Each play will deal, in its own way, with dreams. The first (as we might guess, if we remember Morpheus' aside to his sister a full year earlier) will somehow serve to lure the "faerie" back to the mortal world for one final visit; the last will be a "mirror"-play for the Dreamlord himself, "about a king who drowns his books, and breaks his staff, and leaves his kingdom. About a magician who becomes a man. About a man who turns his back on magic." About a wish-fulfilled Form Shaper, that is, finally (impossibly) freed from his own magic realm, releas ed from what he himself terms — an analogy drawn from this ultimate commission — "my island."

Back in 1589 Shakespeare is asked by Morpheus if what he really wants is to "write great

Fig. 2: Writer: Neil Gaiman Artists: Michael Zulli & Steve Parkhouse "Men of Good Fortune"
Collected in *The Sandman: The Doll's House* [©1995 DC Comics]

plays, create new dreams to spur the minds of men." The young dramatist quickly answers, "It is." "Then let us talk," says Morpheus, leading Shakespeare aside with an arm over his shoulder, as Marlowe remains seated in the foreground, abandoned forever to a lesser greatness. Shakespeare will not enter *The Sandman's* continuing plotline for another nine or ten chapters. He returns in the volume entitled *Dream Country*, where Gaiman's bright inventiveness in the pursuit of fantasy-biography manifests itself in earnest.

Fantasy-biographies of Shakespeare — novelistic, dramatic, and cinematic — have cropped up steadily over the past few generations, and most of them imagine specific episodes in Shakespeare's plays as having been rooted in the experience of the dramatist's life. Indeed, if there *were* a parallel between life and play, this would seem to be the normal ordering; life into play, experience into fiction. To some extent, this is true of Gaiman's Shakespeare as well. The playwright's son, Hamnet, sees it that way when he complains to his friend Tom about his father's inattentiveness to the family: "It's like he's somewhere else. Anything that happens he just makes stories out of it." The fascination and originality of Gaiman's imagining the earlier career of Shakespeare is, however, sometimes quite opposite to this traditional cause-and-effect: against all expectation, play will order life; fiction will factor reality. The relationship is never merely mathematical, never clearly causal, perhaps quite coincidental, but it is still teasingly haunting; what happens in the play will sometimes happen later in the life of the playwright. The price of Shakespeare's gift, the price of that opportunity to go beyond Marlowe and Marston and Middleton, to transcend the "quality" (as Morpheus will remark much, much later) of a minor play like *The Merrye Devil of Edmonton*, may well be a terrible price to pay. Even Shakespeare himself, in later life, will not want to know for sure the precise nature of that price. Suffice it to say, at this point, that the fictions created by the dramatist inevitably suggest — to Gaiman and to the ear-pricked reader — their own toll. The road is not the toll-road we might have anticipated. Shakespeare will not easily master the mis-stress of his passion.

The third chapter of Gaiman's *Dream Country* volume in *The Sandman* is called "A Midsummer Night's Dream." It opens in the afternoon hours of June 23rd (Midsummer's Eve), 1593, some three or four years after the Dreamlord's commission. Richard Burbage, who will become one of the great actors of Shakespeare's day, is leading a provincial-tour contingent of Lord Strange's Men into the countryside (the later play-company for which Shakespeare would become actor, shareholder, and playwright — the Lord Chamberlain's Men — has, of course, not yet come into being). They are headed for the Sussex Downs, south of theater-lively London — three wagons of actors, costumes, and props. Shakespeare's new play, *A Midsummer Night's Dream*, is to have its first performance in this countryside, at the Dream-shaper's command.

The actors are warm friends. They include Shakespeare himself, of course, Will Kemp

(historically, a famous clown-actor during Shakespeare's early career), who is constantly suggesting ad lib stage-actions to the playwright, and a young Henry Condell (historically, he
will be one of the co-publishers of the posthumous First Folio collection of Shakespeare's
plays in 1623), who has been assigned the role of Titania, Queen of the Faeries, in Shakespeare's new play. There is, too, an even younger boy-actor ("Tom") ready to dress for the role
of Helena. Shakespeare has brought along his son Hamnet, too, who will play the speech-
less Indian Boy on stage and serve as prompter behind the scenes.

The Indian Boy never appears as a speaking character in the original Folio text of
Shakespeare's *A Midsummer Night's Dream*. Nevertheless, he is as crucial to Shakespeare's new
play in *The Sandman*, as he was in the real *Midsummer Night's Dream*. It is he over whom the
quarrel between Titania and her husband, Oberon, King of the Faeries, will erupt, impelling
the play's plot. The boy is a "changeling," a mortal boy brought to the faerie world from *our*
world—in this instance the orphaned son of an Indian queen who was Titania's friend. Most
often, a faerie child — also termed a changeling — is substituted for the mortal child, but the
substituted faerie changeling can be mischievous and difficult in his earthly environment. (A
mother angry at the unruliness of her child might accuse it of being just such a changeling
from the faerie kingdom, i..e., "You cannot be a child of mine," etc.) The changeling boy in
Gaiman's imagining of *A Midsummer Night's Dream* would be an excellent apprentice-role for
Shakespeare's young son, Hamnet; the role's requirements lie solely in the realm of physical
charm and beauty, and not at all in verbal acting ability.

The little acting-troupe has been commanded by the Lord Shaper to appear at the base of
"Wendel's Mound," the famous hill-mound on the Sussex Downs that bears the mysterious
chalk outline of the so-called "Long Man of Wilmington" across its green surface. It's a primitive and gigantic figure. The Dreamlord is there to greet the troupe, though Shakespeare and
his company are mystified by the seemingly theaterless surroundings. Lord Shaper assures
them, however, that the Mound "was a theater before your race came to this island." "Before
the Normans?" "Before the humans." Still, there doesn't seem to be an audience for the play's
premiere. But once the players are in costume and ready to go on, the Dreamlord turns to
the Mound with the command "Wendel! Open your door!" The chalk giant *moves,* pushes
a section of the hill aside as if it were a huge door, and lo! the entire entourage of Faerie issues from the hill against a blazing light emanating from within the Mound, as Morpheus
respectfully greets their king and queen, Auberon (*we* know him as Oberon) and Titania. It is
the couple's first venture back to the mortal plane since that moment in the 14th century, already reported in the earlier tavern scene of 1389, when they were about to give up habitation
in this earthly world. The faeries have come because of the Dreambearer's invitation, because
of this last gift that he has commissioned to do them honor, because William Shakespeare
has already imagined them so vividly in his new play before their present return to earth.
They come *because* they have been written about; they do not come in order to *be* written
about. Gaiman's Shakespeare has never seen them before, except in his mind's eye, and then

only with fitful accuracy, though in one respect with terrifying prescience, as we shall see.

Poor Will Shakespeare is nonplussed — a nervous wreck, as he realizes who will be making up the audience this night (and there are hundreds of fairies, goblins, boggarts, nixies, in the entourage of Auberon and Titania, including a ferocious-looking little Puck, waiting perhaps to scoff). These are "groundlings" with a vengeance, and not just *standing* on the ground (as Shakespeare's later Globe Theater "groundlings" will do), but *of* the ground, the spill of Wendel's Mound! Shakespeare is playing the role of Theseus, the Athenian king presiding over the court scenes of *A Midsummer Night's Dream*, but he "dries up" at his very first play-opening lines; his nervousness has escalated into the total forgetting of his lines. He must be cued by Hamnet. After a while, the actors settle into their roles as they try hard to forget the extraordinary circumstances of the evening. The play goes along well, except for the "real" Puck's annoyance at the stage-Puck's performance of him. It isn't long before the *true* Robin Goodfellow renders his actor-counterpart unconscious behind the portable tiring-house (where the actors put on their costumes), and takes on the role himself to lend a modicum of "realism" to the production. Puck will be playing Puck this day.

All goes well for the company. Auberon and Titania are clearly pleased. But young Hamnet's appearance at the stage-Titania's side during her II.i speech about the death of the Indian boy's mother will generate the conceitful *frappe* of this chapter in Gaiman's saga. Hamnet is exceedingly attractive in his Indian costume. The "real" Titania, watching him during the stage-Titania's speech, suddenly turns to the Lord of Dreams: "That child — the one playing the Indian Boy. Who is he? ... A beautiful child ... Will I meet him?" Oh yes, Oneiros assures her, yes, yes, in the interval halfway through the play. (A Housmanian "chill" at this point would not be *inapropos*, as we watch the "real" Titania begin to echo the stage-Titania's obsession with the Indian boy.)

At the first intermission Hamnet is indeed brought to meet Titania, who tempts him with prospects of "bonny dragons that will come when you do call them, and fly you through the honeyed amber skies. There is no night in my land, pretty boy, and it is ever summer's twilight." Before the performance resumes, Hamnet tries to tell his father what has been transpiring, but Shakespeare isn't listening seriously; he has only his play on his mind. (During a short behind-the-scenes respite a bit earlier, Hamnet had confessed to his fellow boy-actor, Tom, that his father hasn't seemed "really there" for a long time and doesn't seem to care about anything but his stories: "I'm less real to him than any of the characters in his plays." He is with his father, now, only because his mother Anne ordered Will to take the child with him for the summer; otherwise, Hamnet seldom sees his father.)

Swelled with the joy of his apparent success, Shakespeare mentions to Morpheus during the interval that this is the best play he has written so far: "Not even Kit Marlowe will be able to gainsay that," Will asserts, quietly, whereupon the Lord Shaper tells him that Marlowe died three weeks earlier, in a Deptford tavern, of a knifewound to the head. Shakespeare is distraught, but guesses that "Ingram Fraser ... [Lord] Cecil's man" was the knife-wielder (this is historically true, of course) and politics was at the root of the killing. "Why did you tell this to me now? This news could have waited. Marlowe was my friend." "I did not realize it would hurt you so." "... No, your kind care not for human lives. Dark stranger, already I half regret our bargain." [*Fig. 3*] At this point we can only agree; this dream-play will exact a terrible price. The Dreamlord is merely giving Shakespeare, as he tells Titania, "what he thinks he most desires," though mortals never seem to "understand the price ... They only see the prize."

The performance continues to the end, and Morpheus explains to the real Titania that he intends this play as a "repayment" for the "diversion and entertainment" the Faerie had afforded the Lord Shaper before they left for their own haunts. It will be a guarantee of fairy-memory through time: "They shall not forget you. That was important to me: that King Auberon and Queen Titania will be remembered by mortals, until this age is gone." When the performance ends and the fairy entourage makes its way back into Wendel's Mound while Lord Strange's Men are lured into a "strange" sleep, the real Puck decides not to return with his king and queen, but to remain among the mortals to "confusticate and vex them ... Puck will stay — the last hobgoblin in a dreary world."

The actors awake in the morning, discover that the "bag of gold" they demanded of Auberon for their performance is merely a bag of yellow leaves, and start on their return journey to London. The final panel of the chapter contains simple black lettering in an orange-tan rectangle: "Hamnet Shakespeare died in 1596, aged eleven." Despite the plot of Shakespeare's play, Titania has taken full possession of her changeling boy after all.

Gaiman will leave Shakespeare to his own devices for most of the rest of the dramatist's career. The pact with the Sandman can only be completed with the last of Shakespeare's non-collaborative efforts, the final dream-play, *The Tempest*. In this conclusion to the Shakespearean material in *The Sandman*, we begin in 1610. Shakespeare, writing in Stratford now, has embarked upon the new play originally agreed upon with Oneiros years before. In the interim he has done much else too, of course. An emissary from the group of scholars commissioned by King James I to retranslate the Bible arrives to thank Shakespeare for his fine work on the Psalms that they had sent him (a delightful Gaiman invention, this!): "'God is our refuge and our strength, a very present help in trouble. Therefore will not we fear, though the earth be removed and though the mountains be carried into the midst of the sea.' Fine phrasing, sir. Fine phrasing." (Did that passage, perhaps, jog Will's memory of the time on the Sussex Downs when he *did* see an instance of earth movement and "mountains" opening?") Shakespeare expresses envy of the visiting scholar's command of Hebrew and Greek, of which he himself has none. "Ah," the scholar replies, with his admiration unabated, "but that is a matter of application, not inspiration."

Where Hamnet had been central to the narrative's concerns in the earlier chapter, it is Judith, Hamnet's surviving twin, who dominates the Stratford world here. She is now 26,

Fig. 3: Writer: Neil Gaiman Artist: Charles Vess "A Midsummer Night's Dream"
Collected in *The Sandman: Dream Country* [©1995 DC Comics]

and cannot read or write (Gaiman's Hamnet was able to read his father's scripts and serve as prompter before he was eight years old), but she is bright, lively, and fully aware of the disadvantages that have accrued to her as a woman and as a playwright's provincial and uneducated daughter. She is not yet married, though young Tom Quiney (some years her junior) seems eager for marriage to her. Shakespeare is deeply disappointed by Judith's poor prospects, especially by a less than advantageous union with the less than bright Tom Quiney. Here is Tom's "small talk" with Shakespeare in the tavern that his mother, Mistress Quiney, now runs. Tom speaks with a self-satisfied smirk on his face: "I saw your Judith this morning, Master Shakespeare," "I am sure that you did." "Well, she says 'Hello, Tommy,' so I says 'Hello, Miss Judith,' and she says ''Tis a fine morning,' and I says 'That it is,' and she says 'But it might rain later,' and I says 'That it surely might.'" "And it did," Shakespeare rejoins, sullenly, clearly bored out of his mind.

Shakespeare has completed only the shipwreck scene, I.i. of *The Tempest*, when this chapter opens, though he already knows that he will include a masque in the play, because "it is the court fashion to include masques, and I am writing this play for the King." Not King James, as Judith first misunderstands her father to mean, but the King of the Dreamrealm, whom he dare not tell her about; he says, simply, that "there are other kings than Scottish Jimmy, Judith." "Oh!," she warns, smiling at her father's indecorous familiarity with their monarch, "You must not call him that." "They call him worse than that at court," Shakespeare assures her: "They call him *Queen* James" (alluding to the king's alleged homosexual liaisons). Anne is so shocked at this loose seditious talk that she shuts her husband up, warning him that Judith might repeat it in town and only trouble can come of it. Then, in a bid for a more unworried and non-domestic atmosphere, Shakespeare sets off in a driving rainstorm for the local tavern, where he will think, perhaps write, perhaps even draw some inspiration from whatever might happen there.

And something *does* happen: two sailors — a bosun and a cook, recently disembarked from a voyage to the New World — enter the tavern with their whore and offer, for a collective sixpence, to show its occupants the wizened corpse of a savage, which they have wrapped in a blanket and brought with them from abroad. The showing of the "monstrous thing" creates the expected commotion, after which the doxy disappears into nowhere and the two sailors go off into the now-rainless night quite drunk, hauling their dead "catch" with them as they sing beneath the full moon. Stephano, Trinculo, and Caliban are ready for Shakespeare's pen.

Many a Shakespeare scholar has noted the degree to which (with a few exceptions) Shakespeare is depicted as writing alone, the sole creator of that grand dramatic romantic edifice, his "canon." Gaiman, on the other hand, starts Shakespeare off with warm fellow-actor friends among "Strange's Men," in the *Midsummer* chapter, many of whom advise, suggest, complain, and sometimes ad lib their lines. At the end of his career, in Gaiman's *Tempest* chapter, Shakespeare is visited in Stratford by another old friend, Ben Jonson, who (despite his cavils about Shakespeare's late play, *Pericles*) encourages Will in his *Tempest*-tossing and actually makes some constructive suggestions about how to handle the first Prospero-Ariel scene by putting Miranda to sleep on stage. Gaiman's Shakespeare is open about the dramatic difficulties he gets into, and always ready to consider the intelligent advice of others. In reminiscing about his process of composing, later, the dramatist will admit to the Dreamlord that sometimes he responded to the moods and exigencies of his individual players, rather than to their intelligent feedback: "*This* speech of mine means *nothing*. I wrote it but to cover while Burbage sank a beer offstage and changed his gown," or "*This* lady's speech is *pretty* but *pointless*—our young lead that week [i.e., the boy-actor playing a female role] sulked until I gave him something to make the pit cheer." Gaiman never gives us a vision of a collaborative "group effort" among the company's actors in working on the text of a play, and in this final Shakespeare chapter, of course, there *is* no company of actors; Shakespeare writes in Stratford now, not in London, and merely entertains advice from visiting friends.

It's worth noting some of the contrasts Gaiman sets up between the figures of Shakespeare and Jonson in terms of their "lived lives." Jonson claims to have moved in circles high and low, among ruffians and among masquing courtiers; he is someone who has been "a soldier, a scholar, a pauper, a duelist, an actor, a translator and a spy." He has killed a man in a duel. He has been imprisoned. He has converted to Catholicism in a dangerously anti-Catholic time. But as for Shakespeare, "What have *you* done, Will? A little tanning, held horses, a little acting, a little writing." "I've lived as much *life* as you, Ben." "But *I* have met *all* sorts of people ... from the lowest to the most high. Thus, I understand 'em." "I would have thought that all one needs to understand people is to be a *person*, And I *have* that honor," Shakespeare finally assures his friend. [*Fig. 4*]

The chief contribution of the *Tempest* chapter to imaginative biography lies in Gaiman's handling of Judith Shakespeare and her relationship to her father. She openly admits resentment over her father's long absences in London during her childhood. She especially resents the fact that Hamnet had a whole summer with his father, while she never had him near her for long. Would that he had been "a smith, or a fletcher, or even a miller," because then he would have been there, with her in Stratford. We learn from Judith that her mother, Anne, wept most of all. Shakespeare can only say "I ... followed a dream. I did as I saw best, at the time," while assuring his daughter and his wife that it will not be long now, just this one last play, which he *has* to write because of a promise.

This last play, however, becomes more than merely a promise kept to the Dreamlord. Gaiman presents us with a Shakespeare uneasy with Judith's memories of paternal neglect, and even more uneasy with the prospect of his daughter's blossoming liaison with the unpromising Tom Quiney ("I wish she would find her a more suitable suitor. He has too much of his father in him. The old devil came to London and spent every penny he had on whores. I had to lend him thirty pounds to get him out of trouble"). In a quiet moment of working on *The Tempest*, Shakespeare looks out the window upon Judith meeting Tom down the path

Fig. 4: Writer Neil Gaiman Artist: Charles Vess "The Tempest"
Collected in *The Sandman: The Wake* [©1997 DC Comics]

from the house just as he himself pens Miranda's first comment upon Caliban: "'Tis a villain, sir, I do not love to look on." Judith is depicted as shy and modest in Tom's presence at the gate beyond the garden, and we are quickly made to feel the ironic perspective behind Miranda's comment on Caliban: it is the force, rather, of her father's feelings toward Tom Quiney.

The combination of Judith's gentle recriminations against her father for his earlier neglect of her, and the unfortunate prospect of her marriage to Tom Quiney, seems to be at once the spur to Shakespeare's lavishing upon Miranda so careful and caring a father as Prospero, and uniting her with a handsome young prince of excellent prospects. Alas, as Samuel Schoenbaum tells us in his *William Shakespeare: A Documentary Life*, Tom was briefly excommunicated for having married Judith during the marriage-prohibitive Lenten season without procuring the necessary special license. Worse still, Tom had earlier gotten Margaret Wheeler with child; a month after his marriage to Judith, and only about two months before his father-in-law's death, Margaret Wheeler and her baby died in childbirth. Less than one month before Shakespeare's death, his son-in-law was brought up on charges of sexual delinquency ("Whoredom and uncleanness") before the "Bawdy Court" of Stratford, and though Tom was sentenced to a humiliating public penance before the congregation, the sentence was remitted to a fine of five shillings. Gaiman never goes into these specific details, of course, but in his story's final panel he does note that this "was not a happy marriage."

The extractor of Shakespeare's "promise" to write this second "dreamplay," the Dreamlord himself, visits Shakespeare *in a dream* in the snowy December of 1610, but doesn't answer his question about why *this* play at the end, and why *this* play for the patron-Lord. Only some time later, when Shakespeare at last pens the final "Exeunt Omnes" on the last sheet of the manuscript, does the Lord Shaper appear once more to him, this time as he sits at home writing at his desk. Now that the play is completed, Shakespeare wants more than a well-wishing "thank you." He wants reassurances that he has not trafficked with pagan gods, with anti-Christian devils. He asks to take a glass of wine with his patron, in his patron's "house." They travel to the Dream Realm, to the great castle of Morpheus. The Dreamlord reminds Shakespeare about what he had once wished for, and why, by flashing before him a replay of his early conversation with Marlowe. "I said that?" He had, for a time, forgotten that wish to "give men dreams that would live on long after I was dead," but now he is forced to recall it once more: "Yes, I did ... I remember. I was so *young*. Five and twenty ... Look at me *now*: a fat old man, lustless and lackluster, with my twoscore years and seven ... I dream of being nobody at all. My every third thought is of the grave."

The playwright does have two important questions he wants answered, however. First, would Hamnet have lived had Will never compacted with the Dreamlord? But no sooner does he ask than he turns his head away, shielding his face with his outstretched hands: "No, do not tell me that. You have said too much already. I wonder ... I wonder if it was *worth* it." The second question's answer he will stay for: Why *this* play? Why this topical subject inspired by a wreck in the Bermudas? Why a mere fairy-story with what Shakespeare himself terms "a cheap happy ending"? Why not a great tragedy, "something lofty, something dark"? The answer is that Morpheus "wanted a tale of graceful ends. I wanted a play about a king who drowns his books, and breaks his staff, and leaves his kingdom" — precisely *because* Lord Shaper cannot ever really leave his *own* "island"; because the Sandman, as Prince of Stories, cannot — does not — change, has no story of his own, craves at least a fictional closure in harmony and release. Shakespeare has earned this answer, and is the first mortal before whom the Form Shaper has ever bared his own burden of fictional, but story-less, infinity. Morpheus thanks the playwright and dissolves into air — into thin air, as *The Tempest*'s Prospero might put it.

Shakespeare writes the great epilogue to the play with his own strength and sympathy, merging the conventionally sentimental superposition of his own release from drama upon the Prospero-actor's release from the stage, but with a newly aware sensitivity to the Dream Shaper's yearning for release from *his* seemingly endless existence. This goes a long way toward mitigating what might otherwise strike us as a merely predictable allegorical-biographical reading of Prospero-Shakespeare's farewell to "art." And to dissolve even further the overly "easy" equation, Gaiman has Shakespeare stress, to the Dreamlord, the "negative capability" aspects of his art. When asked whether he sees himself reflected in his tale, the dramatist responds: "I would be a fool if I denied it. I am Prosper, certainly ... But I am also Ariel — a flaming spirit, crackling like lightning in the sky. And I am dull Caliban. I am dark Antonio, brooding and planning, and old Gonzalo, counseling silly wisdom. And I am Trinculo, the jester, and Stephano, the butler, for *they* are clowns and fools, and *I* am *also* a clown and a fool ..."

The cleverest manipulation of the old, trite equation of Shakespeare with Prospero, however, is that the burden of allegory, the weight of symbol, is borne not by Shakespeare in this recasting of his life and art, but by Morpheus himself. After all, the reason the Lord Shaper commissioned *this* dreamplay as the fulfillment of the original "pact" is precisely that the Prince of Stories wishes to see *himself* as the fictional magus of Shakespeare's last great play. It is Morpheus, not Shakespeare alone, who becomes the symbolic "stand-in" for Prospero in Gaiman's recasting of the tale. The "real" figure behind the magician in *The Tempest* turns out not to be flesh and blood after all, but an allegorical and symbolic figure himself, the very creator of "story," the Prince of Stories, the Dreamlord whose only "release" can be a symbolic release through Shakespeare's art.

One can't say with any certainty that Gaiman makes us understand Shakespeare in any new way. I can say, however, that without the interposition of Shakespeare in this beautiful and complex tale whose serialization spanned almost ten years, I could not have so fully understood the Lord of Dreams. An early and a late Shakespeare play serve as virtual "bookends" for the wider-ranging saga that is Gaiman's seventy-five chapter exploration of the Realm of the Endless and its pained Dream Shaper. That saga has traversed many centuries before and after Shakespeare's, and has done so with an often world-weary melancholy, as well as with wit, charm, and great imagination. This final chapter of *The Sandman* draws us back to the one historical-literary figure in whom Morpheus found a worthy literalist of the Dreamlord's past pleasures, and an even worthier metaphorist of his ever-present pain.

✠✠✠

OF PARENTS AND CHILDREN
AND DREAMS IN *MR. PUNCH*
AND *THE SANDMAN*

by Joe Sanders

✦

"I wouldn't want to gloss over the true facts," says the narrator of Neil Gaiman's first graphic novel, *Violent Cases* (1987), lounging comfortably and looking for all the world like a portrait of Gaiman himself. "Without true facts," he continues, "where are we?" Since *Violent Cases* goes on to demonstrate how few unquestionably true facts there are and how awkwardly they fit together, the answer to that apparently rhetorical question seems to be that we are, without objective certainties to depend on, in a world we build out of our fantasies, a land of dreams. The real question is where, if anywhere, we can go from there.

Violent Cases shows a small boy's fascination with the mysterious, dangerous world around him. Especially as the narrator presents it, the boy lived in a world full of intimations of violence and wonder. For example, the conjurer entertaining at a child's birthday party appears to be somehow allied with the gangsters who spirit away, as the boy watches delightedly, an old man who may have been Al Capone's osteopath. Just so, the angry game of musical chairs played by children at the party may echo Capone's vicious notion of competition as the boy walks around a circle of chairs and bashes in the heads of his "guests." Other dangers and mysteries are closer to home. Before the story begins, the boy's own father settled a disagreement by jerking him along so sharply that he dislocated or at least severely sprained his son's shoulder. "Back then," the narrator says of his father, "he seemed huge. He was my rock and my refuge. But when I read stories of giants fefifofumming their way along rocky castles, the ground echoing to their steps, sniffing for the blood of an Englishman in the way that only giants could — the giants always looked like my father." Obviously, adult readers may say, the boy is exaggerating: His father was neither God Almighty nor a menacing giant. For the boy, however, those fantastic images are not merely the playful products of an innocent imagination, but rather boundary markers within which a weak, uncertain entity can survive. But what did the boy have to do in order to survive? The narrator, looking back as a reflective yet somehow anxious adult, speculates on what was true or important in the child's experience. Since he cannot be sure himself, those questions are left for us readers to decide, based on our own sense of human possibility.

Gaiman and his collaborator, artist Dave McKean, intended to continue their exploration of memory and consciousness immediately (Thompson 71). Instead, it was a few years before they returned to this quasi-autobiographical territory with *The Tragical Comedy or Comical Tragedy of Mr. Punch*, hereafter referred to simply as *Mr. Punch* (1994). This book also is narrated by a man, unseen this time, continuing his youthful efforts to put together bits of information and observation so that he can understand the world in which he must live. Again the task is extremely difficult, and again the adults surrounding the child are of little or no help. They actually try to deny useful understanding. Consider these true facts:

✠ An eight-year-old boy is staying with his grandparents during the last weeks of his mother's pregnancy. His paternal grandfather owns a small, unsuccessful arcade in Portsmouth, one of whose attractions is a mermaid who poses seminude "in the middle of a very small artificial lake." (Even while being scrupulously accurate in describing where she performs, the boy never refer to her as a young woman wearing a mermaid costume; to him, she is simply "the mermaid.")

✠ The boy's grandfather and grandmother sleep in separate bedrooms, and the boy discovers that the man is away, possibly for at least one whole night.

✠ The teenage assistant at the Punch and Judy show that sets up briefly in the arcade comments "knowingly" that the mermaid soon will have to quit her job because the costume won't fit.

✢ The boy sees his uncle, who may be allied financially with his grandfather,
talking with the mermaid. The man is describing how difficult it was to
keep quiet what happened to "the last one." The mermaid replies defensively, "Well, I'm not the last one, am I? And he loves me. He said so."
Before they catch sight of the boy and interrupt their argument, the man
tells her, "He's an old man. He doesn't love anybody."

✢ Professor Swatchell, proprietor of the Punch and Judy show, says that as a
young man the boy's grandfather was "a bit of a lad for the ladies ... That
doesn't lead to a quiet life. And he never understood that it was a sin to
sell fakes as the real thing."

✢ The boy watches his uncle fill an envelope with money and deliver it to a
woman.

✢ Although the grandfather has left him in his car outside the arcade one
night, the boy enters the building. He sees "three men I recognized and
a woman that I didn't" shouting at each other. When the woman laughs
scornfully at one of the men, he picks up a stick and begins beating her in
the face and stomach. As she runs out past the boy, "clutching her swollen
stomach," he recognizes her. Readers see that she is the mermaid.

It is relatively easy for readers to connect these hints and glimpses into a coherent narrative of sexual exploitation and betrayal. For the boy, making the connection seems to be
much more difficult. After the confrontation in the arcade, he walks down to where he saw
the men but finds only his grandfather, "crying in deep gasping sobs. That upset me more
than anything else could have done. Adult helplessness destroys children, or it forces them to
become tiny adults in their turn." The boy does not reveal what sense he has made of what he
witnessed but simply shows himself trying to comfort his grandfather and assist him back
to the car. Once there, behind the steering wheel, the old man has an opportunity to explain
to the boy what happened and to suggest how to cope with the understanding. Instead, now
that he has pulled himself together again, he closes the subject altogether: "'You didn't see
anything,' he said. He was telling me, not asking me." When the authority figures in your life
refuse to help you interpret experience and in fact demand that you deny your senses, what
can you do? For good or ill, the boy has available a set of images by which to understand
people beating and breaking each other: Punch and Judy. As Gaiman describes the puppet
show, during an interview,

> Mr. Punch is a murderous little glove puppet, beloved by children. His
> catch phrase, uttered almost unintelligibly, is ... "That's the way to do it,"
> as he beats to death his wife and the policeman who comes to arrest him.
> At the end of it, he's killed everyone: he's killed the Devil and the guy who

meant to hang him, and he's killed his wife and scared away her ghost ...
[*sic*] and now he's going off to bring happiness and joy to children everywhere. (Thompson 71)

It's fairly clear that the purpose of Punch and Judy shows is not just pleasure but instruc-
tion: "That's the way to do it." Mr. Punch shows children that big people, especially fathers,
can get away with anything. What isn't clear is whether the puppet shows' primary audience
is children or grownups. It may be that adults need constant reassurance about the proper-
ness of their roles. Children, on the other hand, have been *brought* to most of the performanc-
es described in *Mr. Punch*, and the children sometimes appear frightened or actively hostile.
Violence is terrifying to the weak, who realize that they can't defend themselves against it,
and Mr. Punch neatly symbolizes such absolute violence. Early in the book, the boy mentions
that his grandfather eventually went mad, after he wrecked his car, "all his affairs, business
and otherwise" were over, and he stayed home, shouting angrily at his wife. On the page
describing this, the grandfather is pictured with his arms thrust out like a hand puppet's,
his face hidden by a huge mask that combines his anguished, frightening features with Mr.
Punch's.

On the other hand, the first thing shown in *Mr. Punch* is an earlier episode of the boy's
life. As a seven year old, visiting his other grandfather, he goes fishing with the man, but he
gets tired of that and walks alone back up the beach to a forlorn, empty little tent, where suddenly and without explanation a private performance "the tragical comedy" begins for him.
The boy watches as Judy leaves their baby with Punch who, when it begins to cry, "threw it
out the window. Not really. He threw it off the stage. It tumbled down from the stage onto
the beach — and lay there, silent and bleeding." After Mr. Punch's murder of his baby, the
boy immediately runs away from the deserted tent, apparently horrified by what he has seen.
There is no indication, however, that he even mentions the experience to anyone else then
— or ever, until it becomes part of this narrative and until he has become as uncertain about
what actually happened as he is concerned about what it could mean. Though presented as
immediately seen, verified by McKean's illustrations, the boy's/narrator's observations are a
mixture of the factual and the fantastic; for example, he corrects himself that the baby was
not thrown through a nonexistent window but off the stage, but then describes the puppet
lying there "silent and bleeding." But underlying readers' uncertainty about the true facts
of events is the question of how perceptions become distorted in the first place and why
observers fantasize so persistently. In other words, where did that particular Punch and Judy
scene originate, based on the conviction that when one is being bothered by other people,
casting them aside is the best solution, "the way to do it"?

From what the beginning of *Mr. Punch* demonstrates, children already have absorbed that
attitude by the time they arrive at the puppet show. The boy apparently is shipped off to stay
with his grandparents rather frequently. The reason never is explained clearly, for it may not

be clear to the boy, but it appears to have something to do with his mother's disturbing habit of getting pregnant, an awkward process that disrupts living arrangements and family relationships. The boy seems to take little pleasure in the visits, but simply accepts them as the way things are. Docile acceptance is the safest way to behave around adults. When the boy's paternal grandfather notices that the boy is watching him as he waves to the mermaid in her lake, he picks him up and says playfully, "'Shall I throw you in, eh? Shall I throw you in the water?'" The boy mutely shakes his head, and the narrator comments that

> Adults are threatening creatures.
> *Shall I throw you in the water?*
> *I'll put you in the rubbish bin.*
> *I'll eat you up.*
> *I'll take you back and get another little boy.*
> That's what they say. And now matter how much you tell yourself that they're lying, or teasing, there's always a chance maybe they are telling the truth …
> Adults lie, but not always. [*Fig. 1*]

This comment, remember, is the adult narrator verbalizing the child's silent understanding. Powerless, threatened, lied to, a child might naturally feel distrust or even hostility toward the big people around him, even though he would have gained enough cunning to conceal his true feelings. Readers note, later in the book, how the boy's shadow becomes Punch's. And still later, as he watches the argument between the adults in the arcade, his skin changes texture so that his face looks like carved wood as he sees the baby puppet, lying on the edge of the Punch and Judy stage behind which he is concealed, and knocks it to the ground while his grandfather is beating his pregnant mistress.

In fact, the boy and his grandfather are more alike than they appear, far more than either of them could acknowledge. Even as a child, the boy sometimes is forced to act like a "tiny adult," and in any case he is acquiring the skills required to behave like an adult. One such skill is concealment. Adults do not reveal any more of themselves than they must; instead, they create a frozen-faced surface to hide their real concerns. Children realize this and suppose that they must imitate it. When the boy asks his paternal grandfather about his past dealings with Professor Swatchell, he is told that "I should mind my own business; that if I asked no questions I would be told no lies. I wanted to ask whether, if I asked many questions, I would be told many lies, but I held my tongue. Adults do what adults do; they live in a bigger world to which children are denied access." In order to enter that bigger world, where they imagine adults somehow gained the secret of their understanding and power, children try to become like them. To be a "tiny adult," it seems to the boy, is to be stoic and unquestioning of others — and of himself also.

Fig. 1: Writer: Neil Gaiman Artist: Dave McKean *Mr. Punch*
[©1994 Neil Gaiman & Dave McKean]

The advantage of taking on such a role is that one can avoid looking powerless and alone. The disadvantage is that one easily can drift into believing that role. Such belief can prevent a person from being able to function in the real world, and so the boy's grandfather goes insane when his arcade goes bankrupt, he casts off his young mistress, he wrecks his expensive car — in short, when he is unable to deny convincingly that he *is* powerless and alone. It appears to be a circular process: Refusing to understand what is happening in our lives lets us continue to deny understanding so that, with constant rehearsal, our performance becomes both seamlessly polished and dreadfully brittle.

And so we find *Mr. Punch*'s narrator — "lonely now and very far from home," an adult looking back at the adults who surrounded him as a child and at himself studying them. Growing older, one is supposed to know the world better and to be more able to take confident action. Instead, the narrator gropes through his memories, deconstructing certainties and trying to grasp true facts.

Even if facts could be verified somehow, though, what then? The separate facts would have to be fitted together into a whole picture so that we could know where we are and what we should be doing. In *Mr. Punch*, the separate pictures remain separate. The media in different panels vary from altered or enhanced photographs to line-drawings or painted scenes: transitions between panels often are close to what Scott McCloud calls the "non-sequitur," without an immediately apparent relationship. As McCloud continues, however, the very act of seeing panels next to each other leads readers to "find *meaning* or *resonance* in even the most jarring of combinations. Such transitions may not 'make sense' in any traditional way, but still a relationship of *some* sort will inevitably *develop*" (72). Readers of *Mr. Punch* do try to recognize the different versions of the boy himself, sometimes in slashed or torn photographs, sometimes in unemotional line drawings — and once, feeling the inner turmoil after he has watched his grandfather drive away the mermaid, as a fully-painted but featureless "tiny adult" in the same panel with bits of other aspects of himself as a child. *Mr. Punch*'s narrator, however, actively resists making the connections that readers can. He knows how vital it is to do so. As he says, "In a perfect world, it occurs to me now, I would write this in blood, not ink. One cannot lie, if one writes in blood. There is too much responsibility; and the ghosts of those one has killed will rise up and twist the pen down true lines, change the written word to the unwritten …"

Yet, at the same time, he is too involved in the events *Mr. Punch* hints at to let himself look at them directly.

And thus the narrator finds himself trying to reveal truth by using storytelling, the same device that also is used for concealment. "The path of memory is neither straight nor safe, and we travel down it at our own risk. It is easier to take short journeys into the past, remembering in miniature, constructing tiny puppet plays in our heads. That's the way to do it." At first this sounds like an admission of defeat, a surrender to selfish fantasy. Since the narrator has been defeated before he even begins trying to discover or connect true facts, however, it is possible that examining fantasies actually could be a way to grasp the truth. At least we already have been attempting to do so, in our earlier analysis of the book's opening scene in which the boy describes the impossible Punch and Judy performance he "saw." We humans reveal ourselves as we put on the puppets of our choice, just as the boy imagines himself donning the costume head of a badger after seeing a performance of *Toad of Toad Hall*, so that he could "become the badger, a tiny stumbling thing with a huge head, uttering vast truths I dared not think as a child." Later still, Professor Swatchell lets the boy try on the Crocodile hand puppet from his Punch and Judy show, and the boy is thrilled as it comes to life: "I didn't ever want to give it back. I wanted it to sit on my arm forever, brave where I was fearful, impetuous where I held back. I would have taken it to school and scared my teachers, taken it home and made it eat my sister … [*sic*]" In both cases, playing a part allows the actor to reveal desires otherwise unacknowledged. When the boy requests a chance to try on Mr. Punch, however, Professor Swatchell refuses because "'Once you bring Mister Punch to life, there's no getting rid of him.'"

Clearly, the boy knows what he wants, although he knows better than to express his wishes. But the only character in *Mr. Punch* who can admit to such desire is the man who operates the Punch and Judy show. Unable to deal with true facts directly, humans are forced to approach reality indirectly, through fantasy. To the objection that "Things never happened thus," one may reply that "Things need not have happened to be true. Tales and dreams are the shadow-truths that will endure when mere facts are dust and ashes, and forgot" ("A Midsummer Night's Dream" in *Dream Country*). So says Morpheus, Dream, the title character of Gaiman's *The Sandman*, the comics story that ran through seventy-five monthly installments, beginning not long after *Violent Cases* and overlapping the writing of *Mr. Punch*. In fact the form and substance of *The Sandman* show a great deal about the quest for understanding and purpose that fills Gaiman's other writing.

Rather than beginning with the apparent advantage of meeting a protagonist anxious to communicate with us, readers of *The Sandman* start off outside Dream. We must try to figure out what *he* understands and what *his* purpose may be. And even when we don't have enough evidence, we must guess.

Guessing is necessary frequently in *The Sandman*. Gaiman used the interruptions of periodical publication to demonstrate how seldom we see a complete story at one time — or how little even the stories we see as wholes can be understood outside their context. Readers of the monthly magazine sometimes found parts of multi-issue story arcs, sometimes "short stories" complete inside one issue; however, they soon realized that each issue contained only some aspect of Dream, not his essence. This is apparent first of all visually. Gaiman utilized the fact that a monthly comics magazine requires more than one artist and that therefore characters are bound to look different from issue to issue. Beginning a new installment, readers cannot be certain what Dream will look like. It stands to reason that an ancient African queen would see Dream as one of her peers, while a contemporary white teen would see him as a shaggy-haired punk rocker. In the same way, the character would not dress the same in Chaucer's England as in contemporary London. Even within the same series or a single issue, Gaiman requested different artists for different sections, or gave instructions in his script so that Dream looks Oriental to a Japanese storm god while an Egyptian cat goddess sees him as feline.

Beyond that, however, Gaiman reminds readers that there are more sides to Dream's nature than can be reconciled easily. According to an early issue of *The Sandman*, thousands of years ago when Dream's African lover Queen Nada refused to stay with him, Dream responded by condemning her soul to "eternal pain" in Hell ("Tales in the Sand" in *Doll's House*). Just a few magazine issues later, during the 1800s, Dream advises the quasi-immortal Hob Gadling to get out of the slave trade because it means "treating your fellow humans as less than animals" ("Men of Good Fortune" in *Doll's House*). Each of these actions is a true fact, as far as readers can know, but it is hard to see how they can originate from the same person. Dream remains aloof, enigmatic.

Gradually, through several episodes, readers do piece together something of Dream's origin. He is one of the Endless, beings who represent basic conceptual categories. The other members of his family are Destiny, Death, Destruction, the twins Desire and Despair, and finally Delirium (formerly known as Delight). Although the Endless sometimes act as pure embodiments of their names, they also display more personal identities. What readers can guess about Dream himself, based on what he demonstrates and what he says about himself, is that he is in charge of creating or at least potentially monitoring all dreams. He produces both reassuring fancies and nightmares. The focus of his actions is somewhere between those of his cute, perky older sister Death, who removes humans from this level of consciousness, and his younger sister/brother Desire, who operates so much within the world of our present senses that Desire's private citadel is merely an immense replica of his/her own body. Dream is, in short, a being of great power who lives by frequently mysterious rules. He is bigger than readers can estimate, let alone comprehend, but he is too important to ignore, too active in human lives.

Dream sounds, in practical terms, like the adults in Gaiman's *Violent Cases* and *Mr. Punch*, especially the grownup family members. Most especially, Dream resembles the fathers. As with grownups generally and parents in particular, one never can be quite sure whether to expect kindness or pain whenever Dream appears. In the first issues of *The Sandman*, he initially is seen as a prisoner, a victim of foolish occultists who imagined they were capturing Death. This introduction makes Dream appear sympathetic, and when he escapes decades later he takes only what seems appropriate revenge on his captors. As he repairs his realm and reassumes his power, he is sometimes oblivious to mere human concerns. Still, he acts against forces that readers find even less sympathetic, and he is capable of unexpected gentleness, as when he rescues young Rose Walker from the serial killer called Funland and then gives a dream of peace to that tormented man who murdered children because of his frustrated loneliness: "*I'm sorry*, he tells the children. *I'm sorry I hurt you all. Do you forgive me. Of course we forgive you*, they say. *Now let us play some more in these gardens, which are paradise.*" And yet Dream himself prepares, in the last installments of the "Doll's House" story arc, to kill Rose because she somehow unknowingly embodies a "dream vortex" that he believes could break down the barriers between individual dreamers and thus destroy this universe. There seems to be no way to figure out such a character; as the boy in *Mr. Punch* says of adults generally, the Sandman simply does what he does.

That's not altogether true. But before readers can consider how a grownup's mind can be changed, we must try to guess what Dream has on his mind.

What Dream talks about, whenever he wants to explain or justify himself, is Duty. As he tells Rose Walker, he is "the Lord of this Realms [of dreams], and my wishes are paramount. But I am not omnipotent." And so, though he tells Rose he is sorry about having to do it, he will kill her because it is his duty to protect his area of responsibility, the supernatural realm called the Dreaming. As far as Dream knows, all this is unquestionably true. However, fortunately for Rose, her dying grandmother, Unity Kinkaid, appears in the Dreaming to say that she will take Rose's place because *she* should have contained the vortex if she had not been unconscious while Dream was imprisoned. To Dream's bewildered comment that he doesn't understand what is going on, Unity replies, "Of course you don't. You're obviously not very bright. But I shouldn't let it bother you." So Duty turns out not to be the absolute Dream thinks — or at least he may be mistaken about how it is to be carried out.

The real question is whether, or under what circumstances, Dream himself could recognize this qualification. Readers should remember both the Sandman's solemn certainty and Unity's irreverent debunking, indicating Gaiman's own balanced view of the character. Taking himself and his duties with utter seriousness, however, Dream seems unable to see himself except in rigid terms. That certainly is true in his relationship with Nada, in which he is willing to let her sacrifice her people and her world in order to stay with him. In fact, he demands she make that sacrifice, unable to recognize that *she* feels a sense of responsibility stronger than her love. Readers can observe the Sandman's inability to reconcile personal feelings and obligations, camouflaged or denied by resolute belief in public role, in his behavior as a parent. Again, readers become aware of this aspect out of chronological order, after the severed head of Orpheus refers to Dream as his estranged father in a short story set during the French Revolution ("Thermidor" in *Fables and Reflections*). A later special issue of *The Sandman*, set in Ancient Greece, describes Dream's displeasure at Orpheus' rejecting his advice to put aside his grief for the dead Eurydice and stoically continue with life. When Dream refuses to help Orpheus retrieve her soul from the underworld, the boy angrily declares his independence and leaves. After he has failed to save his lover from Hell and still cannot subdue his grief — after, essentially, he has behaved unlike Dream did with Nada — Orpheus is torn apart by the Bacchae. Dream retrieves his son's head on the beach, calmly remarking that he has "come to say goodbye. It seemed the proper thing to do." He has spoken with priests

Fig. 2: Writer: Neil Gaiman Artists: Bryan Talbot & Mark Buckingham "The Song of Orpheus"
Collected in *The Sandman: Fables and Reflections* [©1993 DC Comics]

who agreed to watch over the head from now on. However, he reminds Orpheus that the boy denied their relationship. Therefore, the Sandman will not help his son die, and he will never see him again: "Your life is your own ... Your death, likewise. Always and forever your own. Fare well" ("The Song of Orpheus" in *Fables & Reflections*). And Dream strides away without looking back. [*Fig. 2*]

From what readers have seen of Dream by the time "Song of Orpheus" was published, it is not surprising that his behavior with others is cool and formal. Even with his own son, he appears interested but remote. When affronted by a plea for personal intervention, thus, Dream' idea of punishment is further withdrawal: You did this to yourself, he tells Orpheus, and now you have to live with it. He does not see that by leaving his son in hopelessly mutilated physical condition he has him back under absolute control. He does not admit that he is leaving someone he cares for in helpless imprisonment.

At least, he does not recognize it at the moment.

While he is treating the people around him without compassion, Dream justifies himself by appealing to his role as one of the Endless, his need to execute impersonal duty. Actually, his behavior seems to be based on rigid habit, such a desperate unwillingness to consider change that it denies the existence of alternatives. When Orpheus' uncle Olethros (Destruction) insists that his father does care for him and Orpheus replies that "He has a strange way of showing it," the Endless comments "Aye. But that's his way. He's set in his ways." Orpheus' mother, the muse Calliope, says as much: "He cannot share anything; any part of himself. I thought I could change him. But he does not change. He will not. Perhaps he can not." Centuries later in time — though earlier in the series of comic-book stories — Dream frees Calliope from captivity, and she marvels that he *has* changed; he tells her "I have learned much in recent times" ("Calliope" in *Dream Country*). [*Fig. 3*] He had insisted that he must not and could not change, but now he has. And later, even though he is one of the Endless, nevertheless he dies.

The death of the Sandman, at the end of "The Kindly Ones" story arc, announced the impending end of the regular comic book and set readers debating the reasons Dream accepts the termination of his existence. One difficulty readers have with *The Sandman* is that encountering episodes out of chronological order forces us to put the sequence of events together, so it sometimes is difficult to catch hints of how concerns are related. That probably is why Peter David mistakenly guesses that Dream ultimately commits suicide in reaction to his helpless imprisonment shown in the comic's first issues, a kind of psychic rape that traumatized Dream unbearably because of his obsession with control. It is true that when, during their last conversation, Dream tells Death that he has been making preparations for his passing, she replies, "Hmph. You've been making them for ages. You just didn't let yourself know that was what you were doing" (*The Kindly Ones*). Actually, however, one of the things Dream has been doing since escaping from his imprisonment has been freeing others from confinement, including Calliope, Nada, and eventually even Orpheus. As Dream remarks, he

Fig. 3: Writer: Neil Gaiman Artists: Kelley Jones & Malcolm Jones III "Calliope"
Collected in *The Sandman: Dream Country* [©1995 DC Comics]

has learned from his recent experience. He is not throwing his existence away because it no longer matters. Nor, for that matter, is he simply purging his guilt. He is following a fuller understanding of duty to what he has learned is right.

Freeing Orpheus from imprisonment by finally giving him death is the direct cause of Dream's own death. Like the other Endless, Dream understands that one of the basic rules of their existence is that anyone who spill family blood becomes the prey of the Erinyes, also known as the Furies or the Kindly Ones. Nevertheless, he watches or even nudges into motion the series of events that brings him and Orpheus together again and that leads him to grant his son's plea for release. At a level below full consciousness, the Sandman knows what he is doing, and he knows what the consequences will he: his own extinction and replacement by another embodiment of Dream.

That the Sandman accepts this personal end must show that he has realized that his own past actions have been mistaken, that the way he has carried out his duties has sometimes been wrong. The immediate cause of that realization must be what Dream has learned by his own experience of what it means to be a prisoner. However, his imprisonment appears actually to be culmination of a process of unverbalized reconsideration that had been going on for a very long time. As *Mr. Punch* shows, remember, adults try not to reveal what truly is going on inside themselves for fear of it being noticed by someone else — or by themselves. They must bring out their concerns in fiction, obviously artificial tales that onlookers can hold away at a safe distance. And so in the story "Men of Good Fortune" Dream approaches the eager young hack playwright Will Shaxbeard with the query whether he would like to be able to "write great plays? Create new dreams to spur the minds of men?" A later story reveals that they have come to terms: Dream has given the aspiring writer access to "the great stories," tales that embody basic human fears and desires, and in return William Shakespeare will write two plays for him and have the first performed as his patron desires. Thus, on June 23, 1593, a play about the confusions ensuing when mortals and non-mortals mingle, is performed as *A Midsummer Night's Dream* by a band of human players before an audience the Sandman has invited from the real of Faerie.

Two aspects of Gaiman's script, winner of a World Fantasy Award for best short story, are especially worth noting. For one, the story contains references to subjects from the past that have not yet been shown to readers: Orpheus and his fate. Queen Titania's comment during the play that she "heard this tale sung once, in old Greece, by a boy with a lyre" may be a reference to Orpheus; the play certainly refers to this part of Dream's past, as he watches expressionlessly, when Theseus finds "The riot of the tipsy Bachanals tearing the Thracian singer in their rage" listed among possible subjects for dramatic presentation. More than that, readers note that even centuries before he acts to free Nada or Orpheus, Dream expresses uncertainty about the rightness of his actions. Following her comment just quoted, Titania remarks to Dream, "You are a deep one. I would I could fathom your motives ... ?" Somewhat later in the play, Dream responds to invitation to share confidences by musing,

> I wonder, Titania. I wonder if I have done right.
>
> And I wonder why I wonder. Will is a willing vehicle for the great stories.
>
> Through him they will live for an age of man; and his words will echo down through time.
>
> It is what he wanted.
>
> But he did not understand the price.
>
> Mortals never do. They see only the prize their heart's desire, their dream … [*sic*] But the price of getting what you want, is getting what once you wanted.
>
> And had I told him? Had he understood? What then? It would have made no difference.
>
> Have I done right, Titania? Have I done right?

He gets no answer; Titania has not been listening. The important things for readers to notice about Dream's soliloquy are, first of all, that it shows him questioning himself at all, then than that it shows him questioning himself in mortal terms: He is asking what would be "right" in terms of Shakespeare's welfare, not his own duty. As the capitalized directions in Gaiman's script indicate, "HE'S ASKING HER A QUESTION, TRYING TO SOLVE THE PROBLEM OF WHETHER IT'S RIGHT TO HAVE RUINED SHAKESPEARE'S LIFE, EVEN THOUGH HE DOESN'T KNOW THAT'S WHAT HE'S DONE" (25). Finally, thus, it is worth noting the different levels of the character's thinking, so that he can ponder the rightness of having done something that he "doesn't know" he has done.

Finally, though this never is stated directly, there is the strong possibility that Dream's remarks are caused not just by pondering the rightness of his past actions — especially concerning Orpheus, his only son — but by what he may observe happening in Shakespeare's relationship with his son Hamnet. As a playwright newly aware of his powers, Shakespeare appears to care only about his art. Hamnet feels "distant" from his father, as if he is "less real to him than any of the characters in his plays," and he even repeats his sister's joke "that if I died, he'd just write a play about it. 'Hamnet'." Hamnet's doubts are left as unresolved as the Sandman's, as he must stare at his father from a distance "WITH LONGING, WITH LOVE" (Script 26). As I commented in an earlier essay on Gaiman, watching one self-absorbed father ignore his resentful son might also stir painful uncertainty in another father who has lost his son by letting alienation turn into permanent separation (352).

Even if Dream does not react overtly to all that is happening around and within himself, readers notice what is going on. Events in *The Sandman* demonstrate repeatedly that nothing stays the same forever, that outgrown roles can and must be abandoned. The inhabitants of Faerie cut off connection with the world of humans; Lucifer abandons Hell (*Season of Mists*);

even Destruction, Dream's Endless brother, leaves his role to search for new interests (*Brief Lives*). Also, in the only story included in two reprint albums, Death shows Dream that the end of existence is not necessarily to be dreaded ("The Sound of Her Wings" in *Preludes and Nocturnes* and *The Doll's House*). Moreover, in a story in which Dream does not appear directly, Death even endorses the idea of suicide, telling a disfigured, embittered superheroine that "Your life is your own ... So is your death" ("Façade" in *Dream Country*), virtually the same words Dream speaks, apparently without awareness of their irony, to the mutilated Orpheus. After witnessing all this, readers can reasonably surmise what is going on under Dream's un-emotional exterior. We may accept the final educated guess by Lucien, Dream's librarian, that "he did a little more than let it [his death] happen ... Sometimes, perhaps, one must change or die. And, in the end, there were, perhaps limits to how much he could let himself change ("In Which a Wake is Held" 19). So we may see that it is not simply an insipid euphemism to say that Dream both dies and "passes on."

The wonder, after all, is that a character like Dream could move at all. Even seeing all the evidence that readers see, Dream resists awareness and change even more determinedly than most mere humans could. Why should one of the Endless change? How can one of them change? Dream does not know, at least not consciously. In his last meeting with Will Shake-speare, however, he explains why he chose the subject of the second play Will owed him, *The Tempest*: "I wanted a tale of graceful ends. I wanted a play about a King who drowns his books, and breaks his staff, and leaves his kingdom. About a magician who becomes a man. About a man who turns his back on magic." At the time, he denies that he sees himself re-flected in the characters who leave one condition so they can enter: "I do not. I MAY not. I am Prince of stories, Will; but I have no story of my own. Nor shall I ever." As readers know, hav-ing absorbed *The Sandman* and having watched Morpheus move out of his endless isolation, he is wrong. What makes it possible for the Sandman to escape self-protective role-playing is the experience of fiction. Apparently, as we extend ourselves into other characters and see their confused motives and actions, we become aware — if not fully conscious, even then — of our own. Seeing how they use the possibilities in their lives, we can catch sight of what we might do.

Through fantasies, in other words, we can become aware of our ability to hurt others. We also can become aware that we may be able to choose not to do it.

This is true in *Mr. Punch* too, especially in two important scenes. The first comes midway through the book, between the first and second "true facts" listed above. Earlier in the same night the boy discovers that his grandfather is not sleeping at home, he has a dream of wan-dering through his grandfather's arcade alone in the dark, while he hears the sound of "Croc-odiles and alligators and older, huger reptiles" moving around him. This happens after he has tried on Professor Swatchell's crocodile hand puppet and has felt the sense of primordial power that identity carries with it, how attractive it is to the wielder and how menacing to an outsider. In the dream, he runs toward a lighted Punch and Judy theater, inside which "the doctor was cutting open Pretty Polly, Punch's forgotten girlfriend. Punch stood beside him, looking sad." The idea of illicit sex has barely been hinted at thus far, and the consequences — the pregnancy that a doctor might be operating to terminate — are even farther ahead in the book. However, since people habitually deny understanding of what they have seen, it is quite possible that the boy could have noticed clues that he repressed, before memories that he does show us. As the puppet cuts the empty female puppet open, though, a life-size hand emerges, which the doctor begins to cut with his knife: "Punch laughed, and I wondered who the third hand belonged to," the narrator says. The hand is blank white, not yet marked by use. It is raised in the direction of the doctor and Mr. Punch, as if to defend Pretty Polly, but it does not move once it has emerged. It is present but unable to "grasp" its surroundings. Instead, it is at the mercy of the active adults. In all this, the hand resembles the boy: "I turned to run: but there was nothing anywhere but the darkness. No shelter, no safety. I had lost my way, and I was alone in the night. And already the crocodiles were beginning to roar." Accompanying these words is a pair of panels, one showing the boy as a tiny, indistinct stick-figure, the other filled with the largest picture of him in the book, a photographic montage that merges the boy's features and a crocodile's. It may be that the boy feels threatened and is resisting being swallowed; it may be that the boy is metamorphosing into the powerful reptile. The choice is not clearly made, for it cannot be clearly stated. The boy cannot let himself know what he knows, let alone act on the knowledge.

A somewhat clearer choice appears at the very end of *Mr. Punch*, when the adult narrator attends a celebration of Mr. Punch's birthday, one May in a Covent Garden churchyard. The selfish, murderous Mr. Punch evidently is quite socially acceptable, and the narrator toys with the idea of "abandoning the life I had built for myself" and running a Punch and Judy show, "teaching the children, and those with an eye and a mind to see with, the lessons of death that went back to the dawn times; amusing and delighting both old and young." He even thinks he catches a glimpse of Professor Swatchell in the crowd, though he later realizes that the old man must be dead by now: "Everybody dies but Mr. Punch, and he has only the life he steals from others." When, therefore, he is offered a chance to put Mr. Punch on his hand, he is tempted because "It would have whispered its secrets to me, explained my childhood, explained my life … [*sic*]." However, the narrator appears to realize that those secrets, like the puppet's vitality, would have been stolen from him and distorted before being returned to his conscious self. Triumphant at the end of the play, Mr. Punch exclaims "Hooray! Hooray! The Devil is dead! Now everybody is free to whatever they wish!," but the narrator turns away: "I left the churchyard then, shivering in spite of the May sunshine, and went about my life."

As in *Violent Cases*, the narrator of *Mr. Punch* wants to understand where he is, realizing that most of his certainties are undependable. The very categories he uses to make sense of his world may be too distorted and rigid to do more than keep him in the same rut he began settling into while he was deciding how to become an adult. If that is the case, he may be in danger of passing on false information to the people around him so that they won't know where they are either. Thus parents unthinkingly lie to their children while tacitly daring them to disagree; and thus children learn to disguise their resentment at being lied to as they prepare unconsciously to pass on misinformation to even younger people. As in *The Sandman*, however, *Mr. Punch* suggests that releasing one's inhibitions and exploring apparently remote, fantastic scenarios may be the best way to discover what choices of direction we actually have. We might even begin to share our search for human truth. In any event, since we do live in a world of dreams anyway, the most dangerous thing we could do would be to deny that true fact and refuse to acknowledge our dreams.

WORKS CITED.

David, Peter. "But I Digress" [column]. *Comics Buyer's Guide* #1130 (September15,1995), 82.

Gaiman, Neil. *The Sandman: Brief Lives*. New York: Vertigo/DC Comics, 1994.

—. *The Sandman: The Doll's House*. New York: DC Comics, 1990.

—. *The Sandman: Dream Country*. New York: DC Comics, 1991.

—. *The Sandman: Fables and Reflections*. New York: Vertigo/DC Comics, 1993.

—. *The Sandman: A Game of You*. New York: Vertigo/DC Comics, 1993.

—. *The Sandman: The Kindly Ones*. New York: Vertigo/DC Comics, 1996.

—. *"A Midsummer Night's Dream"* [script].

—. *Mr. Punch. A Romance* [script].

—. *The Sandman: Preludes and Nocturnes*. New York: Vertigo/DC Comics, 1991.

—. *The Sandman: Season of Mists*. New York: Vertigo/DC Comics, 1992.

—. *The Sandman: The Wake*. NY: VertigoDC Comics, 1997.

—. *The Sandman: World's End*. New York: Vertigo/DC Comics, 1994.

—. *The Tragical Comedy or Comical Tragedy of Mr. Punch__*. New York: Vertigo/DC Comics, 1995.

—. *Violent Cases*. Northampton MA: Tundra, 1992.

Groth, Gary. "Neil Gaiman" [interview]. *The Comics Journal* #169 (July 1994, 54-108.

McCloud, Scott. *Understanding Comics: The Invisible Art*. Northampton, MA: Kitchen Sink, 1993.

Sanders, Joe. "Gaiman, Neil (Richard)." In *St. James Guide to Science Fiction Writers*, ed Jay P. Pederson. Detroit: St James Press, 1996. 350-352.

Thompson, Kim. "Neil Gaiman" [interview]. *The Comics Journal* #155 (January 1993), 64-83.

❧❧❧

✠✠✠

IMAGINARY PLACES AND FANTASTIC NARRATIVES: READING BORGES THROUGH *SANDMAN*

by Leonora Soledad Souza e Paula

✦

There is a man with a book, walking through his garden.
The man is blind. The garden is a maze of paths that
divide and branch and recombine.
— *Sandman: Endless Nights,* "*Destiny*"

A FEW WORDS ON APPROPRIATION.

Contemporary artistic manifestations such as literature, visual arts, cinema, music, etc., are in constant communication among themselves. This process of association is especially active in comics, where themes and techniques are borrowed from many sources. Neil Gaiman's *Sandman*, one of the most celebrated recent comics, is an example of such connection. In fact, multiple appropriations of different styles in the graphic narrative, as created by the more than 25 artists working throughout the series, along with sophisticated conversations with literary texts in the plot's structure, have helped make *Sandman* an outstanding comic.

The continuous movement of cultural appropriation in which readings and rereadings are circulating in order to build artistic texts does not necessarily involve subordinating present to past. Actually, the past is no longer seen as a fixed entity but acknowledged for its collective nature. Therefore, such movement depends upon viewing the whole of tradition as available to be accessed and downloaded for appropriation, extending the meaning of previous material while (re)building the new text.

For these reasons, the employment of some topics previously evoked by another artist is not a matter of imitation. More than the simple influence, the transformation of tradition acts as the displacement of former elements, and not as the impersonation of one's earlier style.

Thus, it is taking for granted an act of appropriation that my reading of the presence of Jorge Luis Borges in *Sandman* takes place, as writer and artists rehabilitate the past diction by recontextualizing the referential meaning of some Borgesian imaginary places in the framework of the new piece.

THE FANTASTIC AS SETTING.

As far as that is concerned, the reading of *Sandman* allows the attentive reader to observe an intensive dialogue with some works by the Argentinean writer Jorge Luis Borges, especially his fantastic narratives. Actually, it is possible to assume that Borges is the precursor of a group of writers who, during the 20th century, devoted their attention to fantastic literature. Considering that Neil Gaiman's work in *Sandman* indubitably embraces the fantastic genre as a source, and recognizing *Sandman*'s kinship with the extraordinary narrative, the appropriation of Borges' writing is clear.

Among the several features of fantastic narrative, the limitless space for experimentation in terms of fictional construction is one of the most prominent, as the fantastic enjoys a free relationship with respect to realistic representation. The fictional work of Borges is quite representative of the highly creative and complex narratives that do not follow the rules of realistic creation. In the short story "The Analytic Language of John Wilkins" (to which Michel Foucault devoted a sensitive commentary in his introduction to *The Order of Things*) the writer surprises the readers with a sophisticated classification of animals supposedly existing in a Chinese encyclopedia:

> Animals can be classified as: a. those that belong to the Emperor; b. mummified; c. trained; d. small pigs; e. mermaids; f. fabulous; g. astray dogs; h. included in this classification; i. that shake like a fool; j. innumerable; k. drawn with a very thin camel hair brush; l. etc.; m. that have just broken a pot; n. that, if seen from a distance, look like flies. (Borges, 1964: 85)

This sequence welcomes the variety of fictional elements as a form of approaching fantastic narratives since it surpasses the restrained relationship between language and representation. According to Beatriz Sarlo, "the fantastic fiction offers hypothetical worlds based on the powers of an imagination unfettered by the constraints imposed by representative aesthetics" (Sarlo, 2001:2). Indeed, hypothetical worlds are the substance from which Borges and Gaiman build their fabrics, as both are masters of the woven texts. Moreover, if we consider that the fantastic mode is a creative response to realistic representation of the world, Borges and Gaiman's imaginary places are certainly very sophisticated alternatives.

As I shall demonstrate, three are the main approximations between some of the Borgesian imaginary places and *Sandman's* dreamlike settings: the labyrinth, the book, and the library. Certainly, it is possible to consider the same topic through the observation of differences instead of similarities, but the aim of this essay is to highlight the resignificant appropriation in terms of correspondence.

IMAGINARY PLACES. First, let us consider the amazing garden of Destiny, the oldest of the Endless, which is introduced to the reader of *Sandman* in the first episode of the collection of issues "Season of Mists". There, one can notice the existence of a strong connection with the garden in the short story "The Garden of Forking Paths" ("El Jardín de los Senderos que se Bifurcan"). In fact, the description of Destiny's garden is easily connected to the description of Borges' garden as to its physical characteristics and symbolic content:

> Walk any path in Destiny's garden and you will be forced to choose not once, but many times. The paths fork and divide. With each step you take in Destiny's garden, you make a choice; and every choice determines future paths. However, at the end of a lifetime walking, you might look back and see only one path stretching out behind you; or look ahead and see only darkness. Sometimes you dream about the paths of Destiny, and speculate, to no purposes ... The paths diverge and branch and reconnect; some say not even Destiny himself truly knows where any way will take you, where each twist and turn will lead ... Destiny of the Endless is the only one who understands the garden's peculiar geography, different from time and space, where the potential becomes the actual. Destiny knows. The book he carries is as much a guide to the garden as it is to the minutiae of future-past. (Gaiman, Jones, Jones III, 1991#21:1/2) [*Fig. 1*]

Through this description, we can assume that the garden is a web-shaped place that is situated at an intersection of time and space. Moreover, it is noticeable that the idea of time

Fig. 1: Writer: Neil Gaiman Artists: Mike Dringenberg & Malcolm Jones III "Season of Mists: A Prologue"
Collected in *The Sandman: Season of Mists* [©1992 DC Comics]

is a very relative assumption to this virtual world, in which potentially any situation can be mirrored. The eternal movement of choice and consequence that forms the infinite is central to Destiny's garden.

In the same way, Borges conceived a labyrinthine space of possibilities, which turns out to be at the same time a garden and a book. "The Garden of Forking Paths" is narrated by Dr. Yu Tsun who relates how his ancestor, Ts'ui Pên, had spent the last years of his life on two projects: to write a book and to construct a maze in which anyone would get lost. The book, reflecting the labyrinth, discusses how reality can be divided into different dimensions, suggesting the simultaneous existence of different possible realities. The question of time is a leading question to understand the garden's complexity:

> The garden of forking paths is an incomplete, but not false, image of the universe as Ts'ui Pên conceived it. In contrast to Newton and Schopenhauer, your [Yu Tsun] ancestor did not believe in a uniform, absolute time. He believed in an infinite series of times, in a growing, dizzying net of divergent, convergent and parallel times. This network of times, which approach one another, fork, break off, or were unaware of one another for centuries, embraces all possibilities of time. We do not exist in the majority of these times; in some you exist, and not I; in others, I, and not you; in others, both of us. In the present one, which a favorable fate has granted me, you have arrived at my house; in another, while crossing the garden, you found me dead; in still another, I utter these same words, but I am a mistake, a ghost. (Borges, 1964: 42)

As we can see, the garden is in a limitless and eternal movement of expansion, disregarding concepts of fixed space, and favoring the idea of infinite time. The garden is a place built of multiple reflexes, segments, and fragments, in which the notion of a diverging unity formed by infinite possibilities is evident. All the potential journeys, branches, and bifurcations are organized as a network, indicating the limitless connections that can be traced, since the garden is conceived as "a labyrinth of labyrinths, of one sinuous spreading labyrinth that could encompass the past and the future" (Borges, 1964: 42). So, it does not follow a linear progression, as it is continuously moving without an end.

In a sense, "The Garden of Forking Paths" discusses the possibilities of choices and the parallel universes. The forking paths lead to choices not only in space but also in time, i.e. each time one has to choose among many alternatives and opts for one the others are put aside. But this does not extinguish its possibility of existence since the several forthcoming events also proliferate and branch. Moreover, the chosen alternative is filled with unpredictable forthcoming possibilities.

Likewise, Destiny's garden assumes that the selection is, in fact, another branching point to future possibilities: "Walk any path in Destiny's garden and you will be forced to choose not once, but many times. The paths fork and divide. With each step you take in Destiny's garden, you make a choice; and every choice determines future paths." That is, the future paths, which are also forthcoming possibilities, instead of restraining the alternatives, favor the chance.

Therefore, the notion of infinity is present in the labyrinthine gardens since every chosen path leads to endless possibilities of other choices, successively. In the case of Destiny's garden, the infinity is preserved by the perpetual continuity of choices and alternatives that may be taken, i.e., the notion of time is strongly present and intensively acting.

Furthermore, both spaces contain all the possibilities present in the structure of endless forking paths, which can be explored as a space full of infinite combinations. Sarlo says that "this is one of Borges's preferred visual arrangements of images: the *structure en abîme*, which is at the same time a narrative structure, a trope and a spatial model" (Sarlo, 2001:9). This structure is potentially interminable and deals with the notion of time as a continuous temporal lapse. The infinity is preserved in Borges' garden not by the presence, but by the suspension of time. In this case, the narrative structure *en abîme* defines the visual arrangement and the spatial model of the garden.

In terms of narrative strategy and visual representation, Destiny' garden follows a tautological model of endless continuity as a means to demonstrate the infinite possibilities of different combinations. In Destiny's words, "This place is beyond beginnings and endings" (Gaiman, Jones, Jones III, 1991#21:2). That is, every event, from a blink of the eyes to a relevant historical event, is connected with all past, present, and future possibilities of this same event. In the garden of Destiny, innumerous combinations can be experienced, giving room to the unlimited. Here, the spatial model and the visual arrangement are reflected in the narrative structure, since the garden visual aspect acquires another meaning when transposed to comics.

Though the connections among the imaginary places can be broadly suggested, one of the most intriguing aspects lies in the figure of the book. "Season of Mists" begins and ends with the image of Destiny's garden and his book. There, the garden is as important as the book; in fact, they reflect each other as the book mirrors the garden and, at the same time, the garden gives back the image of the book: "The book he [Destiny] carries is as much a guide to the garden as it is to the minutiae of future-past." Both the book and the garden are symbols of destiny and eternity, reflecting Destiny's function and duties.

Similarly, Ts'ui Pen had the intention to build a book and a maze that could embody each other: "At one time, Ts'ui Pên must have said: 'I am going into seclusion to write a book' and at another, 'I am retiring to construct a maze.' Everyone assumed these were separate activities. No one realized that the book and the labyrinth were one and the same"

(Borges, 1964: 96). In addition, the intricate shape of the place/object is mirrored in its content, which is associated to the idea of totality. The image of books that carry all things is a very recurrent theme in Borges' writings, for instance in "The Book of Sand" ("El Libro de Arena") and "The Library of Babel" ("La Biblioteca de Babel"). In "The Garden of Forking Paths," Ts'ui Pen's book is an infinitive book of choices "a cyclic volume, a circular one. A volume whose last page was identical with its first, a book which had the possibility of continuing indefinitely" (Borges, 1964: 41). That is, the book is a narrative structured like a labyrinth in which everything is there to be chosen as a hypertext of stories where anything can happen.

Also in *Sandman*, the assumption that an end is not necessarily a conclusion is taken for granted in the epilogue of "Season of Mists". There, in a quotation from G.K. Chesterton's imaginary novel, *The Man Who was October*, we can read: "October knew, of course, that the act of turning a page, of ending a chapter or shutting a book, did not end the tale" (Gaiman, Dringenberg, Pratt, 1991#28:24). The unclosed nature of the books gives room to the readers' participation as long as the stories are opened to expansion via an infinite number of possible trajectories that may be created by them. Like the mazes, the books are also activated by the walker/reader who is invited to join the hypertextual game of branching paths/alternative stories.

Moreover, the book to which Destiny is chained is characterized as containing all things in the past, present, and future. In the section dedicated to Destiny in *Sandman: Endless Nights*, the reader is informed of the characteristics of Destiny's book: "He is holding a book. Inside the book is the Universe ... It contains everything that has happened, or will happen, to anyone you've ever met ... Everything is in there, from the beginning of the time to the end" (Gaiman and Quitely, 2003:139-41).

In a Borgesian game, Gaiman tells the reader that inside the book is the whole universe and that this universe is in an unlimited movement of expansion, just like the garden/maze. Ultimately, the book and the maze within the two texts are conceived as settings in eternal transformation, beyond limits, holding the very notion of completeness as a structural element. More than simple images of virtual worlds, the book and maze are congenitally interrelated, i.e., they were conceived as one. For that, it is possible to consider that Gaiman appropriated Borges' concepts of narrative structure and fictional articulation as building strategies to mold the concept and shape of his book/labyrinth.

Totalizing is also an appropriate adjective to describe the imaginary libraries. Indeed, the image of a total library is a device extensively explored in Borges' works and appears in Gaiman's creation as a very interesting appropriation. When first introduced to the reader, the Library of Dreams is portrayed as a place in which all imaginary books[1] are stored: "Somewhere in here is every story has ever been dreamed" (Gaiman, Jones, Jones III, 1991#22:2). [*Fig. 2*]

There it is possible to find a section of imaginary, unwritten, or unfinished literary pieces

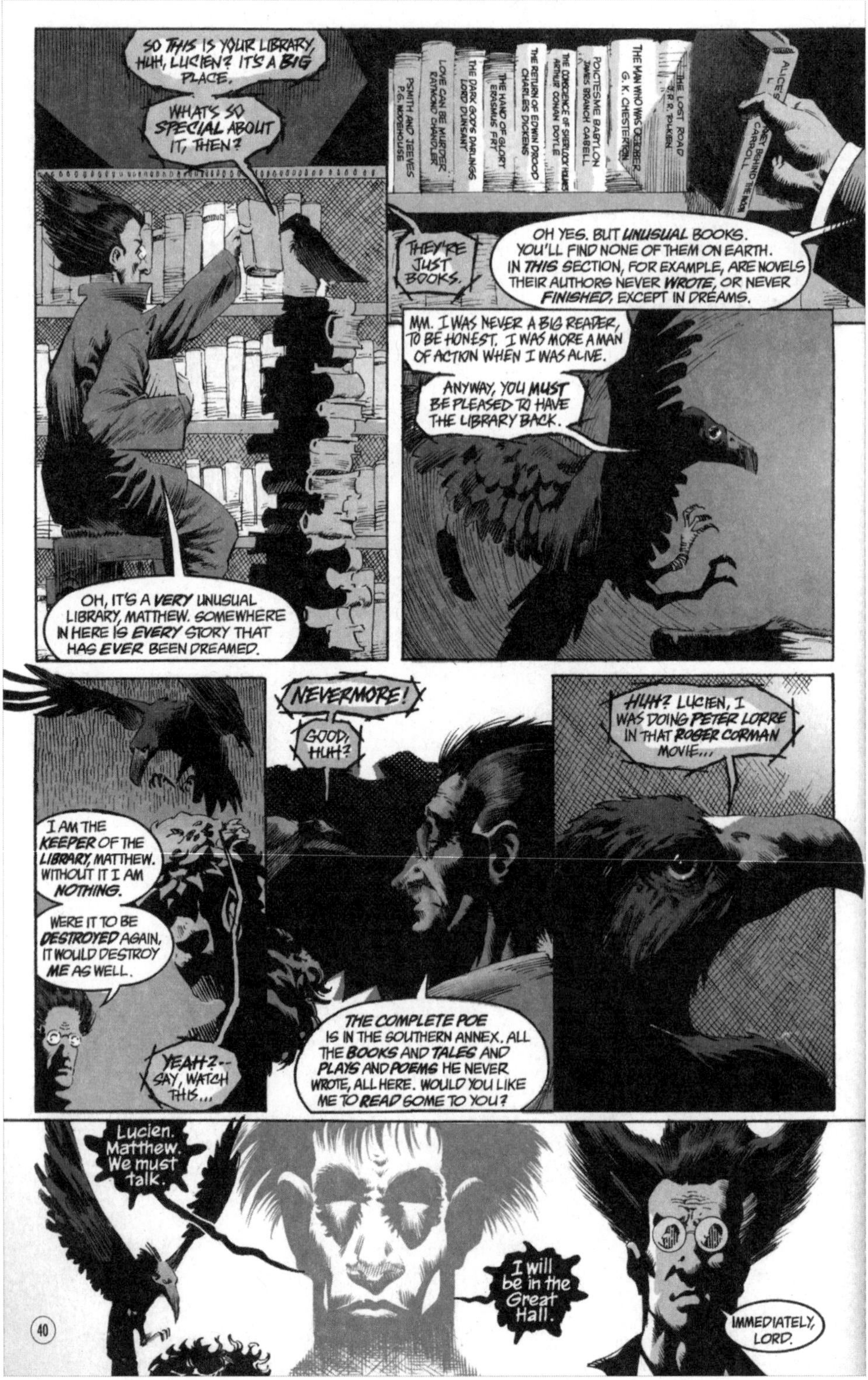
SO THIS IS YOUR LIBRARY, HUH, LUCIEN? IT'S A BIG PLACE.
WHAT'S SO SPECIAL ABOUT IT, THEN?
OH, IT'S A VERY UNUSUAL LIBRARY, MATTHEW. SOMEWHERE IN HERE IS EVERY STORY THAT HAS EVER BEEN DREAMED.
PSMITH AND JEEVES P.G. WODEHOUSE
LOVE CAN BE MURDER RAYMOND CHANDLER
THE DARK GOD'S DARLINGS LORD DUNSANY
THE HAND OF GLORY ERASMUS FRY
THE RETURN OF EDWIN DROOD CHARLES DICKENS
THE CONSCIENCE OF SHERLOCK HOLMES ARTHUR CONAN DOYLE
POICTESME BABYLON JAMES BRANCH CABELL
THE MAN WHO WAS OCTOBER G.K. CHESTERTON
THE LOST ROAD J.R.R. TOLKIEN
THEY'RE JUST BOOKS.
OH YES. BUT UNUSUAL BOOKS. YOU'LL FIND NONE OF THEM ON EARTH. IN THIS SECTION, FOR EXAMPLE, ARE NOVELS THEIR AUTHORS NEVER WROTE, OR NEVER FINISHED, EXCEPT IN DREAMS.
MM. I WAS NEVER A BIG READER, TO BE HONEST. I WAS MORE A MAN OF ACTION WHEN I WAS ALIVE.
ANYWAY, YOU MUST BE PLEASED TO HAVE THE LIBRARY BACK.
I AM THE KEEPER OF THE LIBRARY, MATTHEW. WITHOUT IT I AM NOTHING.
WERE IT TO BE DESTROYED AGAIN, IT WOULD DESTROY ME AS WELL.
YEAH?.. SAY, WATCH THIS...
NEVERMORE!
GOOD, HUH?
THE COMPLETE POE IS IN THE SOUTHERN ANNEX. ALL THE BOOKS AND TALES AND PLAYS AND POEMS HE NEVER WROTE, ALL HERE. WOULD YOU LIKE ME TO READ SOME TO YOU?
HUH? LUCIEN, I WAS DOING PETER LORRE IN THAT ROGER CORMAN MOVIE...
Lucien. Matthew. We must talk.
I will be in the Great Hall.
IMMEDIATELY, LORD.
40

Fig. 2: Writer: Neil Gaiman Artists: Kelley Jones & Malcolm Jones III "Season of Mists: Episode 1"
Collected in *The Sandman: Season of Mists* [©1992 DC Comics]

by different authors, such as *Psmith and Jeeves* by P.G. Wodehouse, *The Return of Edwin Drood* by Charles Dickens, Sir Arthur Conan Doyle's *The Reason of Sherlock Holmes*, J.R.R. Tolkien's *Lost Road*, Lewis Carroll's *Alice's Journey Behind the Moon*, Christopher Marlowe's *The Merry Comedies of The Redemption of Doctor Faustus*, John Webster's *A Banquet for the Worms*. Besides the sections dedicated to literature, there are entire subdivisions dedicated to tales told in other media, such as cinema, painting, and music, where the visitor can find, for instance, some scripts Orson Welles had in mind but could never get the financing to shoot[2].

A library which contains all books that have ever been dreamed, as well as all tales and stories that have ever been imagined may be considered an universe of possibilities, as it is composed of every possible story that can exist in anyone's mind, including the ones committed to the task of writing. For instance, the visitor can find the sole novel imagined by someone who never accomplished the writing as well as the complete work by an illustrious writer: "*The Complete Poe* is in the southern annex. All the books and tales and plays and poems he never wrote, all here" (Gaiman, Jones, Jones III, 1991#22:2).

Borges' echoes in the Library of Dreams are highlighted when we read a short description of the collection of the Library of Babel:

> The minutely detailed history of the future, the archangels' autobiographies, the faithful catalogue of the Library, thousands and thousands of false catalogues, the demonstration of the fallacy of those catalogues, the demonstration of the fallacy of the true catalogue, the Gnostic gospel of Basilides, the commentary on that gospel, the commentary on the commentary on that gospel, the true story of your death, the translation of every book in all languages, the interpolations of every book in all books. (Borges, 1964:12)

By reading this excerpt, we may notice that the *structure en abîme* is adopted as a way to refer to the fact that the Library contains precisely everything. That is, eternity and totality are intimately connected in the image of the Library since it constitutes an endless and interminable universe. The first and foremost characterization of the Library gives support to its total and endless nature: "The Universe (which others call the Library) is composed of an indefinite and perhaps infinite number of hexagonal galleries, with vast air shafts between, surrounded by very low railings" (Borges, 1964:8). Moreover, it is believed that the collection of books present there is one version from all the other possible variations; i.e. each book is nothing but a version of itself. Commenting on this notion, Sarlo acknowledges: "everybody knows that each book has no duplicate, that it is in itself an original. But it is also known that there are in existence indefinite numbers of books that contain slight variations" (Sarlo, 2001:11). In other words, each book brings in itself a countless number of possibilities of meaning and each meaning can vary according to the reader who activates it, infinitely.

Likewise, in the Library of Dreams, the books are conceived as variations on the same theme, every book being nothing but a version of the ideal one. For Gaiman, "Even a professional author typically dreams up a hundred books for every one he publishes ... even a book the author has published is but a sad shadow of the one he dreamed" (Bender, 1999:99). Thus, the idea of an imaginary library, which is at the same time total end eternal, is a subject explored as a device of the fantastic narrative in the fictional writing within Borges and resignified by Gaiman.

FINAL CONSIDERATIONS. The activity of appropriation observed in *Sandman* can be considered a legitimate practice of circulation of cultural productions where there is no place for the authoritian tradition, as already discussed. Instead, such practice involves the displacement of older art to viewers of a different mentality and cultural makeup, refiguring cultural codifications from the past (Hoestery, 2001). In this sense, the rehabilitation of fantastic themes in recent works of art ends up to bring different perspectives to the contemporary audience who will produce new readings of it.

Finally, the labyrinth, the book, and the library are some of the Borgesian fictional motifs, which, for being part of the broad gallery of cultural material, are susceptible to an endless plasticity. Through the reconfiguration of the imaginary places in *Sandman* the readers are invited to walk along them in a nonlinear way indicating that each reading may lead to a particular story. Assuming that conclusion are endless, and bearing in mind the measureless space of fictional creation, as skillfully presented by Borges and Gaiman, we may assume that each labyrinth, book, and library may keep their existence not only in books and comics, but also in places far beyond.

ENDNOTES.

1. According to Neil Gaiman, all actually published books are also part of the collection, and they can be found in a distant annex of the Library of Dreams, "a very small annex".
2. An interesting curiosity is visiting *The Invisible Library* website and finding some other books of the Library of Dreams. http://www.invisiblelibrary.com/

WORKS CITED.

Bender, Hy. *The Sandman Companion*. New York: Vertigo DC Comics, 1999.

Borges, Jorge Luis. *Labyrinths: Selected Stories and Other Writings*. New York: New Directions, 1964.

—. *Obras Completas*. Buenos Aires: EMECE, 1974.

Gaiman, Neil. *Sandman: Season of Mists*. New York: Vertigo/DC Comics, 1991.

—. "Destiny". *Sandman: Endless Nights*. New York: Vertigo/DC Comics, 2003.

Hoesterey, Ingeborg. *Pastiche: Cultural Memory in Art, Film, Literature*. Bloomington: Indiana University Press, 2001.

Sarlo, Beatriz. "Imaginary Constructions." *Borges, a Writer on the Edge. Borges Studies on Line.* On line. J. L. Borges Center for Studies & Documentation. Internet: ‹http://www.hum.au.dk/romansk/borges/bsol/bsi5.htm›

ΦΦΦ

REINVENTING THE SPIEL:
OLD STORIES, NEW APPROACHES

by Stacie Hanes and Joe Sanders

✦

Tell me, are you a goddess or are you a mortal woman?

— *Homer*

INTRODUCTION.

Whether goddess worship ever was the basis of a primitive culture, the concept of the goddess — especially in her threefold embodiment as maiden, mother, and crone — certainly exists now for writers who want to explore human lives, especially with regard to gender roles. The witches of Terry Pratchett's Discworld and the female triads in Neil Gaiman's *Sandman* series, with the ghosts of immemorial myth and the newer spirits of Wiccan revival behind them, are all a part of an ancient literary tradition and a developing archetype that "makes visible to us the very depths of what is humanly possible," (Ulanov, qtd. in Adler 41).

Research turns up no solid evidence of utopian matriarchies in recorded history, or much substantiation of the literal historicity of what Isaac Bonewits called "the Unitarian, Universalist, White Witchcult of Western Theosophical Britainy," (Adler 45). While many cultures in every era and many lands have practiced goddess worship in one form or another, the sociopolitical structure seems never actually to have been controlled by women; nor did ancient matriarchal religious traditions survive unadulterated and undiluted to the modern age. Thus the claims of invocation in Robert Graves's *The White Goddess* are generally questioned by scholars who argue that the goddess-paradigm operates metaphorically rather than historically (Wood 22); in other words, stories about her are not a literal record of magic, or any one time and place, but a way of thinking about the common experiences of women and the force of belief in creation. For that reason, stories involving her continue to have compelling force, so that Pratchett and Gaiman use the triple goddess to explore the power of stories, and all of the roles an individual may play in the course of a lifetime.

THE MAIDEN, THE MOTHER, AND THE ... OTHER ONE: THE GODDESS OF TERRY PRATCHETT. The tale

of the triune goddess has taken different shapes over the many centuries, but Terry Pratchett has refined it into a story-shape so elegant that it may be, at last, the true shape of the myth. As Granny Weatherwax tells the elf Queen, people make their own gods, and then "take 'em to bits for the parts when we don't need 'em anymore," (*Lords and Ladies* 281). After thousands of years, during which innumerable storytellers have used stories as tools to examine the kaleidoscopic aspects of humanity, Pratchett and other modern fantasy authors have taken shards of the Goddess and assembled from them something wonderful, bringing this particular myth, if not to a logical conclusion, then to a place of stability. As described by Pratchett and others, the triune goddess illuminates the pattern of feminine life with a soft but revealing light; his characterizations fit Everywoman just as surely as the crystal slipper fit Aschenputtel.

She is a moon goddess, with triple aspects. The most common names she has traveled under are Artemis, Selene, and Hecate. Connections are alluded to as far back as the 15th century in a French poem called *Des astres, des forêts* by Étienne Jodelle (1532-73). Edith Hamilton, widely regarded as the first lady of myth, presents a memorable synthesis of earlier sources in her 1940 work *Mythology*. Hamilton wrote that Artemis is identified with Hecate in the later poets, and quotes a passage from one of them:

She is "the goddess with three forms," Selene in the sky, Artemis on earth, Hecate in the lower world and in the world above when it is wrapped in darkness ... She was associated with deeds of darkness, the Goddess of the Crossways, which were held to be ghostly places of evil magic ... It is a strange transformation from the lovely huntress flashing through the forest, from the moon making all beautiful with her light ... (31-32)

This figure recurs frequently in modern fantasy fiction as Maiden, Mother, and Crone. In antiquity, Artemis was the virgin huntress; Selene was the fertile moon goddess; and Hecate was the dark personification of lightless, forsaken night. However, as Pratchett claims, the treatment of the myth today is perhaps much more important than what has been done with it in the past. Although he is not the only author who might be considered a modern myth-maker, Pratchett's Discworld series contains one of contemporary fantasy's most impressive and cohesive presentations of the goddess myth today, in the form of three witches: Magrat, Nanny Ogg, and the extraordinary Granny Weatherwax.

The Discworld witches are not cast in the maiden, mother, and crone mold in any superficial sense, but as Nanny Ogg explains to Agnes Nitt in *Carpe Jugulum*, "that ain't really important, because it ain't down to technicalities, see? Now me, I don't reckon I was ever a maiden ment'ly," (87). Karen Sayer observes that "There is an adherence to the (reproductive) pagan model of maiden, mother, crone, yet women's sexuality is not constructed simply — there are various models of motherhood (Magrat and Gytha), maidenhood (Granny, Agnes, and Magrat), and of being a crone (Gytha and Esme)," (97).

Magrat Garlick is the virginal figure, and her part is to learn and evolve. She has never walked where the elder two have, but she must grow into the roles she will later play. Magrat acts the part of the reader, asking the sometimes naïve questions a reader might ask. Without Magrat, the elder two witches would have no one to teach, and teaching is a very important part of their purpose.

Nanny Ogg is the Mother of the trio: three times married, with fifteen living children and others among the dead. Her fertility is an important illustration of another concept vital to rural life: the continuance of the community. Her excesses of character further her outward image as the ultimate maternal figure. Her deep interest in men and sex, and even the "Hedgehog Song," she sings after a few pint glasses of some liquor normally sold by the ounce are core manifestations of the fertility concept of which she is a symbol.

Esmerelda Weatherwax, or Granny as she is known in the Ramtops, is the most complicated personality in the group. Her proper place in the arrangement is to be the crone, but in truth she is all three. She remains a maiden, but she acts as a mother to all of the people under her protection. They fear and respect her; they may mutter against her at times, but that is how children behave toward stern parents, no matter how loving they really are.

Jungian psychology indicates that these three characters are all aspects of the mother archetype. The goddess, even in her triune form, is in truth the ultimate mother of all things: she is everything that any woman can be. She embodies every function the female, or in some cases even the male, soul can perform in a lifetime. In his *Four Archetypes*, Jung refers to the Hindu goddess Kali, whom he calls the "loving and terrible mother," as an elaboration of the mother archetype. He invokes terms of Sankhya philosophy in his explanation: "the three *gunas* or fundamental attributes [of the mother archetype are] *sattva, rajas, tamas*: goodness, passion, and darkness. These are three essential aspects of the mother: her cherishing and nourishing goodness, her orgiastic emotionality, and Stygian depths" (16).

According to this system, we can call Magrat the incarnation of emotionality because she has not yet matured sufficiently to keep her impulses in check. This state pertains for her at least until *Carpe Jugulum*, wherein she and King Verence, whom she weds in *Lords and Ladies*, have a baby daughter. Clearly, she is no longer technically a maiden, although she is not as experienced as Nanny Ogg and thus does not fully represent the mother aspect of the trio. In *Lords and Ladies*, Agnes Nitt makes her first appearance. As Magrat moves toward motherhood, Agnes is being groomed to become the maiden of the coven.

By Jung's standards, Gytha Ogg is the one of whose "cherishing and nourishing goodness" we see evidence most often. Nanny can provide comfort, whereas Magrat is apt to say the wrong thing, and Granny's sort of help isn't often comforting. In conversation, Pratchett explained that while Granny is the most intelligent of the three, Nanny is by far the wisest. Further, despite having the clearest parallels to the id, which does not enjoy a reputation as the storehouse of wisdom, Nanny Ogg commands the insight to (sometimes) manage both Granny and Magrat effectively. She has "emotional intelligence," (Goleman xii). The concept of emotional intelligence embraces both the "gut instinct" of the id and the nurturing warmth of *sattva*; whereas Granny and Magrat think, Gytha Ogg acts. What she does is usually correct because her instincts spring from a loving understanding of people. This comforting wisdom is what makes Nanny the popular witch. She is called in for births and similar happy occasions, when new lives are in need of cherishing warmth to begin properly.

Conversely, it is Granny whom the people of the Ramtops call out for the dying. At first glance it may seem unfair that Granny is connected to disturbing subjects and left to be Jung's representation of darkness and Stygian depths. Then again, says Nanny, "there's always been a bit of the dark in the Weatherwaxes ..." (*Carpe Jugulum* 88). However, dark does not always mean evil. Pratchett raises this point in *Witches Abroad* with mention of a witch of bygone Discworld days called Black Aliss: "Even Magrat knew about Black Aliss. She was said to be the most powerful witch who ever lived — not exactly *bad*, but so powerful it was sometimes hard to tell the difference" (126).

The distinctions between power, darkness, and evil are important, because in the same book Granny notably exceeds Black Aliss by moving the entire kingdom of Lancre fifteen years into the future. Granny is now the most potent witch who ever lived on the Discworld, and the scope and power of her actions make it difficult for ordinary people to realize that they are those of a "good" person. The title of the short story "The Sea and Little Fishes" refers directly to Granny: Pratchett explains that it means that Granny is the sea and the rest of the witches are the little fishes. Her complexity and intelligence often lead her to do things that the people to whom she ministers do not understand. In this passage from *Carpe Jugulum*, she speaks to a rural midwife who does not approve of Granny's choice not to consult a man whose pregnant wife has been gravely injured, before deciding which life she will save, that of the mother or the child:

> It was doubtful that anyone in Slice would defy Granny Weatherwax,
> but Granny saw the faintest grey shadow of disapproval in the midwife's
> expression.
>
>   'You still reckon I should have asked Mr. Ivy?' she said.
>
>   'That's what I would have done ...' the woman mumbled.
>
>   'You don't like him? You think he's a bad man?' said Granny, adjust-
> ing her hatpins.
>
>   'No!'
>
>   'Then what's he ever done to me, that I should hurt him so?' (24-25)

This passage shows the depth and complexity of Granny's compassion, and gives the lie to the idea that she might be evil. A.S. Byatt notes that Granny "makes the practical choice, and doesn't ask the husband, who would have made the sentimental one" (par. 7). By choosing to save James Ivy's wife, Granny also chooses to let his unborn son die. She might have evaded the awful responsibility by asking the man whether he would prefer to be a father or a husband, but by her strength she spares him further and ultimately pointless pain. Her choice preserves the Ivy family; the parents will grieve, but together they will be able to carry on. The rural community, which would have been weakened by the destruction of an entire family, remains intact even in the face of a painful loss. Granny knows this, although she might not articulate it; she also knows, and accepts, that the community under her protection will never thank her for what she has done. She has inflicted pain and caused distress: it is against human nature to be grateful for that, even if some degree of suffering admits the possibility of being spared worse. Most of the Ramtops villagers will never embrace Granny with warmth; their perspective from inside the narrative does not allow it. From outside, we see that measuring Granny by conventional, unthinking standards doesn't work, as readers recognize better than the people around her. The crone's role has traditionally included standing "at the gateway of death, welcoming those about to enter, easing their passage" (Gardner 160), which is often difficult to identify as the mercy it really is. All that lives also dies, and the choice is only between fear and solace.

Granny provides the practical help a remote rural village needs, but she does so most often without using magic. Magic is an easy fix but one that works only superficially, and in the end does more harm than good. In *Maskerade*, when a man comes to her door seeking a remedy for the pain in his back, she is compelled to resort to certain tricks. Before he knocks, her door swings open. Sitting in her rocker with her back to him, Granny greets Jarge Weaver by name and says, "let me give you something for that back of yours," (13). Knowing that he expects a magical potion, she has prepared one; as she describes it, a mixture of rare herbs and suchlike ... including sucrose and akwa,"(14). Then she tells him to walk three times around a chestnut tree and put a board from a twenty-year-old pine beneath his mattress. He believes the pine board is prescribed so that the knots in his back can be magically transferred to it. After assuring him that all of the necessary "dancin' and chantin' and stuff"(14) was done before he arrived, Granny shows him to the door: "Weaver was never quite certain about what happened next. Granny, usually so sure on her feet, seemed to trip over one of his sticks as she went through the door, and fell backward, holding his shoulders, and somehow her knee came up and hit a spot on his backbone as she twisted sideways, and there was a *click-*" (15).

Weaver leaves then, believing that Granny is a clumsy old woman who, despite being rather daft, makes fine potions. As Granny watches him go, the intimate knowledge of human nature she has gained through her long years of service is evident in her thoughts: "People were so *blind*, she reflected. They preferred to believe in gibberish rather than chiropracty" (15).

Granny gives people what they need, not what they want or think they ought to get. What they want is often an easy, absolute answer to the many troubles a human being may experience while living a normal life, especially a rural, farming life. For aches of the flesh and the more abstract pains of the heart and spirit, the villagers of the Ramtops crave cures that will settle the trouble for once and always. Granny is powerful enough to provide such supernatural cures, but she knows that taking the easy way brings grief more often than not. Her wise-woman therapies, which involve some discomfort and trouble for the patient, work as well as magic but without the troubling side-effect of a community-wide dependence on occult forces — a condition most would agree is probably unhealthy.

Granny's intellectual solutions dovetail nicely with Nanny's intuitive, comforting remedies, as well as Magrat's practical medicine. How the three work together is well demonstrated when elves return to Lancre. The elves of the Discworld, though beautiful, are not the frolicking sort of faerie-kin depicted in porcelain gift shop sculpture and some insipid modern children's stories; the comparatively bland Disney elves are the debased heirs of the Seelie Court. Nor do they resemble Tolkien's elves; despite individual weaknesses, the elves from *The Lord of the Rings* are firmly planted in the benevolent tradition of the Seelie Court. The elves of the Discworld bear more resemblance to the much colder, crueler fey of the Unseelie Court; whether they are actually evil is debatable, but that they are nasty, capricious, sadistic, and not possessed of empathy is not. In *Lords and Ladies*, a young would-be witch, Diamanda (Lucy, to her mother) Tockley, in seeking a shorter route to power than the path of long years — decades — of practice traveled by the elder witches, makes a pact with the Queen of the Elves; such pacts seldom end well, and so it happens in this case. Her foolish effort to get something for nothing ties the land of the elves to the mortal world, and gives the elves access to Lancre; she receives the power she is promised, but still loses a contest of witchcraft to Granny Weatherwax, whose power isn't borrowed. After the contest, in a fit of humiliated rage, Diamanda flees through the standing stones to the kingdom of the elves. She encounters the Queen with whom she bargained and learns what elves are really like. Granny comes after the girl, rescuing her, and herself, from death at the hands of the Queen's warriors; the elves give chase, and Diamanda is wounded by a poisoned arrow. Granny, though powerful, does not know how to cure her. Neither does Nanny Ogg, whose comforting, matronly magic is suited more to midwifery than to battlefield surgery. The kind of knowledge and power that allowed Granny to haul Diamanda bodily from the elven kingdom is of no use once they are out. Granny is unable do anything about the arrowhead lodged the girl's shoulder, but she knows someone who may be able to do what she cannot: Magrat. The youngest witch, who believes in studying herbal lore and medicine, may be able to help. She knows which herbs can heal infection, provide antidotes to poisons, or bring down a fever. If someone needed a potion calling for Love-in-Idleness, Pratchett explains, Magrat would know which of the many species of plants known by that name was actually required. The following selection from *Lords and Ladies* illuminates the difference between Granny's talents and Magrat's:

> The reason that Granny Weatherwax was a better witch than Magrat was that she knew that in witchcraft it didn't matter a damn which [plant] it was, or even if it was a piece of grass.
>
> The reason that Magrat was a better doctor than Granny was that she thought it did (128).

To help the injured girl, they need both types of magic. Magrat's medicines begin to heal Diamanda's physical wounds; unfortunately Magrat, who does not believe in the old wives' tale that cold iron blocks fey interference, disdainfully removes the bars of iron with which the elder witches have surrounded the sickbed. Without the protection of iron, Diamanda falls under the influence of the elves, causing herself further harm and bringing the kingdom of Lancre close to ruin. Working together seamlessly, Magrat and the two elder witches would have wrought a successful cure; because they did not work together, they nearly failed — the price of that failure would have been high indeed.

Representing all aspects of the triple goddess, Granny, Nanny, and Magrat are the basic trinity of womanhood and, indeed, of humanity. Sets of three work well in fairy-tales, possibly because long-dead storytellers realized, centuries or millennia ago, that the simple dichotomy of pairs did not always provide an adequate, satisfactory explanation for the complexities of life. To explain why the human mind is drawn to trinities, Freudian psychologist Bruno Bettelheim claims that the number three represents the id, ego, and superego (102). It is quite easy to see Magrat as the superego, Granny as the ego, and Nanny unquestionably as the id. The purity of higher, superego thinking is equivalent to Magrat's lofty, if misguided motives; our conscious intelligence directs us as Granny directs the Ramtops' tiny coven; we all have an id whose directives, like Nanny's earthy pronouncements, are often hard to interpret as wisdom or waywardness.

Obviously, this Freudian characterization supported by Bettelheim's analysis differs slightly from the Jungian viewpoint offered earlier, just as one goddess story differs from others in various respects. This apparent contradiction is just that, an apparition. Both schools of thought offer ways to think about why human lives flow and develop as they do, rather than fixed meanings.

Again, besides being aspects of the goddess, the Lancre witches are mortal women. As such, they all carry within themselves the seeds of what they will become and never completely shed the husks of what they were. It would be passing strange if each did not occasionally exhibit traits more closely identified with one of the other two. Magrat, Nanny, and Granny change during the courses of their lives, just as we all must. But consider: Magrat's emotionality, mentioned in the Jungian analysis, does not conflict at all with naming her the personification of the superego later on. The high-flown motives she has may be attributed to her idealism, which is something she retains *because* of her emotional nature. The elder two have seen too much of a sometimes harsh world to keep that quality; they have learned to compromise and to use their heads rather than only their hearts. And yet, Magrat will grow old one day; the idealism of her youth, though adhered to by the heart, is intellectual in nature. She has the potential to be very much like Granny in time.

In *Carpe Jugulum*, Magrat becomes a mother and gains new power in the evolution, but it upsets the trinity. With the birth of the infant Esmerelda, Granny leaves Lancre because she must wrestle with whatever follows cronedom and face the darkness. She is no longer bound by the threeness, so she is free to find out whether she does have darkness in her soul; she is not sure, herself. Near the end of the novel, Granny says to her priest companion, "This is where you find out ... To the fire we come at last ... This is where we *both* find out" (252). It may be personally necessary for Granny to face her own soul, but readers know that the other witches want her to stay. Her temporary departure may have been necessary when the vampires flew into town, but once they are defeated, it is not actually necessary for her to leave Lancre or the mortal plane because the trinity has expanded to become ... more.

Three works well in fairy-tales, but there *are* other numbers. Witches don't have to come in threes, literally, or when it's time to abandon a metaphor. "Course not," said Nanny. "You can have any number up to about, oh, four or five." Five is exactly the number of personalities, if not bodies, left when the survivors are tallied at the end of *Carpe Jugulum*. Pratchett has gone outside the frame of the physicality of three and into an exploration of the trinity unbound by mortal flesh. He retains the goddess in the device of the coven, but he allows the coven to expand and include other personalities the better to illuminate the aspects of the goddess not easily shown by means of his established characters.

Besides expanding the cast of the witches' story arc, Pratchett re-examines their roles. The original three are all what most people would call good, even though Granny's brand of goodness is difficult for many to understand. The terms *good* and *evil* did not always apply to the divine figures of antiquity, either: Artemis, with her brother Apollo, slew Niobe's children, but Magrat just isn't that sort. She does not have the darkness, but she has the core of stone and steel that is Granny's entire substance, or near enough; readers glimpse it in *Lords and Ladies* when Magrat punches the Queen of the Elves between the eyes.

Pratchett further explores cronedom in *Witches Abroad* by means of Granny's sister Lily. [*Fig. 1*] Lily Weatherwax went bad and tried to make Genua, a New Orleans-style city, into a fairy-tale kingdom more like Disneyworld than a real city. She used her power to force people into roles that did not fit, in direct opposition to Granny's basic existence as a crosser of boundaries. Lily wants people to lead scripted lives; Granny, who embraces tradition while rejecting stereotypes, sees no reason to do something just because it would make a good story. Ironically, this attitude is one reason the Discworld books are good stories. This con-tra-narrative defiance is important for several reasons, both inside and outside of the books themselves. Granny's perverse nature is more intriguing to readers than the wicked witch template everyone has seen before, and as Pratchett explains, it keeps him interested in writing about her: "The reason I like writing about Granny Weatherwax is that she's so twisted up. All her power comes from denial and refusal — she'd just love to let rip, but she won't because that wouldn't be Right. She's wicked by instinct but good by choice. [...] you could argue that she's so frightened about what she *could* be that she's always testing herself, just to check" (Gay, par. 8).

Her contrary divergence from the script makes her powerful: from the inside, as a person, and from outside, as a character. Her disinclination to play nicely with destiny makes her the woman and the witch that she is. There is something in Granny that doesn't love the walls placed around people by outside forces. Her sister, on the other hand, has no compunctions about using her power to stuff people into the molds of her choosing. Lily Weatherwax sees herself as good, but her despotic interpretation of the fairy godmother theme is very close to the Discworld definition of wickedness. Granny causes suffering only when suffering is unavoidable; when her choices must affect other lives, she disturbs those lives as little as pos-sible. Lily inflicts pain with her stories, believing that people ought to want for themselves the lives she envisions for them; she scruples at nothing in pursuit of her vision, turning lives upside down to bring about Procrustean "happy endings" that only she really wants. Where-as Granny chooses what she will be, her sister tries to choose for others: there is a world of difference between the two. That is why Lily is only a temporary character; a truly evil person-ality has no place in this trio.

The character who does permanently expand the coven by one body and two personali-ties is Agnes Nitt. Agnes is, according to Pratchett, more intelligent and more powerful than Magrat. However, she is still relatively subdued. It might be to accommodate a newer, more modern style of maiden that Pratchett introduces Perdita, Agnes Nitt's inner voice. Agnes herself is necessary to play the part of the apprentice, but she is as practical as Magrat is ear-nestly fanciful. When Magrat loses some of her dreaminess in her transition to motherhood, Perdita's gothic fancies fill the resulting gap. Perdita is an edgy, dominant personality, with an

Fig. 1: Cover illustration to Terry Pratchett's *Discworld: Witches Abroad*: Josh Kirby [©1993 Josh Kirby]

inherent darkness that neither Magrat nor Agnes possesses. That darkness might be necessary in a world that will not always have a Granny Weatherwax.

The presence of a new, sharper maiden frees Granny, in a way. She has been pushed out of the crone role, or rather *beyond* it. Now that Agnes is the Maiden and Magrat is a Mother and Nanny is the right age to be the Crone, what the script has in store for Granny is death. The trinity is complete without her; she feels the influence of the myth of which she is no longer an integral part. She feels unneeded because the coven is complete without her, unwanted because her invitation to Magrat's daughter's christening never reached her, and worn out from a lifetime of hard work and harder choices; believing herself beaten by the vampires who have invaded Lancre, she departs for a cave on the moors. Eventually, Granny confronts the vampires and wins. She resumes her life. Why should she lie down and die simply because it would make a tidy narrative? She is the first person on the Discworld to confront the After. All of us wonder what comes After. After *everything*. Granny is no doubt nearer the end of her mortal coil than the beginning, but she is still a maiden, acts as a mother to her people, and has the accumulated experience of the old. Since she has always been all of them, she is now free to expand on all of the roles she has played in her long life. She is no longer subject to labeling because there is no name for what she has become. She is so profoundly powerful that she might be called the universal female principle. She is the culmination of a female life but without any obligation to die. She creates a new class beyond classification.

The entire series of Discworld novels dealing with the Lancre witches has been the story of each witch learning and growing in each novel, and Granny Weatherwax is the end product of that process.

Although, as Pratchett insists, the Lancre witches are mortal women and not divine personifications, their presence in modern fantasy is a vital indication of the enduring nature of the goddess story. People need these models to begin seeing what is possible in life. Even Lily Weatherwax gives readers a valid blueprint for a human life — not a desirable one, but we need counterexamples, too; Catherine Aird might almost have been referring to Lily when she wrote, "If you can't be a good example, you'll just have to be a horrible warning" (196). Her shadow allows us to better see what is implicit in Granny's kind of darkness. In her time, Esmerelda Weatherwax has effected hurt and death, but the Great Mother has her destructive aspect, and it would be foolish and naïve to pretend she does not. Her apparent darkness is deceptive, representing the painful aspects of life and death, rather than evil. As Ruth Gardner explains, perceived destruction is not always true destruction: "The Crone stands at the gateway to death — to rebirth. To begin life again, there must first be death ... the new moon goes on to waxing, and then to full. Death is part of the continuing cycle of wholeness. The Crone closes one cycle so that another can begin" (40). Nanny Ogg, too, has been tested in the course of a long life; Magrat and Agnes will face their own heavy responsibilities as they grow older, each in turn.

These modern characters, with all the force of thousands of years of legend behind them, can only help us to better understand what it is to be woman, and human.

ALWAYS CONSTANT, ALWAYS CHANGING: THE TRIPLE GODDESS AND NEIL GAIMAN. The triple goddess's

presence also pervades Neil Gaiman's *The Sandman*. Only in the eponymous *The Kindly Ones* do Maiden-Mother-Crone become major actors in the plot; otherwise, they appear briefly to offer cryptic comments or warnings. Beyond that supporting role, however, the goddess's three personae are embodied in many characters who are important within the main plots and who cluster in sets of three. But a closer look shows that, although the triple goddess appears many times as herself and as analog characters, an individual maiden, mother, or crone keeps surprising us by performing actions inappropriate to that role. It appears that Gaiman, like Pratchett, wishes to show how useful the concept of the triple goddess is in understanding human behavior and interaction — yet simultaneously to show how seldom the concept sums up a person.

The three aspects of the goddess are part of a swarm of otherworldly beings encountered by the Sandman, otherwise known as Dream, one of the Endless. Readers eventually observe enough to make a rough classification of the supernatural characters.

Gods, first of all, are the most immediately recognizable supernatural beings because they have individual names, physical characteristics, personality traits, and demands for specific rituals. Their worshipers give them reality and power by the tribute of belief. This vivid individuality is also their weakness. As time passes, believers empower new gods, and the old ones disappear.

Members of the Endless, the Sandman's family, may seem less powerful than a particular god at a particular time; however, the Endless do not fade away, as gods do, because they come from a more basic level of humanity than belief. The Endless are born in the act of classifying concerns about the purpose and conduct of life, the process that later will lead to religions. Thus, the Endless never will be outmoded, because they are re-imagined every time someone thinks reflectively. Each of the Endless has a distinct personality, but each has had many names.

The characters who represent aspects of the triple goddess — Maiden, Mother, and Crone — are even more physically fluid than the Endless and have even more names. If the Endless represent categories of conscious thought, the aspects of the triple goddess embody a less individual, less intellectual level of mental activity. [*Figs. 2 &3*] The Kindly Ones' mission — punishment of anyone who spills the blood of a family member — supersedes *any* other consideration. It doesn't matter that the reason the Sandman kills Orpheus, his son, is that the young man is hopelessly maimed and has begged for death; once family blood is shed, the Kindly Ones instinctively become instruments of vengeance. They don't stop to consider a situation's ambiguities. They can't.

Fig. 2: Writer: Neil Gaiman Artists: Sam Keith & Mike Dringenberg "Imperfect Hosts"
Collected in *The Sandman: Preludes & Nocturnes* [©1995 DC Comics]

Fig. 3: Writer: Neil Gaiman Artists: Sam Keith & Mike Dringenberg "Imperfect Hosts"
Collected in *The Sandman: Preludes & Nocturnes* [©1995 DC Comics]

If this is true — if the triple goddess represents womanhood at an absolutely fundamental level; if Maiden, Mother, and Crone embody the goddess; and if the Kindly Ones are just Maiden, Mother, and Crone working together — the unthinking ferocity shown in *The Sandman* suggests severe limits for women. The goddess seems to be part of the unconscious, silent, emotional — in short, "female" side of humanity. In fact, Gaiman has spoken of deliberately writing Sandman sequences that move from male- to female-focused stories:

> *Preludes & Nocturnes* is a guy's tale — it has a male hero, The Sandman, who triumphs over various challenges. The next book, *The Doll's House*, is fundamentally Rose Walker's tale, and it deals with women, relationships, and the tearing down of walls. The following book, *Season of Mists* is again a Sandman story, in which the Sandman uses his courage and wits to deal with a problem of diplomacy. And then there's *A Game of You*, which is about women, fantasy, and identity. (in Bender 117)

Someone who took this at face value might conclude that being a "guy" is about courage and wit, heroically overcoming challenges, while women concern themselves with touchy-feely relationships. If fact, someone who accepted this superficial Guy-Girl distinction might scan *The Sandman* and conclude that women are happiest when barefoot, pregnant, and inflicting terrible vengeance on anyone who has shed family blood.

The Sandman as a whole demonstrates that this is nonsense. However, Gaiman recognizes that such stereotypes can control the actions of individuals who insist on believing they must live up to their assigned sexual-social roles. Some men *do* take decisive action in the exterior world even while they are disconnected from their own inner lives. Some women *do* submerge themselves in small, emotional concerns even when that leaves them groping, without long-range plans in the hard-edged world. The results frequently are disastrous. But people don't have to accept these stereotypical limits as "natural" or absolute. In fact one of the major themes of *The Sandman* is the difficult, uncertain progress of a few individuals — including the Sandman himself — toward recognition that they can escape what they imagine to be their roles.

The problem seems to be that people take the process of conscious reflection too far, too fast. They are so anxious to have stable identities that they seize something immediately satisfying, then ignore new possibilities. As the Sandman comments, "Mortals ... see only the prize, their heart's desire, their dream ... But the price of getting what you want is getting what once you wanted" ("A Midsummer Night's Dream," 81). Although he does not recognize it at the time, he is describing himself too, self-assured and powerful within his realm but apparently trapped there.

A Game of You is one of *The Sandman*'s "women stories" in which the triple goddess is especially active. The central character is a young woman named Barbie who looks like a plastic doll. She even was married to a man named Ken when she was introduced as part of the supporting cast of the earlier "women's story" *The Doll's House*. Now she is divorced and living alone in a shabby New York apartment decorated with photos of bizarre tattoos and piercings that she has not yet had done to her own body because she can't make a commitment at any level of life. Her best friend is Wanda, *ne* Alvin, a pre-operative transsexual. Barbie is drifting aimlessly, and she insists that she never dreams. But she did in *The Doll's House*. Then, showing Barbie's incompatibility with her sleeping husband Ken's brutal power fantasies, Barbie dreamed of being a princess in The Land, a magical place where she heroically undertook dangerous but significant tasks and where marvelous, loyal friends were eager to look after her.

In *A Game of You*, Barbie's waking world is invaded by creatures from her dreams, and she is drawn back to The Land because its very existence is threatened by the mysterious Cuckoo. She is at first happy to be back. She had forgotten that experience could be so vivid, fresh and full of possibilities as her dreams when she was a little girl. However, when one of her wonderful friends betrays her to the Cuckoo, Barbie discovers that monster is *herself* as a little girl. At least that is what it looks like, and Barbie is so hypnotized by its appearance of helpless cuteness that she agrees to aid it in destroying The Land even though that will mean her own death.

The story never explains what the Cuckoo actually is, so readers must revert to analogy. A baby cuckoo bird is weaker than other birds but can intrude into another species' nest and take the place of the owner's young until it grows big enough to fend for itself. In *A Game of You*, the Cuckoo is a creature that has found refuge in the little dreamworld Barbie has never quite relinquished. But now the Cuckoo is ready to move on, and it needs help to break The Land open. In our world, a cuckoo fools the parent birds because it can imitate their babies. Gaiman's Cuckoo overcomes its adversaries because it represents whatever they cherish most about themselves; it takes the form of something they want to protect because it seems to be the keystone of their identity.

From Barbie's bedazzled surrender to the Cuckoo, it follows that people should be careful about basing their identities on some superficial quality. She is not the only vulnerable person. When she begins dreaming of The Land, before the Cuckoo traps her, Barbie's body lies in a trance while the Cuckoo tries to manipulate the dreams of others in her apartment building to destroy her there. One other tenant, however, is "Thessaly," an ancient witch currently masquerading as a nerdy young art history student who takes this magical tampering as a personal attack. She has not survived for centuries by letting anyone bother her. Thessaly carefully conceals her true nature from the people around her, but consciousness of her long life is a private talisman of her superior wisdom and power. Accordingly, she gathers her fellow tenants to form an expedition into the dreamworld and kill the Cuckoo — and also, though this is much less important to Thessaly, to save Barbie. In order to do this, the witchwoman draws down the moon so that she can command the triple goddess's aid; she also organizes the war party to represent the triple goddess's aspects: She sees herself as the wise-woman, the crone; Hazel, a lesbian who naïvely has become pregnant, is the mother; Fox-glove, Hazel's lover, is the maiden. Wanda/Alvin, the person most concerned about rescuing Barbie, can't be part of the group because Thessaly decrees that he is not a genuine woman and so cannot walk on the moon's road.

As maiden, mother, and crone walk into the dreamworld, they experience the merging of personalities shown elsewhere in *The Sandman*. In The Land, however, they revert to separate roles, so Thessaly, witchwoman Crone, again becomes the leader. She has brought them this far, and she is certain that she knows where to go and what to do next. Her encounter with the Cuckoo does not go as anticipated, however, because Thessaly's pride-based self image makes her vulnerable. Still the guise of a little girl, the Cuckoo runs up to Thessaly and pleads for help. Thessaly agrees immediately, certain that — being Thessaly — she is too clever to make a mistake. [*Fig. 4*] She thus winds up as entranced as Barbie. Only the arrival of the Sandman himself interrupts the Cuckoo's triumph and restores the humans to their senses. The Land is old, so the Sandman accepts its dissolution, but he gives Barbie, its last dreamer, one wish. She could have The Land restored and continue as Princess Barbie, but she now recognizes the limits of that role. She also could take a somewhat more adult attitude and get revenge by having the Cuckoo punished. That is what Thessaly demands, trying to take control again. But Barbie refuses to accept Thessaly's authority. She realizes that the one necessary goal is to get them all home safely. As a direction in Gaiman's script says, "There's a new Barbie here, sharper and more cause, less effect, than she was before" (Script, 266). And so Barbie, who apparently was trapped in the role of maiden, rebukes the naïve egotism of Thessaly, the crone.

This happens within the dream. After it is over, back in our world, Barbie continues to demonstrate the unreliability of fixed roles. She does not remember what happened while she was unconscious, the three women won't talk to her about it, and Wanda is dead, crushed when their apartment building collapsed during a hurricane caused by Thessaly's tampering with the moon. And so Barbie must go alone to Wanda's family home in Kansas for the funeral. Wanda's aunt appreciates the trouble Barbie went through to get there, but she warns her to refer to the deceased only as "Alvin." After all, she explains, "God gives you a body, it's your duty to do well by it. He makes you a boy, you dress in blue. He makes you a girl, you dress in pink. You mustn't go trying to change things" (176). After the funeral, however, Barbie says her private farewell by canceling "Alvin" on the tombstone with a huge "WANDA" scrawled in "tacky flamingo" lipstick (183). This renaming is validated by a dream she remembers having during her ride out to Kansas; falling asleep in the back of a Greyhound bus, she sees her friend *as* Wanda, no longer a pre-op transsexual but the woman she always has claimed to be: "perfect, drop-dead gorgeous. There's nothing camp about her, nothing artificial. And she looks happy" (186). Even if Thessaly and the triple goddess herself would disagree, Wanda *has* been able to recreate herself.

Fig. 4: Writer: Neil Gaiman Artists: Shawn McManus, Bryan Talbot & Stan Woch "Over the Sea to Sky"
Collected in *The Sandman: A Game of You* [©1993 DC Comics]

Barbie herself, at the end of *A Game of You*, doesn't look especially happy. Alvin's aunt has just dropped her off outside a bus station, and she is uncertain about where to go or what to do next. She has no place to live and no one to look after her; no support and no illusions — but also no limits.

There are worse things than alert uncertainty. One is the befuddled listlessness Barbie endures at the story's beginning. Another is the smothering certainty that one *must* grow beyond unbreakable limits. That's why, despite the pain the Cuckoo causes, readers can sympathize with its need to destroy The Land so that it can fly away.

Leaving an established role isn't easy; there is no certainty that one's new condition will be happier, and the new condition itself may as yet be impossible to visualize. However, the devastating effects of keeping fixed, limiting roles are shown in the longest Sandman story arc, *The Kindly Ones*, in which the Sandman interacts directly with three women:

> Nuala, the elf maiden who has been his servant since *Season of Mists* and who yearns for him to love her;
>
> Lyta Hall, mother of two-year-old Daniel, preoccupied with dread of losing her son since *The Doll's House*, especially afraid that the Sandman will steal the little boy;
>
> Thessaly (now calling herself Larissa), the youthful-looking crone familiar from *A Game of You* and more recently the Sandman's lover, who still lives for and by her own schemes.

Awareness of the characters' roles help readers understand how they see themselves, not just what actions they imagine as desirable but as *possible*. Yet *The Kindly Ones* also shows how a role confuses each character and leads her to actions that actually work against her interests.

Nuala, for one, behaves like a romantic heroine by calling the Sandman to her when she hears he is being attacked. She imagines they can run away from the Furies together, as lovers, but she actually brings the Sandman's doom closer by summoning him away from the protection of his realm. The Sandman literally cannot imagine going away because he won't let himself think of giving up his responsibility, his own role. When she apologizes, "I did not mean to harm you," the Sandman replies, "I know that Nuala. But, as has recently been pointed out to me, intent and outcome are rarely coincident."

It is Thessaly who recently rebuked the Sandman in those words for not being a more attentive lover. And so, because her feelings were hurt, Thessaly becomes an ally of the Furies against the Sandman. She uses her wisdom to do their will, and she rationalizes this by telling herself that she is bargaining for more years of life; she actually is motivated by pique and by a need to prove that *she* controls the situation. In a dream after the Sandman's passing, she remembers their love affair/relationship — from, of course, her perspective and displaying a great deal of emotional projection. He is described, for example, as "rather brooding and self-absorbed" (*The Wake* 60), adjectives that could describe Thessaly herself. Each blames the other for their bitter parting; each sees the other through a self-distorted lens. But anger is easier than reflection. Thessaly states that when he left The Dreaming for "real life," full of rage, she "swore I would never shed another tear for him" (61). As she speaks, she is crying.

Lyta Hall is the character most closely connected with the three aspects of the goddess. She even talks directly with them several times while she is working herself into the role of avenging mother, and the Furies use her in that persona. Because she is sure that the Sandman stole Daniel from her and then killed him, Lyta focuses totally on attacking the Sandman. Her body under Thessaly's magical protection, Lyta's spirit takes the form of a warrior, enters the Sandman's realm, and begins destroying whomever she encounters there. When the Sandman recovers Daniel safely from the real kidnappers, Lyta pauses. Standing in her shining armor, she tells the Furies, "We have to rescue Daniel. Bring him back. We don't have to hurt anyone anymore." By that time, however, she no longer has a choice. As the Furies tell her, "We don't rescue. We revenge." And so, at the end of the story, when she becomes fully conscious of herself again and dazedly says "I was looking for Daniel ..." Thessaly replies, "As I understand it, your actions have ensured that you will never see Daniel again."

Each of these women sets immediate goals for herself and succeeds. Each is disappointed with the results. Getting what she wants turns out to be getting what once she wanted — because that was what she expected to want because she identified herself as a lovelorn maiden, a protective mother, or an arcane crone. Working separately but serving the aim of the Furies in the background, what Nuala, Lyta, and Thessaly actually bring about is the end of the Sandman; when he cannot protect the beings for whom he is responsible, fulfill his role as lord of dreams — in short, be the individual *he* expects himself to be — he ceases to exist in that identity and is replaced by another Dream.

Giving up his existence as Dream by "dying" means that the Sandman literally passes away, moves on to another existence beyond our vision. He is like Barbie in that respect. Or the Cuckoo. The characters still in readers' sight at the end of *The Sandman* show varying degrees of this potential to grow into uncertain, unpredictable freedom.

Lyta seems the least likely to take a chance. She has been so damaged by her experience as Mother that she advises Rose Walker to get rid of her unborn child: "Kill it before it breaks your heart" (*The Wake* 58). Daniel has been transformed into the new Dream, so Lyta truly has lost her son forever and is in danger of losing her self in an unhealthy way by clinging to fragments of her shattered role. While she is asleep, however, the new Dream summons her to give her protection from vengeance and a chance to at least reassemble herself.

Thessaly is last seen before she wakes, tears streaming down her face as she remembers the Sandman and what she did with and to him. If she can see herself as readers see her, she could realize that she needs to change. However, Thessaly's past dreams show how she has overcome such emotions in the past. She has not displayed much ability to reflect on the rightness of her actions. In the last installment of *The Kindly Ones*, Thessaly speaks of punishing Lyta for helping destroy the Sandman. But this is not the same thing as accepting responsibility for what she herself has done; rather, it is exactly the vengeful reaction readers would expect from Thessaly whenever she is bothered. So it is uncertain what she will manage to do with this new evidence that she has done something wrong.

Of these three women, however, Nuala certainly refuses to return to her familiar place. When she goes home after spending time in the Sandman's castle, she chooses to be less glamorously seductive than before, and she refuses to be bullied by Queen Titania. And eventually she does choose to leave her home and her kin. After the Sandman's passing, finding herself among the group of beings who are remembering him in their dreams, she fully accepts the consequences of her actions that led to his demise. As she tells her brother, "I have left Faerie, certain of but one thing: That the words of your poem will come true for me, 'Be sure your sins will find you out'" (*The Wake* 51). When she wakes, she is shown in the act of rising from a table in an inn, tossing coins on the table and moving on.

As for Maiden, Mother, and Crone themselves, the Kindly Ones, at the end of that story they are shown absolutely unchanged. They have no increased understanding of what has happened, no larger self-awareness. Unlike the women who represent them, they are unable to begin understanding what they have done, let alone digesting it; they just do what they do. When they change, it is by exchanging one familiar identity for another in an endless loop.

If this feels like an anticlimactic end to the longest *Sandman* story arc, the characters' incomplete self-recognition and transformation does illustrate one of *The Sandman's* continuing themes: What happens to us is determined both by what we're given and by what we do with it. The goddess and her avatars certainly exist; the concerns they represent are parts of each woman's life. That does not mean that we are ruled by them. People can change. They can incorporate what is permanent and unchangeable in themselves into larger wholes; they can move from smaller into larger roles. Our temptation always is to stop, to say, "This is what I am, all I ever can be." *The Sandman* tries to demonstrate otherwise. Gaiman believes that we should recognize what we are but not stop there. Rather, we should try to discover the uncertain hope of what we may become.

CONCLUSION. The myth of the Goddess has persisted through history, making her presence felt all over the world. Myths, legends and fairy-tales have been passed on by elders to teach those who come after, since the far distant time when our kind developed the capacity to plan. Even after literal belief faded, people continued to tell these stories, finding in them examples both negative and positive. The bloody nature of some earlier versions of supposedly familiar fairy-tales (mistakenly thought to be well-known) supports this because they arose from and reflected the harsh realities of life in the past. Yet the same stories show up again and again, serving as inspirations — or warnings — every time. This process works so well because, although people are capable of committing stupid acts, selfish acts, and now and again kind or beautiful acts, the entire catalogue of human behavior is somewhat repetitive. Within the normal scope of human behavior, and even in the depths of the distinctly abnormal, there are only so many possible actions. Our lives are palimpsests; the faint traces of the paths of earlier lives, real of fictitious, may evoke insight into our own.

This doesn't, however, mean that a contemporary audience will easily recognize — or find applicable — the old myths. Athena may have been exactly what the ancient Greeks needed, but what has she done for us lately? Vital as an awareness of historical myth is in understanding how we got to where we are, we need new interpretations of those myths. That is what Pratchett and Gaiman offer readers today.

The most immediately striking thing about the two writers' use of the myth of the Triple Goddess is how different the results are.

Pratchett is concerned with community, the combining of distinct individuals into an active, productive harmony, however imperfect and temporary that must finally be. His characters must maintain their own distinctive selves but also learn to adjust themselves to other people — and sometimes to learn how to adjust the other people non-destructively. Awareness of their mythic roles actually aids their personal self understanding so that they are able to cooperate without compromising their identities. Trying to impose old plots on living people, as in *Witches Abroad*, is momentarily amusing to readers, but they soon realize how stultifying it is and how the literally deadly the results could be. As Granny says, people can disassemble old myths and salvage the parts they want to use in new stories. They can discover new roles by working together, supporting and challenging each other.

Gaiman shows the stifling control of old stories but stresses even more the possibility of escaping from them. His characters begin and end alone, separated by conflicting aims. The triads that form during his work are genuine but much more temporary than those of Pratchett's witches. Thessaly must identify Fox and Hazel as parts of a triad; they are unconscious of their mythic roles and confused about how to fill them. Moreover, at the end of *A Dream of You*, that triad has dissolved, forgotten. The triad the Furies create in *The Wake* also dissolves, its members free to move on, probably sadder but possibly wiser. What readers learn from Gaiman's use of the Triple Goddess by and large is respect for individual differences and non-interference in other people's affairs.

Yet, despite the differences in how Pratchett and Gaiman picture the effects and lasting significance of the Triple Goddess, both writers have discovered and used the myth in creating impressive, memorable fiction. Readers who notice this will see female triads elsewhere in stories they read — as in the suspicion that Barbie, Death, and Wanda form at least a momentary triad at the end of *A Dream of You*. Both writers agree that the myth expresses the way human concerns are structured, and they have found new ways to bring it to contemporary readers' attention.

WORKS CITED.

Adler, Margot. *Drawing Down the Moon*. Boston: Beacon Press, 1986.

Aird, Catherine. *His Burial Too*. New York: Bantam, 1981.

Bettleheim, Bruno. *The Uses of Enchantment*. New York: Vintage-Random House, 1989.

Byatt, A.S. "A Comforting Way of Death." 2002. *Guardian Unlimited Books*. <http://books. guardian.co.uk/reviews/sciencefiction/0,6121,836250,00.html>. 04 April 2004.

Gay, Anne. "The Line One Interview with Terry Pratchett." 1999. *Anne Gay: The Website*. Available: < http://herebedragons.co.uk/gay/>. 22 March 2004.

Gardner, Ruth. *Celebrating the Crone*. 1st ed. St. Paul: Llewellyn, 1999.

Goleman, Daniel. *Emotional Intelligence*. New York: Bantam, 1995.

Graves, Robert. *The White Goddess*. New York: Noonday Press-Farrar, Straus and Giroux, 1948.

Hamilton, Edith. *Mythology*. New York: Mentor-Penguin, 1942.

Jung, Carl. *Four Archetypes*. Bollingen. Ed. William McGuire. 1st paperback edition ed. Vol. 9. Princeton: Princeton, 1970.

Pratchett, Terry. *Wyrd Sisters*. New York: Roc-Penguin, 1990.

—. *Witches Abroad*. New York: Roc- Penguin, 1993.

—. *Lords and Ladies*. 1st mass market paperback ed. New York: HarperPaperbacks-HarperCollins, 1996.

—. *Maskerade*. New York: HarperPrism, 1997.

—. *Carpe Jugulum*. London: Doubleday-Transworld LTD, 1998.

—. "The Sea and Little Fishes." *Legends*. Ed. Robert Silverberg. New York: Tor, 1998.

—. "Witches of the Discworld." Plain Dealer Book & Author Series. Conversation with Stacie Hanes & Joseph Sanders. Cleveland, OH, March 28, 2000.

Sayer, Karen. "The Witches." *Terry Pratchett: Guilty of Literature*. Ed. Edward James Andrew Butler, Farah Mendlesohn. Reading, United Kingdom: The Science Fiction Foundation, 2000.

Wood, Juliette. "The Concept of the Goddess." *The Concept of the Goddess*. Ed. Sandra Bullington and Miranda Green. London: Routledge, 1996. 8-25.

✠✠✠

OMNIA MUTANTUR: THE USE OF ASIAN DRESS IN THE APPEARANCE OF DREAM FROM *THE SANDMAN*

by Lyra McMullen

✦

Neil Gaiman's closing comments in the first collection of his *Sandman* stories, originally published as individual comics from 1989-1996, describe how the main character, Dream, got his distinctive mode of dress:

> The inspiration for his clothes came from a book of Japanese design, of a black kimono, with yellow markings at the bottom which looked vaguely like flames; ...[1]

By the close of the 20th century, fans of popular media based SF and fantasy productions have become accustomed to fictional characters appearing in Asian-inspired costume. Familiar examples of this phenomenon are some of the costumes from various branches of the *Star Trek* Franchise and the costumes of the Jedi knights from George Lucas's

Star Wars films. Certainly the ever-increasing popularity of Japanese anime-style, in films, TV and comic books has exposed Western audiences to Eastern fantasy and clothing styles over the course of the last two decades. Asian styles of traditional dress, most notably the Japanese kimono and Chinese court dress, continue to be recycled in fantasy and science fiction productions produced by American authors and media conglomerates. Through an in-depth analysis of the relationship between choices used in costume illustration and the themes of these stories, it becomes clear that common stereotypes of Asian costume and culture have deeply penetrated the Western psyche.

The only difficulty present in analyzing Asian influences upon the illustration of *The Sandman*, are that these influences are much more subtle than they may appear. One of the ironies behind the proceeding quote is that without Neil Gaiman's own commentary on the subject, the source of inspiration for Dream's distinctive costume may well have remained unguessed. As a being of incredible power, Dream has the power to mold and shape his environment and his person to his liking, pretty much at will; this includes his clothing. At some points in the series, his garb closely approximates the kimono Gaiman has cited as a model. [*Fig. 1*] At other points in the progression of the comic book series however, Dream's robes appear more like a toga or oversized bathrobe; it trails on the ground behind him like the Heian court dress of medieval Japan, and flames, or faces, flicker in the patterns of its hem. Dream also goes about in something more closely approximating modern garb and the kimono becomes a toga, cape, or trench coat. Sometimes he goes without but it remains one of his favorite styles throughout the series.

It is important to remember that Western Civilization's fascination with all things Asian goes back several hundred years. One aspect of Asian fashion that is remarkable to Western eyes is its continuity. Where trends in European art, architecture, and fashion change and then disappear completely relatively quickly, traditional Eastern styles like the Japanese kimono seem to hang on for centuries. Although certainly worn much less in modern times, Asian styles of traditional dress remain much same even in the face of Western colonization, and the more recent mass exportation of our modern material culture to the Far East.

It may be this factor of timelessness that influences the choice of Asian-inspired costume for many modern works of science fiction and fantasy. Valerie Steele, in her introduction to the catalogue from the recently produced exhibition *China Chic*, reflects on a Western misperception of China as a place where nothing changes:

> A surprising number of people have the impression (without
> thinking about it very much) that China changed hardly at all
> during the long traditional era from the time of Confucius to
> the fall of the last emperor.[2]

Like many stereotypes, this perception of Chinese dress and the perception that Asian

Fig. 1: Writer: Neil Gaiman Artists: Mike Dringenberg & Malcolm Jones III "Lost Hearts"
Collected in *The Sandman: The Doll's House* [©1995 DC Comics]

fashion in general is "static" is somewhat incorrect. A rapidly changing silhouette does not convey fashion in the East like it does in Western costume. In Asian costume, the age, gender, fashion-consciousness, and status of the wearer are frequently expressed through quality and quantity of garments, choice of textile materials and applied decoration, while the actual silhouette remains relatively stable over time.

This mutability disguised by continuity makes Asian costume especially appropriate in *The Sandman* where Gaiman's main protagonist, Dream, belongs to a mythic-quality group of beings called the Endless. Gaiman's own inventions, The Endless are embodiments of various aspects of the human or living condition: Destiny, Death, Dream, Destruction, Desire, Despair, and Delirium formerly known as Delight. As such they have existed since the beginning of time and will continue to exist until the end of the universe. The very term "Endless" implies a static existence without end so that birth, death, love, and even change itself become more difficult states to attain. Yet, because they are supposed to embody all the characteristics of the living existence of the Universe so, The Endless should also embody the more mutable states of life, as we know it. Ordinary people dream about being omnipotent or immortal, but put into this context, being a member of the rather exclusive club known as "The Endless" sounds more difficult than it may first appear as petty interpersonal conflicts reverberate over centuries rather than months or years.

The idea of change — to change or not to change and the risk one takes of being somehow left behind in time — is one of the ongoing themes of *The Sandman* comic book series. Dream, or Morpheus, as he is sometimes called, is oft critiqued both by fellow characters within the series and the various contributors of the introductory texts to the bound volumes of this work, as someone who is unable or unwilling to change, or to even acknowledge that he has changed. It is ironic that a being who lives in such a mutable world, and has such ability to morph it to reflect his wishes cannot acknowledge the changeable nature of both himself and the universe around him.

What we know about the character of Dream better explains the choice of a kimono as costume in the comic-book illustrations when viewed in light of Ms. Steeles' comments. It confirms Ms. Steele's hypothesis that Western culture views Asian dress as static, and broadens the scope of the stereotype she describes beyond Chinese dress to reflect attitudes held by Western culture toward Asia as a whole.

THE WAKE. Moving very close to the end of the series, in the last collected volume of the original series, entitled *The Wake*, very obvious and intentional Eastern elements in the illustrations of Dream's costume merit exploration. To give a little background information, at this point in the series the Dreamworld has been reduce to a wasteland, many of its inhabitants have been killed, and Dream is dead — well sort of.

As one of the characters in *The Wake* puts it, "How can you kill an idea? How can you kill the personification of an action?"[3] For that is all Dream is really, an anthropomorphic incarnation of the act of dreaming. Dream in his incarnation of Morpheus is dead, however Dream of the Endless continues. Dream may be immortal; but he is certainly not invincible. At the climax of the series, in the bound volume entitled *The Kindly Ones*, Dream lays down his own life (or commits suicide) only to be replaced by another aspect of himself.

It is in this incarnation, the metamorphosed form of Daniel Hall, that the new Dream King makes his first appearance in *The Wake* on the original cover art drawn by Michael Zulli.

As reincarnation is a notion closely associated in the West with the Eastern philosophies and theology, perhaps it is no coincidence that in his first re-appearance after the death of the old Dreamking, Dream is dressed in robes derived, in large part from non-Western sources. His dress shows an unmistakable resemblance to Japanese kimono, not only in terms of style but also in terms of patterning with its all-over design of gold flowers trimmed in red. The shoulder projections of the sleeveless over-robe mimic the effects of a kamishimo, a sleeveless jacket often seen in Sharaku's prints of kabuki actors.

The long tight undersleeves, although apparently composed in this instance of wrapped bands, have a distinctive horseshoe shaped curve to the wrist cuffs, a feature found in Manchu court robes from China. [*Fig. 2*]

Since American society lacks the tradition of titled nobility, it has no appropriate cultural symbols for this type of authority figure including attire, and must therefore borrow from other sources. Since Western culture has become much more familiar with the costume of both Japan and China in recent decades it becomes ready inspiration for a fictional character in need of regal attire.

The imperial grandeur of Dream's new white robes provides an interesting visual contrast to the child or adolescent-like physical presence and emotional openness of the new Dreamlord. The underlying contradiction is that the new Dream is both a continuation of the old Dream within the conception of the Endless (i.e. never-ending), and the new reality that Dream/Daniel prior to his transformation was a very young human boy, who is now seems somewhat awkward and inexperienced in his new position of incredible power. Ironically, and perhaps intentionally, Daniel's abduction from his mortal mother propels a chain of events that ultimately leads to the old Morpheus's demise.

Also new is Dream's acknowledgement that things have not remained the same as they always were, the change in his clothes is symbolic of a greater change in character (Morpheus's robes whatever their shape were always black. Daniel's are always white). In a conversation with his sibling Destruction (another member of the dysfunctional family of the Endless) Dream acknowledges a fact that is so obvious it can no longer remain ignored; that things do not always remain the same.

> "Things change, don't they?" Destruction asks.
> "Yes, they do." Dream replies.[4]

Fig. 2: Writer: Neil Gaiman Artist: Michael Zulli "Chapter One: Which Occurs in the Wake of What Has Happened Before" Collected in *The Sandman: The Wake* [©1997 DC Comics]

It is no coincidence that Dream shares this conversation with his brother Destruction. Their talk is a reflection on another conversation between the old Dreamlord and his brother where Morpheus denies that things change[5] — for change is, in essence, what Dream's brother Destruction is all about.

EPILOGUES. This theme of change is followed through all three of the closing stories in *The Wake*, vignettes covering both earlier and later timelines of Dream's existence. The first of these, "Exiles," is the most directly Orientalist of any of the tales in the original *Sandman* series and uses Asian-inspired costume, here Chinese, to its most dramatic effect (I am discounting here one of the more recent additions to the *Sandman* epic, *The Dream Hunters*, for reasons that will become apparent shortly).

"Exiles," tells the story of a Chinese official, who having angered the Emperor through no good fault of his own, has been sent into exile in the far Western reaches of the Chinese empire. To reach his new post he must cross the great desert, and on his way he becomes lost in the sand and has a dream, or hallucination, in which he encounters the Dreamlord in both his past and present incarnations. [*Fig. 3*]

Dream frequently changes his appearance to fit into the cultural context of those with whom he is communicating. It is fitting then that the new Dream reappears in the same costume first drawn by Michael Zulli in *The Wake*, here rendered in John J. Muth's carefully crafted imitation of Chinese ink-brush painting. In this context, the chinoiserie of Dream's robes seem to fit the pseudo-Chinese illustrative style and the cultural context of the story — the action takes place in an imagined version of the western Chinese desert. Here, the Dreaming and our reality collide and a changing state of reality is as frequent as a shift of the sands.

Aided by his often-laconic speech patterns, the empty spaces devoid of words speak volumes more than Dream's meager allotment of dialogue. Dream himself becomes an eerie apparition that blends in with the desert sands on which the story takes place. Perhaps this is why Master Li initially mistakes the first apparition of the Dreamking for a Demon.

Master Li talks to Dream about his troubles, and rejects an offer to come to Dream's realm as an advisor, to escape from both the desert and his impending exile. Before parting ways, Li watches Dream free a group of riders, "barbarians" as Li terms them, who have been trapped in this netherworld between The Dreaming and the real world for centuries. Li asks for a translation of their last words to the Dreamking before being sent on to an unknown fate:

> "Lord — what was it the barbarian said, as the riders vanished?"
> "Omnia mutantur, nihil interit. 'Everything changes, but
> nothing is truly lost.'"[6]

The new Dreamlord bids Li farewell; his white robes blend into the sand, and he is gone.

Fig. 3: Writer: Neil Gaiman Artist: Jon J. Muth "Exiles"
Collected in *The Sandman: The Wake* [©1997 DC Comics]

Again the theme is that of change. Perhaps the message here is that change is neither good nor bad, but inevitable in all things, a fitting epilogue to one of the most engaging fantasy series in recent memory.

ASIAN STYLISTIC ELEMENTS MEET COMIC BOOK LIMITATIONS.

Before the term "manga" referred to Japanese comic-book art, it referred to books of cheap woodblock prints in the *ukiyo-e* style. Gaiman said he took his inspiration from an image in a book of Japanese-style prints; it is easy to imagine that he may have been looking at work in this style when he conceived of the character Dream.

It is interesting to note here that Dream's costume, as portrayed in the comic book, more closely resembles artistic renditions of Japanese dress than actual garments worn at any time by the Japanese. The dramatic elements in Dream's costume reflect liberties taken in artistic representation in both two and three-dimensional forms. The Japanese print artist, Sharaku, was working for a very brief period of time at the close of the 18th century producing woodblock prints of kabuki theater actors in costume. An aspect of Sharaku's prints that deserves to be remarked upon is his ability to capture dramatic action or emotion in his subjects, while working within the very stringent material limitations of the woodblock medium. Likewise the comic-book format limits the range of emotion or action that can be shown to a rather narrow frame-by-frame field, a finite number of pages and the diminutive size of each frame limits the amount of detail that can be shown in each one. A convenient tool to convey emotion used by Japanese artists like Sharaku and the many illustrators of *The Sandman* series over its nine-year run is the movement of drapery.

The use of movement of drapery is a pictorial technique of telling a story in lieu of words that is common to both Western comic books, Japanese manga, and traditional Japanese art, where its use goes at least as far back as the Heian period. A good example of this is the design from the back of this kosode (kimono) robe from the Nomura collection in Japan. The rustling screens and drapes are meant to suggest the recent passage of someone — a lover — from one interior space to another.[7]

It is appropriate for Dream from *The Sandman* stories to have an equally dramatic mode of dress. He is often known by one of his many names as the Prince of Stories; in this guise he is the inspirer of artists and writers. He also has the aforementioned ability to morph his garments and his world, The Dreaming, to reflect his emotions, which don't show on his face as well as they show in the rain endured by the denizens of his realm after his latest lover has left him for good at the beginning of the collection of stories entitled *Brief Lives*.

Is it a coincidence that the illustration of Dream's robes so closely mimics the movement of the curtains on the kosode? Possibly, but it is indicative that the illustration of Dream's agitated costume and the decoration of this 19th century kimono share a common aesthetic intent, and perhaps a common cultural source of inspiration.

THE DREAM HUNTERS. A very intentional West to East cross-cultural interplay takes place in *The Dream Hunters,* one of several additions to the *Sandman* literature since the completion of the original series in 1996. It would be impossible to talk about the use of Asian costume in *The Sandman* without at least mentioning the book *The Dream Hunters.* The story is based on a traditional Japanese tale Gaiman adapted to include in its cast of characters well-known faces from *The Sandman* comics, including Dream, Cain, Abel, and a particular raven who used to be a poet.

Japanese costume appears in *The Dream Hunters* for the most simple of reasons, one of the same reasons it appears in "Exiles," the story takes place in the Far East (medieval Japan) and it is culturally appropriate to the setting of the story. In addition, the book *Dream Hunters* is entirely illustrated by a Japanese artist whose work Neil Gaiman admired prior to asking him to collaborate with him on this story. The fact that *The Dream Hunters* is an illustrated book and not a comic came about because Yoshitaka Amano declined to produce comic-book illustrations, but agreed to illustrate Gaiman's story.[8]

The limited support the costume in the illustrations plays in *The Dream Hunters* highlights the essential distinction between a comic book and an illustrated story. In comic books, the pictures are an integral part of the story, since text is effectively limited to dialogue. Essential characteristics of character, plot, and setting are conveyed solely by the use of pictures. Dream's costume in the comic series portrays characteristics and emotions of the character that are not conveyed through dialogue or descriptive text. In a comic book there is no story without the pictures. In an illustrated book, the pictures are there as a supplement to the story (if I can say this without diminishing the skill and talent Yoshitaka Amano used to complete his illustrations for the book; they are lovely). The use of illustrations in *Dream Hunters* tells us very little that is not already conveyed through the text of Gaiman's short story.

Dream (the "old" Dreamlord Morpheus) is a relatively minor character in *The Dream Hunters.* The plot revolves around the emotional triangle of the Monk, the Fox, and the Onmyoji who wants the monk's contented soul. Of course there are several of the comic stories where Dream manifests himself only briefly, if at all, but Dream always returns to play a greater role in the next installment, or the one after that. Dream is the main connecting character and plot element throughout the entire comic series. The reader, if already familiar with the comic books, knows how that story is going to end, so there can be very little said about Morheus's appearance in *The Dream Hunters.* The reader gets to witness a rare moment of empathy on the part of the Dreamlord, but aside from that the insertion of the story at an earlier point in the timeline after the completion of the original comic series precludes further development of Morpheus's character.

CONCLUSIONS. If the argument is accepted that through many points in the series Dream's costume is based very clearly, and at other times more loosely, on the Asian models of the Japanese kimono, and Chinese (Manchurian) Court dress, where does this discussion of Oriental influences in the costume of *The Sandman* end? Back at the old paradigm that nothing we create is truly original since every thing man makes, every piece of art is based on other sources of inspiration that came before? How does one define originality when a lot of creative energy is expended in retooling what is in essence a Western stereotype concerning the deeper meaning of Asian traditonal attire — the conveyance of a certain timeless, ultimate authority, and emotions, by means of dress?

There are volumes written in art history about Chinoiserie and Japonisme, the blending of artistic styles and design influences when Western (European and then later American) culture first met the great powerhouses of Asia. The politically correct 21st-century thinker too easily shrinks from any hint of a discussion suggesting that anything positive comes from Western cultural colonialism.

An attempt to ignore the more bittersweet aspects of human political history ignores the truth that a lot of really good art happens in those "soft places" where two cultures meet, whether it be in the decorative arts, architecture, costume design, or illustration. A lot of good literature happens too, particularly if we can expand the definition of literature to encompass media beside traditional printed books, thing like comics (manga) and anime. A plethora of good art far greater than the number of imaginary people from different cultures who appear in that desert in the story "Exiles" (which coincidentally takes place along that ancient route of cross-cultural fertilization known as the Silk Road). Originality often happens when a fresh set of eyes, without the same baggage of shared cultural history, gaze on something they have never seen before, even if what those eyes see and absorb initially are merely stereotypes, gross generalizations of and misinterpretations of meaning.

The result is often better, more original, if the work resulting from cross-cultural fertilization is the product of many hands, if that creation is a collaborative work — like the 16th century palampores where the design is an Indian interpretation of a western pattern that a European traders brought over to have the natives paint in their indigenous technique for colorfast dying of cotton and linen fabric. The results were textiles that were neither truly Asian nor European, and the impact they have had on Western Decorative Arts over the last four centuries has been substantial.

Gaiman conceived of *The Sandman*, Dream, and The Endless. He drew on a multiplicity of literary sources: mythology, folklore, fairy-tales, and comic books for his inspiration. He is the one who originally thought of the kimono as a suitable costume for the King of Dreams. Like his character Dream, Gaiman was the connnecting unifying factor behind the work. After the initial conceptual phases, he turned those ideas over to a series of artists who made Dream into a physical reality on the pages of a comic book. Each time a collection of stories was completed, work on *The Sandman* was turned over to another set of artists, so the visual development of the character of Dream was undergoing continual reworking, revision and reinterpretation. Those images of Dream from the original comic series build up into a character over the course of the original series run. They become a more powerful part of the story than they would have had *The Sandman* been published as a book in prose form. They become an essential aide in the portrayal of Morpheus as a stubborn bulwark standing in the stream of time resisting, in an ultimately futile gesture, the change of the tide.

ENDNOTES. Author's note: Giving properly paginated citations for *The Sandman* is problematic, for two reasons. Original comic issues are hard to come by, and not shelved at most libraries. Some stories were not issued as regular installments in the original run of comics and others have been edited/expanded for the bound collections. I have an incomplete collection of miscellaneous editions of bound volumes at my disposal. Pagination is inconsistent at best. Some collections like, *The Wake* are numbered front to back. In those cases, I have stuck with it, as it seems simplest. Other collections retain issue to issue numbering, which I have had to stick with. *Brief Lives* is a good example. Chapter/issue designations should line up with the appendix in Bender's *The Sandman Companion*.

1. Gaiman, *Preludes and Nocturnes*, afterword, 2.
2. Steele, *China Chic*, intro, i.
3. Mikal Gilmore's intro to *The Wake*, iv.
4. Gaiman, *The Wake*, 75.
5. The earlier conversation about change takes place in *Brief Lives*, chapter 8 pp.8-16.
6. Gaiman, *The Wake*, 142.
7. Stinchecum, *Kosode*, 188. I am relying solely on the description of the symbolism and story implied by the decoration on this kosode (kimono) from the description given here.
8. Gaiman, *The Dream Hunters*, afterword, 128.

WORKS CITED.

Bender, Hy. *The Sandman Companion*. New York: DC Comics, 1999.

Dickenson, Gary and Linda Wrigglesworth. *Imperial Wardrobe*. London: Bamboo Publishing Ltd., 1990.

Gaiman, Neil. *The Sandman: The Dreamhunters*. New York: DC Comics, 1999.

Gaiman, Neil. *The Sandman: Preludes and Nocturnes*. New York: DC Comics, 1992.

—. *The Sandman: The Doll's House*. New York: DC Comics, 1990.

—. *The Sandman: Dream Country*. New York: DC Comics, 1991.

—. *The Sandman: Season of Mists*. New York: DC Comics, 1992.

—. *The Sandman: A Game of You*. New York: DC Comics, 1993.

—. *The Sandman: Brief Lives*. New York: DC Comics, 1994.

—. *The Sandman: World's End*. New York: DC Comics, 1994.

—. *The Sandman: The Kindly Ones*. New York: DC Comics, 1996.

—. *The Sandman: The Wake*. New York: DC Comics, 1997.

Henderson, Harold G. and Louis Ledoux. *Sharaku's Japanese Theater Prints: An Illustrated Guide to His Work*. New York: Dover Publications, 1939 (1984 ed).

Keyes, Roger S. and Keiko Mizushima. *The Theatrical World of Osaka Prints*. Boston, MA: David Godine and The Philadelphia Museum of Art, 1973.

Steele, Valerie and John S. Major. *China Chic: East Meets West*. New Haven, CT: Yale University Press, 1999.

Stinchecum, Amanda Meyer. *Kosode: 16th-19th Century Textiles from the Nomura Collection*. New York: Harper and Row Publishers, 1984.

❦ ❦ ❦

LESBIAN LANGUAGE, QUEER IMAGININGS, AND *DEATH: THE TIME OF YOUR LIFE*

by Joe Sutliff Sanders

✦

How does the way people talk change the way they see themselves? How does it change the way strangers see them? How do people reveal themselves not just in the words they say, but in the *way* they say those words?

I want to look closely at two characters, Hazel and Foxglove, who were only minor in the *Sandman* series, but went on to star in a later miniseries Neil Gaiman set in the same universe. What I'm interested in here is how the way in which these two characters talk opens up a world of secrets, love, and oppression in which lesbians live. There is something familiar about the kinds of words Hazel and Foxglove use to represent themselves, something that operates in a matrix of gender and power. By very careful attention to the subtleties of speech, Gaiman has managed to show how masculinity and femininity can infuse the language of lovers and frustrate their — our — attempts to form private communities of equality and respect.

We first meet Hazel and Foxglove in the "A Game of You" story arc that runs near the middle of the *Sandman* series. They are part of an insular and fascinating community of women: a pre-op transsexual, an ancient mystic, a gorgeous blonde named Barbie, and themselves. [*Fig. 1*] Their world is stable, almost disturbingly complete. The story follows the dissolving of boundaries of privacy between the women, the tightening of the community, and then, at the moment of victory, that community's dissolution. Throughout my analysis of *Death: the Time of Your Life*, the later miniseries I will study at length, I will be considering the importance of community, and it is possible that this early treatment of the theme of community is what suited Hazel and Foxglove for the kind of story that Gaiman wanted to tell later. Moreover, it begins a character arc that will work out smoothly through the two *Death* miniseries, both of which feature Hazel and Foxglove. This character arc is one of gender, the actions and decisions that we use to demonstrate where in the spectrum of feminine to masculine we want to exist. In "A Game of You," the lesbian couple is a near-stereotype of butch lesbianism, both of the women rude, slovenly, and abrupt. Their apartment is dingy and even a bit dirty. They smoke in bed, wear traditionally masculine haircuts, and generally seem intent on distancing themselves from conventional ideas of femininity. In their next appearance, though, the *Death: the High Cost of Living* miniseries that comes between "Game of You" and *Death: the Time of Your Life*, Foxglove has begun a career as a musician, and Hazel is no longer quite so stereotypically butch. Though she still openly defines herself as a lesbian, she has allowed her hair to grow out, she wears make-up, and she giggles when she speaks on the phone. The story in *Death: the High Cost of Living* is not about these two characters, and they receive little space in the text. However, there is a clear implication that something has begun to change between Foxglove and Hazel, that their relationship and the private, two-member community they shared in *Sandman* is no longer the same. The theme of community developed in the ongoing series and the subtle transition, at least on Hazel's part, away from a butch lesbian persona, set up nicely the way that language reveals the power dynamics of gender in *Death: the Time of Your Life*.

My original hypothesis was that Gaiman's use of American lesbian language in this miniseries would be flawed. I anticipated that the reason for such shortcomings would be that his background as a (born) British heterosexual male would necessarily inhibit his efforts. To a large extent, the hypothesis proved to be true, but the reason I had concocted was not. The language of the miniseries does not reflect some demographic handicap on Gaiman's part, but a subtle and even queer goal for the story. I found that, apart from an occasional nod to lesbian language, the language spoken by lesbians in this miniseries works to construct a narrative of difference not between straight and lesbian, but a difference *within* a lesbian community: the difference between butch and femme. This schism in the community, the miniseries reveals, is a holdover from and tool in heterosexual oppression of queer life.

Fig. 1: Writer: Neil Gaiman Artist: Shawn McManus "Slaughter on Fifth Avenue"
Collected in *The Sandman: A Game of You* [©1993 DC Comics]

Though there has been little research on language as explored by lesbians, many scholars have uncovered links between language and community. Sapir, for example, says that "Such categories as ... gender ... are systematically elaborated in language and are not so much discovered in experience as imposed upon it because of the tyrannical hold that linguistic form has upon our orientation in the world" (68). How exactly does linguistic form shape our view of gender? Arnold M. Zwicky has asserted that

> Since people are in fact quite good at discriminating the sexes on the basis of speech alone, it follows that dykes and faggots should be detectable by a disparity between their appearance and their speech, or in fact merely by contradictory signals in their speech. In actual practice this practice seems to be restricted to men; for straight people, there appears to be no female equivalent to The Voice. (26)

Here Zwicky refers largely to phonological variances which have come to be associated, through generations of stereotyping, with homosexual men. Since the subject of our study is a comic book, in which phonological representations are limited by the skill of the person who draws the letters in the word bubbles, the argument against a lesbian Voice is largely unimportant, but Zwicky's caveat is just the first of many for the would-be student of lesbian language. In fact, Zwicky has claimed that "... it is not even clear that lesbians are distinguishable in their speech from straight women ..." (29). Further, Barrett has argued against the use of one ideal speaker as subject for linguistic study of any group, saying, "By removing social variation from the system of language, formal linguists have reencoded the very prescriptive norms they claim to reject" (182-3). Barrett's telling criticism complicates the study of lesbian language, so we must go back to the concept of the imagined community for help. Instead of prescribing attributes to an ideal speaker and then measuring other texts/utterances against the attributes of that speaker, we must ask, as Anna Livia has asked in her study of butch/femme speech, "How do lesbians *think* they talk?" (245, Livia's emphasis).

It is with an observation by Birch Moonwomon-Baird that we begin our study of the text's use of linguistic conventions. We have already seen that the phonological differences between lesbian speech and feminine speech are slight, but Moonwomon-Baird says that "We are heard as lesbians, at least by ourselves ..." implying that there must be something a linguist can point to and say, "That is typical of lesbian language." What's more, *Death: the Time of Your Life* was granted a 1997 GLAAD Media Award by the Gay and Lesbian Alliance against Defamation, so we can assume that there must be something in the story that the larger homosexual community recognized as positive, perhaps even authentic. Moonwomon-Baird goes on to give a clue as to where to look. "The authentic lesbian voice," she reports, "is characterized not by intonational peculiarities or, for the most part, by use of special lexicon but by implication, inference, and presupposition that reveal a speaker's stance within the territories of various societal discourses" (203).

When Moonwomon-Baird speaks of "various societal discourses" important to lesbian communication, one can assume that feminism and the feminist movement are among those discourses. In a flashback near the end of the story, Hazel and Foxglove are in bed, and Hazel is trying to relate to her lover the scene earlier in the day when she made her deal with Death. Foxglove, who is reading a magazine while Hazel talks to her, says, "So what are you telling me, hon? Last week Alvie was dead, and this girl gave him *back* to you?" Hazel responds, "*Woman. Not Girl*" (75). Hazel's correction works to remind her partner of their stance within a community of feminists, that they are antagonists to the ancient practice of devaluing women through language. Later, Foxglove invokes an allusion to another discourse, this one perhaps closer to the heart of the lesbian community. Foxglove reveals that her identity as a homosexual will soon become public knowledge, that a former lover of hers is "going to the papers about it. I *didn't* want to be outed," Foxglove says, "I *don't* think I ever wanted to be inned" (77). Foxglove's invention of the word "inned" shows both an understanding of the lexemes utilized by the queer and queer-friendly communities as well as a "presupposition" that her audience, a lesbian, will be able to decode the new word. As Moonwomon-Baird has said, "I have come to think that language use among lesbians, at least across ethnicities and social classes of English-speaking American lesbians, is peculiarly lesbian in that interlocutors assume shared knowledge about many extradiscoursal matters touching on both gender and social-sexual orientation" (202).

In this way, Gaiman's use of lesbian language is accurate.

However, there is little else in the script of *Death: the Time of Your Life* to indicate that Gaiman has any special facility with lesbian language. Thus far, my original hypothesis has proven correct. And yet, I have found that it is not sufficient to point out a lack of lesbian language and insinuate that Gaiman's characters therefore revert to using dominant language. In fact, as it became more clear that scholars disagree on what precisely lesbian language might be, I realized that it is problematic to condemn a text for failing to adhere to a classification that linguists themselves find difficult to make. Further, Gaiman has said in an interview with Patrick Daniel O'Neill that "One of the sweet things about *Sandman* is that very few people seem to turn around and say, 'This comic has lesbians in it'; what they tend to say is, 'This comic has really good people in it'" (36). Gaiman's comment was made in the context that he has been surprised by the lack of outrage over his use of marginalized people in his mainstream book, but it also points out that Gaiman's readers have not perceived the lesbian characters as defined primarily by their sexual orientation. Since the lesbian characters to which Gaiman refers in this comment are also those who appear in *Death: the Time of Your Life*, it became clear to me that there is something more at work in Gaiman's construction of his characters' lesbianism as rendered by their language. I began researching again to find out what that something more might be.

Perhaps the most successful analysis of lesbian language in comic books has been Robin

M. Queen's "'I Don't Speak Spritch': Locating Lesbian Language." In her study, Queen looks at a variety of comic books written by and for the lesbian community, demonstrating plausibly that lesbian language seen from the perspective of lesbian-oriented comic books is constructed by drawing from the stereotypical language of a diversity of communities. Queen delineates a series of attributes for four different speech communities, then demonstrates their presence in her texts, most notably the independent comic book *Hothead Paisan: Homicidal Lesbian Terrorist*. However, it became clear to me upon comparison that Gaiman does not utilize all four of the speech communities represented in Queen's study; he in fact only uses two: that of stereotypical women's language and stereotypical men's language. One explanation is, of course, that Gaiman's attempt at lesbian language is simply a failure. Another, more rewarding explanation is that Gaiman is explicating a lesbian couple in terms of a butch (a woman speaking stereotypically masculine language) / femme (a woman speaking stereotypically feminine language) relationship.

Therefore, the focus of the research tightened, not just to analyze the language as lesbian/ non-lesbian, but to look closely at the two lesbian characters themselves and see how their language utilizes what linguists have identified as butch/femme tropes. In order to define butch language versus femme language, I have made use of studies of masculine and feminine language. Fortunately, though there have been few studies on lesbian language, in the years since Lakoff's *Language and Woman's Place* there has been an explosion of studies of how women and men communicate. Indeed, Lakoff is still an excellent source for enlightened opinion on gender language, particularly feminine language.

As we study the use of feminine language in *Death: the Time of Your Life*, we find that Gaiman repeatedly ascribes the most feminine attributes to Hazel. One example of feminine language Gaiman gives to Hazel is the prolific use of tag questions, which Lakoff has noted is most common among women (14-15). The first use of a tag question in the narrative is spoken by neither Hazel nor Foxglove, but by a minor female character. She tells Foxglove that Foxglove's first album "was like my favorite CD of the whole year. I just *played* it and *played* it. It gave me the strength to walk out on this guy" (14). When Foxglove asks the woman her name, she responds, "Jude. Like 'Hey Jude,' y'know?" Thus the reader is aware that Jude, a woman, was at least recently heterosexual, and is in the habit of using tag questions. Hazel uses a tag question only pages later, as she implores her son, who has climbed out on to a balcony, to "go back — carefully — into the house, okay?" (22). Here the reader witnesses Hazel using a tag question in a maternal context, encouraging the perception of Hazel as similar to a heterosexual female character. Then, when the child survives a fall from the second story unharmed, a friend of Hazel's asks if she doesn't think they should take the boy to a hospital. Hazel responds, "Well, I think if he'd *hurt* something, we'd *know* about it, y'know? Kids are resilient" (23). Hazel's intent in this utterance is to play down the miraculous nature of Alvie's survival, which she knows is because he has been granted extra life by Death. But regardless of the purpose of the tag question, Hazel's use of it again recalls a parallel with the first heterosexual woman in the story.

Lakoff has also pointed out that women often structure their language to imply that the speaker is not sure of the validity of what she is saying, even when the speaker has no reason to doubt her own opinion. In Gaiman's narrative, this most often manifests as Hazel's use of the word "like." She tells Death that Foxglove's disappearance into the public arena "was like she was going up in a balloon," which is merely an expression of a simile. However, she uses the word again shortly thereafter in what seems to be not a comparison but an effort to couch the strength of her assertion. She says, "And [Foxglove] was getting further and further away from me. And I just felt stupider and stupider, and I mean I *am* pretty stupid, I mean, I'm *not*, but I never knew much except cooking … I felt like I was an embarrassment. And I was *so* good: I lost weight. And I started to read stuff, and I tried to, like, broaden my *mind*" (56).

Hazel knows that she was trying to broaden her mind; no one else could possibly know better than Hazel what Hazel's intentions were when she "started to read stuff." However, Hazel finds that she must phrase the sentence in such a way that it becomes less assertive, probably in an effort to avoid sounding vain. Therefore, she adds the word "like" to detract from the assertiveness of her opinion. Conversely, when Foxglove attempts to couch her words during a photo/interview session, the interviewer — who mentions that she has a boyfriend, thus distancing herself from the homosexual subculture — forces her to be more specific. The interviewer first asks, "So, do you have a steady boyfriend at present?" to which Foxglove responds, "… I don't have anyone steady in my life." The interviewer observes, "You sound a little doubtful," and, as Foxglove smiles for the camera, she rephrases her language so that it is more masculine. "No," she says. "There's nobody special" (20). Whereas Hazel has spoken in deliberately couched terms, Foxglove revises her evasion into an outright — and direct — lie. As we will see in a moment, it is also significant that her revision in favor of more masculine language takes place under pressure from a marked heterosexual.

As Foxglove's career and the narrative progress, other scenes also highlight the widening gulf between the lovers, and again a linguistic analysis of the gendered language in those scenes helps reveal the changes. Fern L. Johnson and Elizabeth J. Aries have determined that "Females engage in more intimate, one-to-one relationships involving mutual exploration, understanding and security, showing less concern for the relational aspects of friendship and putting more stress on activities" (216-7). If we view the use of language by these two characters in the context of a masculine/feminine duality, we find rich material in another scene which explores Foxglove's attitude toward her career and Hazel's place in it. In the scene, Foxglove is seen signing autographs as she prepares to leave in her limousine. Her bodyguard hands her a portable phone, over which Hazel begs her lover to return home, saying, "*I need you. Alvie* needs you." Foxglove tells her, "For fuck's sake, Hazel. This is serious. I'll be back in a few weeks. Now *if* you'll excuse me I have a career to be getting on with" (31). [*Fig. 2*] The exchange is reminiscent of that classic exchange between workaholic father and stay-at-home mother in its content, but Hazel's phrasing of her request — "*I* need you. *Alvie* needs

Fig. 2: Writer: Neil Gaiman Artist: Chris Bachalo, Mark Buckingham & Mark Pennington "'Things You Just Do When You're Bored'" Collected in *Death: The Time of Your Life* [©1997 DC Comics]

you"— also highlights Hazel's belief that the most persuasive argument is one which invokes a threat to security and the shared relationship. When Foxglove hangs up on her, Hazel explains to Death that "She said no. I mean, I can understand it. She's got to go to the premiere. She did the title song. And she wants to meet the director — he says he might have a part for her in his next movie. And then she has to go to Europe for the album. She has to" (32).

Hazel paraphrases Foxglove's opinions, and it becomes clear that Hazel recognizes Foxglove's motivation as activity-oriented, just as Johnson and Aries might have predicted. In fact, not only does Hazel recognize activity as a motivation for Foxglove, she sees it as a necessity: "And then [Foxglove] has to go to Europe for the album. She has to." Foxglove is playing the role of bread-winning husband, Hazel the part of martyred but understanding wife. Again, the drift in language toward either end of the spectrum of gender coincides with a growing rift in the couple's relationship.

Janet Holmes has also demonstrated that "Women tend to use linguistic devices that stress solidarity more often than men do" (468). Gaiman uses this pattern of gendered language also in his representation of butch/femme speech. When Hazel elaborates on the deal she made to postpone Alvie's death, she says, "Well, sooner or later, she'll come back. And then we'll *all* go to her — you, and me, and Alvie. And then. Um. One of us will stay with her. And the other two will come back. Fox, honey? You aren't *mad* at me, are you? It was all I could think of" (75).

Hazel is most concerned with solidarity in this passage. She relates her tale in terms of what "we" will do. She stresses the word "*all*." Then she ascertains whether the comradeship of their relationship has been violated by asking if Foxglove is "mad" at her. Foxglove's response, however, is unconcerned with the maintenance of solidarity. "You want to know what *I* think?" she asks. "I think you aren't getting out of the house enough. I wish you'd learn to drive or something." Foxglove changes the grammatical subject of the sentence to singular, denying Hazel's preference for the inclusive plural. She changes the conversation to focus on herself and her own opinions, then mocks Hazel's inability to drive. Hazel's response, though spoken in anger, reaffirms her inclusive perception of the exchange. "For God's sake, Fox," she says, "this isn't *about* driving. It's about *us*. And [about] Alvie …" (75). Again Hazel stresses the use of the plural pronoun to indicate that she is worried about security, the solidarity of the family unit.

Another tool Gaiman utilizes in constructing Foxglove's masculinity is her use of foul language. Lakoff has commented that the use of vulgarity is most commonly considered men's speech (17), and there are many examples of such usage in the miniseries. Foxglove uses the word "fuck" multiple times, such as when she refuses to return home at Hazel's request and when joking with her bodyguard (27). When Foxglove tells her manager that she has changed her mind concerning what song she will play on national television that night, her manager responds with an uncomfortable, "Mm. It's your decision," and Foxglove grunts, "Damn right" (16). Later, when Foxglove pleads with her manager to change his mind and allow her to reveal her homosexuality to her fans, he says, "Y'know, it's not a simple thing, Fox." "It's a *very* simple thing," she argues. "I'm a *dyke*. I like girls. I've *always* liked girls. Since I was a little girl I liked girls. When I play with myself I *think* of girls" (17). Foxglove maintains her dominance over her self-definition through the use of first person pronoun, and her repetitive use of simple sentences in retelling her lesbian history acts like a bludgeon, as Foxglove attempts to force her manager to see things from her point of view. She also chooses vulgar euphemisms, such as "dyke" and "play with myself." She talks easily with her male manager, actually outperforming his own masculinity through her masculine use of language. The linguistic constructions these characters use serve to communicate to the reader that Foxglove is masculine and Hazel is feminine.

The question of why Gaiman chooses to present his lesbian characters along lines of traditional masculinity and femininity may be answered in various ways. For example, it may be that Gaiman is attempting to make a nontraditional pair of protagonists more palatable to his largely male audience. He therefore would be concerned with rendering his characters in terms familiar to the readers, which would also explain the many ways in which Hazel and Foxglove's relationship parallels conventional stereotypes of married couples (such as when Foxglove reads a newspaper rather than listen attentively to her lover and when she chooses to pursue her career rather than indulge what appears to be Hazel's whimsy). However, as Gaiman insinuated in the interview cited above, he expected his rendering of homosexuals to stir up controversy amongst his audience. Therefore, it is unlikely that he was trying to make Hazel and Foxglove more palatable.

A more reasonable explanation for the butch/femme dichotomy in his text is that Gaiman wants to show a lesbian couple undergoing the trauma of oppression at the hands of the mainstream. Our first example comes in Foxglove's conversation with her manager. It is in this early scene that we first realize both that Foxglove has not come out to her audience yet and that her decision to remain in the closet is motivated by her career. In fact, as Hazel later points out, it was not until Foxglove's manager "told her to be in the closet" that Hazel and Foxglove began pretending they were anything other than lovers (56). Then, in the discussion with her manager quoted above, a conversation with great implications for her career, Foxglove begins to swear and assert her point of view. Shortly thereafter, the reporter forces Foxglove to take a stand on her current dating status, and Foxglove must abandon a feminine response for a masculine assertion in order to keep her career safe. Likewise, Foxglove curses and denigrates her lover when Hazel tries to convince her to come home rather than pursue her career, and Hazel assumes a submissive stance though she knows that her very life is threatened by Foxglove's refusal to return home. It is Foxglove's career as a masquerading straight entertainer in an industry dominated by heteronormativity that is the reason for the growing disparity in the lovers' personalities.

Although it is hardly revolutionary to conduct a study of words on the page, comics and linguistics share a common ground that has been inaccessible to mainstream literary studies.

Because language in comics is no less a tool of visual art than are color and line, there is an emphasis on language in comics that demands methodical attention, attention perhaps best given according to strategies of linguistics. In this miniseries, for example, linguistics allows us to detect the whispers of a lesbian language in mainstream comics as well as in comics such as *Hothead Paisan* marketed for lesbians. Further, it reveals the critique of heteronormative society — which threatens Foxglove and Hazel with economic and creative disenfranchisement if they reveal their membership in the lesbian community — implicit in Gaiman's miniseries. An understanding of the growing butch-femme split between Foxglove and Hazel, as flagged by their language drift toward either end of the spectrum respectively, helps to reveal not only the careful characterization at work in the story but also the developing subplot of homosexual characters under assault by heterocentric pressures, pressures that endanger their relationship, lives, and language.

At the narrative's close, Foxglove decides to abandon her career in show business. An epilogue gives the reader a glimpse of the pair's lives a few years after the close of the main story. There is very little spoken dialogue, but what the reader hears is largely genderless. Foxglove and Hazel find happiness as a family unit again, doing their shopping at a local supermarket, with little Alvie in tow. They have forsaken the wider, heterocentric community for a new imagined community of their own, wherein they are content and empowered. The lesbians form their own nation, limited to their exclusive membership, and in which they are sovereign.

WORKS CITED.

Anderson, Benedict. *Imagined Communities: Reflections on the Origin and Spread of Nationalism.* Revised Edition. London: Verso, 1991.

Barrett, Rusty. "The 'Homo-genius' Speech Community." Ed. Anna Livia and Kira Hall. *Queerly Phrased: Language, Gender, and Sexuality.* New York and Oxford: Oxford University Press, 1997. 181-201.

Chesebro, James W. Introduction. Ed. James W. Chesebro. *Gayspeak: Gay Male and Lesbian Communication.* New York: The Pilgrim Press, 1981. ix-xvi.

Coates, Jennifer. Introduction. Ed. Jennifer Coates. *Language and Gender: a Reader.* Oxford: Blackwell Publishers, 1998.

Eckert, Penelope and Sally McConnell-Ginet. "Constructing Meaning, Constructing Selves." Ed. Anna Livia and Kira Hall. *Queerly Phrased: Language, Gender, and Sexuality.* New York and Oxford: Oxford University Press, 1997. 469-507.

Gaiman, Neil. *Death: the High Cost of Living.* Illus. Chris Bachalo, Mark Buckingham, and Dave McKean. New York: DC Comics, 1994.

—. *Death: the Time of Your Life.* Illus. Chris Bachalo, Mark Buckingham, and Mark Pennington. New York: DC Comics, 1997.

—. "The Master of Dreams, Lost Loves, Old Gods and Unanswered Riddles...." By Patrick

Daniel O'Neill. *Wizard: the Guide to Comics* May 1992: 32-37.

—. *The Sandman: a Game of You*. Illus. Shawn McManus et al. New York: DC Comics, 1993.

Holmes, Janet. "Women's Talk: the Question of Sociolinguistic Universals." Ed. Jennifer Coates. *Language and Gender: a Reader*. Oxford: Blackwell Publishers, 1998. 461-483.

Johnson, Fern L. and Elizabeth J. Aries. "The Talk of Women Friends." Ed. Jennifer Coates. *Language and Gender: a Reader*. Oxford: Blackwell Publishers, 1998. 215-225.

Lakoff, Robin. *Language and Woman's Place*. New York: Harper Colophon Books, 1975.

Livia, Anna. "'I Ought to Throw a Buick at You': Fictional Representations of Butch/Femme Speech." Ed. Anna Livia and Kira Hall. *Queerly Phrased: Language, Gender, and Sexuality*. New York and Oxford: Oxford University Press, 1997. 245-277.

Moonwomon-Baird, Birch. "Toward a Study of Lesbian Speech." Ed. Anna Livia and Kira Hall. *Queerly Phrased: Language, Gender, and Sexuality*. New York and Oxford: Oxford University Press, 1997. 202-213.

Mühlhaüser, Peter and Rom Harré. *Pronouns and People: The Linguistic Construction of Social and Personal Identity*. Oxford: Blackwell, 1990.

Queen, Robin M. "'I Don't Speak Spritch': Locating Lesbian Language." Ed. Anna Livia and Kira Hall. *Queerly Phrased: Language, Gender, and Sexuality*. New York and Oxford: Oxford University Press, 1997. 233-256.

Sapir, Edward. "The Status of Linguistics as a Science." Ed. D.G. Mandelbaum. *Selected Writings of Edward Sapir*. Berkeley: University of California Press, 1970.

Zwicky, Arnold M. "Two Lavendar Issues for Linguists." Ed. Anna Livia and Kira Hall. *Queerly Phrased: Language, Gender, and Sexuality*. New York and Oxford: Oxford University Press, 1997. 21-34.

❖❖❖

CONTRIBUTORS

✦

DAVID BRATMAN is married to a woman who reads more comics than he ever did, and who points him to the good stuff, like Neil Gaiman. In the waking world, he alternates lives as a librarian and a classical music reviewer with bouts as a literary critic and historian specializing in Tolkien. He has compiled an authorized bibliography of Ursula K. Le Guin and edited *The Masques of Amen House* by Charles Williams. This paper was originally presented at Mythcon XXXV in Ann Arbor, 2004, at which Gaiman was Guest of Honor.

JOAN GORDON is a professor of English at Nassau Community College and an editor of *Science Fiction Studies*. She recently co-edited, with Veronica Hollinger, *Edging into the Future: Science Fiction and Contemporary Cultural Transformation*.

STACIE L. HANES is a Teaching Fellow at Kent State University, where she is pursuing a doctorate in 19th century British Literature. Her essay "Death and the Maiden" was published in the second edition of *Terry Pratchett: Guilty of Literature*. Her critical interests include ethics, satire, and queer theory in the context of science fiction and fantasy. Interested parties may read more of her work at http://exmeraldus.blogspot.com/, a site which also features pictures of her cat.

✢✢✢

K. A. LAITY is an Assistant Professor of English at the University of Houston-Downtown where she teaches medieval literature, creative writing, and film. Clive Barker has called her fiction "full of fluent style and poetic dialogue." Her first novel *Pelzmantel: A Medieval Tale* (Spilled Candy Books) was based on a Grimm fairy-tale and was nominated for the 2003 Aesop Award and the International Reading Association's Children's Book Award. She has published articles and delivered papers on medieval literature and culture, comics, speculative fiction, mythology, folklore, and modern paganism. She's working on her second novel, set in contemporary New England and 14th century Ireland, as well as on *Unikirja*, a collection of short stories inspired by Finnish mythology. "Free time" remains only a theoretical concept to her.

ALAN LEVITAN taught Shakespeare and early modern poetry and drama at Brandeis University from 1960 to 2000. He also taught courses in classical Japanese poetry, fiction, and drama. His publications include many reviews of theater, ballet, Asian dance, and Japanese *noh*, *kabuki*, and *bunraku*, as well as scholarly articles on Dante, Chaucer, and Shakespeare. Gaiman's book-signing many years at Comicopia, in Boston, was the only book-signing for which Alan was happily willing to stand on line (he was in seventy-fourth place that day). Alan is an avid amateur pianist and loves playing Mozart and Hayden, though he assures us that "they always win." He lives in Cambridge, Massachusetts.

LYRA MCMULLEN is an independent scholar with a lifelong interest in the meaning and construction techniques of costume and dress. Cross-cultural influences, the use of Asian dress in the West, and Western Dress in the East have always held a particular fascination for her. She holds an M.A. in Museum Studies in Costume and Textiles from The Fashion Institute of Technology in New York and also is an alumna of Bard College, where she studied Art History. Current research interests include the use of costume in Japanese manga illustration and learning the Japanese language. Hobbies include reading science fiction and fantasy, making art, and collecting dolls because they make the perfect models for her sewing.

B. KEITH MURPHY is a Professor of English at Fort Valley State University in Georgia. He holds a Ph.D. in rhetoric from Ohio University and has taught college level courses in English, Composition, Speech, Mass Communication, and Philosophy. Keith also has worked as an actor in radio, a magician, and a cave guide. His research areas include comics, for which he was awarded a grant from the National Endowment of the Humanities, conspiracy theory, and ancient literature. He and his wife Kathy run bunniwerks, a domestic rabbit rescue. For more information, see www.keithmurphy.info

RENATA SANCKEN in an English/history major at Grinnell College. (That's Grinnell, not Cornell.) Her website about the mythology in Neil Gaiman's *American Gods* , http://frowl. org/gods/, was recently released as a companion to Hill House Publishers' Lettered Edition of *American Gods*. In Renata's spare time, she has single-handedly brought international villainess Carmen Sandiego to justice on multiple occasions.

JOE SANDERS in a professor emeritus at Lakeland Community College, Kirtland OH, where he instituted courses in contemporary fiction, science fiction, fantasy, and graphic fiction. He is a former president of the Science Fiction Research Association and received the SFRA's Clareson Award for service in 2001. During a long career as an SF critic, he has written countless book reviews, many essays, and books on Roger Zelazny and E. E. "Doc" Smith; he also edited a volume of conference proceedings from an International Conference on the Fantastic in the Arts and a collection of essays about sf fandom.

JOE SUTLIFF SANDERS is a professor of literature at Illinois Wesleyan University, where he teaches courses on comic books and U.S. literature and culture. His reviews, scholarly articles, and fiction have appeared in various venues around the world since 1998, including a monthly graphic novels review column for a major book distributor and regular contributions to the journal *VOYA*. His ongoing research focuses on gender, discipline, and children's literature.

Originally from Belo Horizonte, LEONORA SOLEDAD S. PAULA recently got her M.A. in Comparative literature at UFMG, Brazil. The several readings of *The Sandman* led her to an extensive study in which she discussed the continuous recycling of cultural material present in contemporary graphic novels. Despite her affinity with postmodernist perspectives, she still likes drinking coffee in real cups and feeling the ink while reading the newspapers.